Your College Experience

Strategies for Success

CONCISE MEDIA EDITION
SIXTH EDITION

JOHN N. GARDNER

Distinguished Professor Emeritus, Library and Information Science
Senior Fellow, National Resource Center for The First-Year Experience and Students in Transition
University of South Carolina, Columbia

Executive Director, Policy Center on the First Year of College, Brevard, North Carolina

A. JEROME JEWLER

Distinguished Professor Emeritus, College of Journalism and Mass Communication
University of South Carolina, Columbia

AUSTRIALIA • CANADA • MEXICO • SINGAPORE • SPAIN • UNITED KINGDOM • UNITED STATES

Your College Experience: Strategies for Success, Concise Media Edition, Sixth Edition

John N. Gardner, A. Jerome Jewler

Executive Manager, College Success: *Carolyn Merrill*
Development Editor: *Cathy Murphy*
Assistant Editor: *Amy Hurd*
Technology Project Manager: *Joe Gallagher*
Advertising Project Manager: *Linda Yip*
Project Manager, Editorial Production: *Lianne Ames*
Senior Print Buyer: *Mary Beth Hennebury*
Permissions Editor: *Chelsea Junget*
Production Service: *Lois Lombardo, Nesbitt Graphics, Inc.*
Text Designer: *Diane Beasley*
Photo Manager: *Sheri Blaney*
Photo Researcher: *Deborah Nicholls*
Cover Designer: *Laurie Anderson*
Cover Printer: *Coral Graphics*
Compositor: *Nesbitt Graphics, Inc.*
Printer: *Courier Corporation*
Cover Art: All: © *Index Stock Imagery:* Left *top to bottom:* © *Stewart Cohen;* © *Ed Lallo;* © *Stewart Cohen;* © *Chris Rogers;* Right: © *Len Rubinstein*

Printed in the United States of America
1 2 3 4 5 6 7 09 08 07 06 05

For more information about our products, contact us at:
Thomson Learning Academic Resource Center
1-800-423-0563
For permission to use material from this text or product, submit a request online at **http://www.thomsonrights.com.**
Any additional questions about permissions can be submitted by email to **thomsonrights@thomson.com.**

Library of Congress Control Number: 2004115027

Student Edition: ISBN 0-534-64521-6

Loose-leaf Edition: ISBN 1-4130-1364-3

Credits appear on page 193, which constitutes a continuation of the copyright page.

Thomson Higher Education
25 Thomson Place
Boston, MA 02210-1202
USA

Asia (including India)
Thomson Learning
5 Shenton Way
#01-01 UIC Building
Singapore 068808

Australia/New Zealand
Thomson Learning Australia
102 Dodds Street
Southbank, Victoria 3006
Australia

Canada
Thomson Nelson
1120 Birchmount Road
Toronto, Ontario M1K 5G4
Canada

UK/Europe/Middle East/Africa
Thomson Learning
High Holborn House
50–51 Bedford Road
London WC1R 4LR
United Kingdom

Latin America
Thomson Learning
Seneca, 53
Colonia Polanco
11560 Mexico
D.F. Mexico

Spain (including Portugal)
Thomson Paraninfo
Calle Magallanes, 25
28015 Madrid, Spain

Brief Contents

Contents

Preface to Students

Any person of any age who is admissible to college and reads this book has the potential to succeed and graduate. The trick is to be prepared for the many things that can confuse you, distract you, and undermine your goals in the first year. Knowing what to expect in college—and being prepared with strategies that help you overcome whatever obstacles you encounter—are the keys to success and the basis for this textbook.

Our belief in your ability to succeed is not based in faith. As founders and dedicated supporters of the First-Year Experience movement, we have many years of experience working with students just like you and training instructors who then go on to teach students just like you.

Strategies for Success

Research conducted at our institution—The National Resource Center for The First-Year Experience and Students in Transition at the University of South Carolina, Columbia—and others continues to show that students are more likely to succeed if they follow the strategies in this text.

These **Strategies for Success** inform each chapter. You will find them in the Introduction to the text and on the accompanying CD-ROM, as well as on the convenient perforated card attached to the cover of this book. In this new edition, these 20 strategies are grouped into three categories to help clarify the major concepts in this book:

Get Ready: The Basics

Among the most important things you must learn in college is how to be prepared. This means knowing how to manage time to avoid cramming for exams, getting too little sleep, or studying day and night with no breaks. Without planning, college can turn into a threatening maze of due dates that creep up too soon, missed classes, and sheer exhaustion.

Get Set: Study, Study, Study

You will discover that the best ways to study aren't any harder than the bad ways. We'll help you uncover new thinking skills and classroom strategies. Active participation is one of the key talents for taking charge of learning and life. Learning is more exciting and productive for both students and instructors when students confidently speak up in class.

Go: The Extra Mile

It is critical in college that you establish and maintain connections. There are numerous benefits to participating in campus life, studying with a group, meeting with teachers outside of class, and choosing a good advisor or counselor. Such connections can lead to some wonderful friendships as well as success in classes. At the same time, we offer some tips on how to take care of yourself, mentally, emotionally, and physically.

Text Features to Help You Succeed

College textbooks typically include "features"—sections, boxes, or design elements that are written specifically to help you learn the material effectively. *Your College Experience: Strategies for Success, Concise Media Edition*, Sixth Edition, is no exception. In fact, the features in this book are deliberately designed to make learning and understanding interesting, relevant, and efficient.

Each chapter opens with a **Self-Assessment**. This short questionnaire invites you to inventory your knowledge of, confidence or capability in the topics covered in the chapter.

At the end of each chapter, the **Reassess Yourself** section asks you to revisit your initial responses to the chapter-opening self-assessment after completing each chapter's reading assignment. Taking a second look at the self-assessment serves as a mini-review of the chapter's key concepts and gives you a chance to evaluate what you've learned and how it has affected you.

Also at the end of each chapter, you will find a variety of **exercises**. The CD-ROM that accompanies this book contains additional exercises as well as all the exercises from the textbook. In addition, each chapter includes at least one exercise specifically designed for group collaboration. These are labeled **Working Together Exercises.**

Other features that appear in every chapter of the text include:

- **Setting Goals for Success** boxes, each of which asks you to set a goal and create a plan for achieving it. This feature ties in with the CD-ROM, which includes chapter-by-chapter lists of online resources for working on these important goals.
- **Critical Thinking** boxes, which invite you to work through a tightly focused problem or question, either as a mental exercise or work to turn in to your instructor. These sections address situations or problems that are personal, but require a critical approach.
- **Examining Values** boxes—brief sections that ask you to consider your values, viewpoints, and opinions on important topics related to each chapter's content.
- **Where to Go for Help** boxes—sections in each chapter where you can turn for ideas, support, and resources, both on and off campus, in person, and online.
- **Going Forward/Looking Back** paragraphs—these point/counterpoint sections pair a contemporary student voice reflecting on current experience with the recollections of one of the authors on his college days. These appear at the beginning of each chapter.
- **Speaking of Careers** boxes, which focus on careers and career-planning issues.

Technology That Supports Your Learning

An interactive CD-ROM accompanies new copies of this edition of *Your College Experience.* The CD-ROM includes both Internet-based and InfoTrac® College Edition exercises that invite you to explore resources beyond the textbook. Using the CD-ROM lets you complete exercises electronically, instead of on a hard copy. You can even e-mail your homework to your instructor! Also on the CD-ROM are self-assessments designed to personalize the learning process, a "Where to Go for Help" section with links to resources, goal-setting resources tied to chapter content, all the exercises from the textbook, bonus exercises, additional readings, and journal writing activities.

Additional Resources for Student Success

A free companion Web site is available at: *<http://www.success.wadsworth.com/gardnerconcise6e/>*. Containing many useful assessment exercises, practice quizzes, and other useful tools, the site is organized by chapter so that you can use it in conjunction with your book and CD-ROM to make the most of your learning opportunities.

Your new copy of this text may include a four-month subscription to InfoTrac® College Edition, a powerful online library. InfoTrac® College Edition offers an easy-to-search database of the latest news and research from over 5,000 academic journals and popular magazines.

So, Get Ready, Get Set, and Go Begin Your College Experience!

John N. Gardner
A. Jerome Jewler

Preface to Instructors

Some years ago, we decided to write a book that would help new college students overcome the problems which might cause them to drop out. The book was a natural outgrowth of the first-year seminar course we had been teaching for a number of years.

We began to list some topics that would be appropriate to the task. We believed then, as we still believe today, that practically anyone of any age who is admissible to college can make it as long as he or she is prepared for the many factors that can turn that first year into a catastrophe. That's what our book was designed to do: to convince readers that, by following the examples in these chapters, they will complete their first year successfully and open the door wide toward graduation.

As founders and dedicated supporters of the First-Year Experience movement, we are pleased to present this new concise media edition of *Your College Experience: Strategies for Success*, which continues to focus on these vital goals. We have received tremendous assistance in this major revision from instructors who have used this text before, reviewers, Wadsworth Publishing Company's editorial staff, experts who assisted us in the preparation of many of the chapters in our newest edition, and of course, students.

Enhanced Strategies for Success

Research from the National Resource Center for the First-Year Experience and Students in Transition at the University of South Carolina and at other institutions continues to show that students are more likely to succeed if they follow the strategies in this text.

These Strategies for Success inform each chapter. You will find them in the Introduction to the text and on the accompanying CD-ROM, as well as on the convenient perforated card attached to the cover of this book. In this new edition, these 20 strategies are grouped into three categories to help clarify the major concepts in this book:

Get Ready: The Basics

Among the most important things a student must learn in college is how to be prepared. This means knowing how to manage time to avoid cramming for exams, getting too little sleep, or studying day and night with no fun breaks. Without planning, college can turn into a threatening maze of due dates that creep up too soon, missed classes, and sheer exhaustion.

Get Set: Study, Study, Study

Students will discover that the best ways to study aren't any harder than the bad ways. We'll help them uncover new thinking skills and classroom strategies. Active participation is one of the key talents for taking charge of learning and life. Learning is more exciting and productive for both students and instructors when students confidently speak up in class.

Go: The Extra Mile

It is critical in college to establish and maintain connections. There are numerous benefits to participating in campus life, studying with a group, meeting with teachers outside of class, and choosing a good advisor or counselor. Such connections can lead to some wonderful friendships as well as success in classes. At the same time, we offer students some tips on how to take care of themselves, mentally, emotionally, and physically.

New Features of the Student Media Edition CD-ROM

The interactive CD-ROM that accompanies this edition of *Your College Experience, Concise Media Edition*, Sixth Edition, has been significantly revised. The CD-ROM includes both Internet-based and InfoTrac® College Edition exercises that invite students to explore resources beyond the textbook. Also on the CD-ROM are enhanced self-assessments designed to personalize the learning process, a "Where to Go for Help" section with links to resources, goal-setting resources tied to chapter content, the full set of exercises from the textbook, bonus exercises, additional readings, and journal writing activities.

New Features in the Concise Sixth Edition

Each chapter continues to open with a **self-assessment inventory**. A new **Reassess Yourself** section asks students to revisit their initial responses to the chapter-opening self-assessment upon completion of each chapter's reading assignment. Taking a second look at the self-assessment serves as a mini-review of the chapter's key concepts.

In response to requests from users of the book, we've included **more exercises** for each text chapter. All chapters have at least one new exercise. Each CD-ROM chapter offers more exercises as well. In addition, each chapter now has at least one exercise specifically designed for group collaboration. These exercises are labeled **Working Together**.

A new feature, called **Setting Goals for Success**, appears in every chapter. Students will set a goal and create a plan for achieving it. This feature ties in with the CD-ROM, which includes chapter-by-chapter lists of online resources for working on these important goals.

The **Critical Thinking** boxes in each chapter now ask students to work through a tightly focused problem or question, either as a mental exercise or work to turn in to the instructor. The sections address situations or problems that are personal but require a critical approach.

The sixth edition also includes **Where to Go for Help** boxes, sections in each chapter where students can turn for ideas, support, and resources, both on and off campus, in person, and online.

In **Going Forward/Looking Back**, point/counterpoint sections pair a contemporary student voice reflecting on current experience with the recollections of one of the authors on his college days. These appear at the beginning of each chapter.

Given the importance students place on securing a good job, **Speaking of Careers** boxes continue to be a feature of this text, but many of them have been revised to tighten the focus on careers and career-planning issues.

In addition, we've continued to include **Examining Values** boxes, and have revised and updated many of them.

New Chapter Coverage

Every chapter has been revised with contemporary statistics, revised features, and new exercises.

Chapter 1 is now completely devoted to time management. The Gardner/Jewler Strategies for Success and the book plan appear in a new Introduction. This new organization has allowed us to expand coverage of important time management issues, and strategies such as avoiding procrastination and building a "to do" list.

Chapter 5 has been revised to enhance coverage of memory, including more on mnemonic devices, organization tips, and visualization. In Chapter 6, we've added new sections on taking open-book, short answer, machine-graded, and take-home exams. The goal-setting box focuses on succeeding on standardized tests. In Chapter 7 (Values), we've added an extensive discussion of Service Learning.

Chapters 9 (Creating Diverse Relationships) and 10 (Staying Healthy) have been substantially revised. Chapter 9 now concentrates on diversity, relationships, and sexuality. In addition, you will find a revised section on students with disabilities and updated statistics throughout. Chapter 10 brings together information on wellness, including stress management, diet, sexual health, alcohol and other drugs, safety, and maintaining balance in your life. Specifically, you will find a new chart on sexually transmitted infections, updated information on the dangers of heroin, new material on methamphetamine, a new section on depression and suicide, coverage of eating disorders, and an expanded discussion of nutrition.

Instructor's Resources

A complete supplements package for instructors accompanies this text. For additional advice and information about College Success products and services that will help you teach the course, call the Toll-Free Consultation Service: 1-800-400-7609.

Instructor's Manual/Test Bank

Each chapter of this flexible and unique Instructor's Manual/Test Bank contains additional exercises, test questions, tips on teaching, a list of common concerns among first-year students, and a case study relevant to the topics covered.

ExamView® Computerized Test Bank

ExamView is a premiere test-building program that allows instructors to quickly create tests and quizzes customized to individual courses. ExamView's Quick Test Wizard guides you step by step through the process of creating and printing a test in minutes. Tests can contain up to 250 questions using 12 unique types of questions.

WebTutor Toolbox™ on WebCT and Blackboard

WebTutor Toolbox is a web-based teaching and learning tool that offers instructors the opportunity to track student progress, hold virtual office hours, and post syllabi online using the WebCT or Blackboard course management systems. To find out more about WebTutor Toolbox, visit <*http://webtutor.thomsonlearning.com*>.

New MultiMedia Manager 2.0

This easy-to-use, one-stop lecture tool helps you assemble, edit, and present custom multimedia lectures for your college success course. Organized into 13 common college success topics, the MultiMedia Manager contains PowerPoint® slides, digitized CNN video clips, full-color images from our textbooks and other sources, and live Web links. The MultiMedia Manager is available **free** to adopters of this text.

JoinIn™ on Turning Point® *for truly interactive lectures!*

Transform any lecture into an interactive experience for students with JoinIn on TurningPoint software—our book-specific content created specifically for use with personal response systems. Combined with your choice of several leading keypad systems, JoinIn turns an ordinary PowerPoint application into powerful audience response software. With just a click on a hand-held device, your students can respond to multiple-choice questions, short polls, interactive exercises, and peer-review questions.

You can take attendance, check student comprehension of difficult concepts, collect student demographics to better assess student needs, and even administer quizzes without collecting papers or grading. This interactive tool is available to qualified college and university adopters. For more information, visit *http://turningpoint.thomsonlearningconnections.com*.

Video Presentation Resources

Ask your local Wadsworth sales representative for details.

- **CNN Today: College Success Video Series.** An exclusive series of video clips have been created specifically for use in college success courses by Wadsworth and CNN, the world's leading 24-hour global news network. Tapes are updated yearly and serve as provocative "lecture launchers."
- ***New:* 10 Things Every Student Needs to Know to Study.** This sixty-minute video covers such practical skills as note-taking, test-taking, and listening.

Custom Publishing Options

Faculty can select chapters from this and other Wadsworth College Success titles to bind with your own materials into a fully customized book. For more information, contact your Wadsworth/Thomson Learning representative or visit <*http://success.wadsworth.com*>.

Loose-leaf Version of *Your College Experience, Concise Media Edition,* Sixth Edition (1-4130-1364-3)

Students can easily create their own course-specific binder using this three-hole-punched version of the text. The unbound format allows students to create their own customized reference guide by adding material how and when they choose.

College Success Workshops

Wadsworth offers on-campus regional training designed to focus on the demands of teaching college success courses as well as **Web E-seminars**. These workshops and E-seminars provide active learning exercises you can use to enhance your course and provide an opportunity for instructors and administrators to exchange ideas. See <*http://www.success.wadsworth.com*> for more details regarding the locations of the live workshops and the schedule for the E-seminars.

Student Resources

Interactive CD-ROM

The CD-ROM that accompanies each new text gives students the option of doing exercises electronically and provides links to valuable resources on college success topics. Rich with additional self-assessment exercises, the CD-ROM is the perfect complement to the text.

Companion Web site

A free companion Web site is available at: *<http://www.success.wadsworth.com/gardnerconcise6e/>*. Containing many useful assessment exercises, practice quizzes, and other useful tools, the site is organized by chapter so that students can use it in conjunction with the book and CD-ROM to make the most of their learning opportunities.

InfoTrac® College Edition (0-534-40449-9)

You can order a new copy of this text that includes a **free** four-month subscription to this online library. InfoTrac® College Edition offers an easy-to-search database of the latest news and research from many well-known academic journals and popular magazines.

College Success Factors Index (0-534-40440-5)

This unique online assessment tool allows students to easily identify the behaviors and attitudes that will help them succeed in college. Available via a purchased Pincode that can be bundled with a new textbook, see *<http://www.success.wadsworth.com>* for more information.

Premiere College Success Academic Planner (1-4130-1549-2)

Wadsworth offers inexpensive planners designed specifically for college students. Available with the purchase of a new text for a small additional fee, the planner is updated annually.

Acknowledgments

Although this text speaks through the voices of its two editors, it represents contributions from many others. We gratefully acknowledge those contributions and thank these individuals whose special expertise has made it possible to introduce new college students to "their college experience" through the holistic approach we deeply believe in:

Chapter 1: Jeanne L. Higbee, University of Minnesota, Twin Cities
Chapter 2: Tom Carskadon, Mississippi State University
Chapters 4–6: Jeanne L. Higbee, University of Minnesota, Twin Cities
Chapter 7: John M. Whiteley and James B. Craig, University of California, Irvine, and Edward Zlotkowski
Chapter 8: Philip Gardner, Michigan State University, Linda Salane, Columbia College, and Stuart Hunter, University of South Carolina, Columbia
Chapter 9: Tom Carskadon, Mississippi State University; J. Herman Blake, Iowa State University; and Joan Rasool, Westfield State University
Chapter 10: Bradley H. Smith, Rick L. Gant, Georgeann Stamper, JoAnn Herman, Danny Baker, and Sara J. Corwin, University of South Carolina, Columbia

We would also like to thank Joseph Cuseo, Marymount College, for his thoughts on collaborative learning. Special thanks are also owing to these reviewers whose wisdom and suggestions guided the creation of this text:

Jennifer Kalligonis, *Delaware County Community College*
Patsy Taylor, *Chowan College*
Pamela Niesslein, *College of Charleston*
Robert Eves, *Southern Utah University*
Carol Sweetser, *Northern Virginia Community College*
Colleen Courtney, *Palm Beach Community College*
David Goss, *College of Charleston*
Sonya Hildreth, *California State University—Fresno*
Kim Smokowski, *Bergen Community College*

Finally, all this could not have happened without the support of the Wadsworth team, without whom this book would never be. Special thanks to Cathy Murphy of Editrix for her superb guidance and to Carolyn Merrill, Executive Manager of College Success, who helped us through the tough times.

Our special thanks also go to Susan Badger, CEO of Thomson Higher Education; Sean Wakely, President of Wadsworth Publishing; Amy Hurd, Assistant Editor for College Success; Lianne Ames, Senior Production Project Manager; Lois Lombardo, Project Manager, Nesbitt Graphics, Inc.; Constance Staley, Workshop Facilitator; and Ilana Sims, Workshop Coordinator and College Success Consultant.

We could have done it without you, but it wouldn't have been anywhere nearly as good.

John N. Gardner
A. Jerome Jewler

Part 1

Get Ready

(The Basics)

Introduction
Succeeding in College

© Spencer Grant/PhotoEdit

Going Forward: Student Voices

I just stood in line for two hours and spent over a hundred dollars for two books. And I realized I have three exams during the same week in October. First week of college and I'm already stressing out. At least I've met a few interesting people. Wish I had time to talk to them.

Looking Back: Author Voices

Frankly, I didn't want to go to college, and I hated my first semester. Few friends. No real attachment to campus, since I lived at home. Then I enrolled in a required math course, knowing I would flunk. But I made a B, one of the highest grades in the class, which was reputedly #1 on the campus "flunk list." Math! I didn't care about math. I wanted to be a writer. Jerry Jewler

In this chapter, YOU WILL LEARN

- Important strategies for college success
- Why some students don't graduate
- The impact of college on your future earnings
- Typical questions first-year students ask
- Some differences between high school and college
- How to set your own goals for success

No matter your age, no matter your background, the fact that you were admitted to college means you have the motivation to follow through and eventually earn a degree. Yet the sad fact is that many entering students drop out or flunk out. And the highest college dropout rate occurs during the first year.

What can go wrong so quickly? Well, take the student who left campus before the first day of classes because she was intimidated by the social activities the school had arranged for new students. Or the guy who wanted to meet other students so much that he went out every night and never cracked a book. Or the first-year student who maxed out his credit card the first week of the term and had no money for food. Or those who lacked clear goals for college or couldn't manage their time or never learned how to study for an exam or use the library, the Internet, and other sources to research a topic. Or the student of color who felt out of place on a predominantly white campus. Or the returning student who found it was nearly impossible to balance the responsibilities of work, family, and studies.

This book, as you will see, is a game plan for succeeding in college, a package of strategies that, if followed, can help you achieve more than you ever dreamed possible. We've grouped those strategies under three categories that we call Get Ready (The Basics), Get Set (Study, Study Study), and Go (The Extra Mile).

On the perforated card inside this book, you have probably already found the "Strategies for Success." We've printed these on a durable, portable card for a reason. We want you to keep the card with you, or post it someplace where you will see it often (like your bathroom mirror!). These 20 strategies, which correspond to sections of this book, will help you succeed in college. Many of the ideas may strike you as common sense, and many of them are. Nonetheless, you will benefit from carefully reading them and thinking about what they mean to you.

Here are the 20 strategies, with an explanation of how we think they can help you.

Strategies for Success

Get Ready: The Basics

1. **Show up for class.** When you miss even one day, you're missing something. You're also sending your instructor a message that you don't care. If you know you are going to miss class because of an appointment, sickness, or emergency,

Self-Assessment
Succeeding in College

Check the items that apply to you:

1. _______ I feel nervous about college. Now that I'm finally here, I wonder if I can make it through.
2. _______ I think I chose my major way back when I started high school, and I'm still comfortable with it.
3. _______ I chose a major because I had to, but I don't really have any clear goals in sight.
4. _______ I'm sure I won't change my major.
5. _______ I'm certain I will change majors, and that's probably not a smart thing.
6. _______ Since classes don't meet every day, I'm going to have no trouble studying.
7. _______ I aced high school. College should be no different.
8. _______ I don't need to ask for help with my study skills.
9. _______ I feel stressed, but I'd rather deal with it myself than ask for help.
10. _______ I haven't set any short- or long-term goals for the time I'm in college.

contact your instructor as soon as possible and certainly before the next class meeting. The most dangerous classes to miss are those at the start of the term.

2. **Complete work on time.** Not only may you face a grade penalty if you don't, you will most certainly irritate some of your teachers if you are perpetually late with assignments. Some instructors may have a policy of not accepting late work or penalizing you for it. Ask to be certain. If your work is late because of illness or an emergency, let your instructor know. It may help.
3. **Set up a weekly schedule.** And stick to it. Learning how to manage your time can make the difference between success and frustration. Get a portable appointment calendar from your campus bookstore this week or a PDA (Personal Digital Assistant) and always keep it handy. Consider using a computer calendar program as a backup to your written one.
4. **Give yourself a realistic workload.** If you are a full-time student, limit your workweek to 15 hours. Most students begin a downhill slide after that. Need more money? Consult a financial aid officer. Try to find a job on campus. Students who do and who work less than 15 hours have a higher graduation rate than those who work off campus and/or more than 15 hours. If you're stressed, enroll part-time. Stress is the enemy of learning.
5. **Discover how you learn best.** Explore learning style theory, which suggests that we are all individuals with differing approaches to the world around us, the information we receive, the decisions we make, and the way we choose to live and to learn. Perhaps you'll understand why you hate being alone and love to plan things in detail, while your best friend—or more important, your instructor—is just the other way around. You'll also discover how to accommodate your weaker learning preferences.

6. **Have realistic expectations.** At first you may be disappointed in the grades you make, but remember that college is a new experience and things can, and probably will, improve. Remember you are not alone. Millions of other students have faced the same uncertainties you may be facing. Hang on to that positive attitude. It makes a difference.

Get Set: Study, Study, Study

7. **Improve your study habits.** Starting with a time management plan, make every minute of every day count. Master the most effective methods for reading textbooks, listening, and taking notes in class, studying for exams, and using information sources on campus. If your campus has an academic skills center, visit it whenever you need help with your studies.
8. **Develop critical thinking skills.** Challenge. Ask why. Seek dependable information to prove your point. Look for unusual solutions to ordinary problems. Never accept something as fact simply because you found it on the Internet or someone tells you it's true. And don't be swayed by your emotions; keep your logical thinking powers at work.
9. **Participate in class.** Research indicates that students who involve themselves in class discussions usually remember more about the discussion than students who do not. As a result, they usually enjoy the class more and earn higher grades. Seek teachers who favor active learning; you'll find learning is also more fun this way.
10. **Learn how to remember more from every class.** Effective listening not only results in better notes but also helps you improve memory techniques—an important skill as exams approach.
11. **Learn from criticism.** Criticism can be healthy. And helpful. It's how we all learn. If you get a low grade, ask to meet with your instructor to discuss what you should do to improve your work.
12. **Study with a group.** Research shows that students who collaborate in study groups often earn the highest grades and survive college with fewer academic problems. If you have family responsibilities, consider inviting several other students to your home for a study group session.

Go: The Extra Mile

13. **Get to know at least one person on campus who cares about you.** It might be the teacher of this course, some other instructor, your academic advisor, someone at the counseling or career center, an advisor to a student organization, or an older student. You may have to take the initiative to establish this relationship, but it will be worth it.
14. **Get involved in campus activities.** Visit the student activities office. Work for the campus newspaper or radio station. Join a club or support group. Play intramural sports. Most campus organizations crave newcomers—you're their lifeblood.
15. **Become engaged in campus life and work.** You can do this by engaging in a practicum, an internship, or a field experience. Or you can perform community service as a volunteer. Or work with a faculty member on his or her research. Or enroll in a study abroad program. Going the extra mile is what engagement is all about. And students who are more engaged with their studies report that they have a more beneficial college experience.
16. **Find and use campus helping resources.** Academic, personal, and career services are usually free and confidential. Successful students use them. If you're a minority student, a student with a disability, or a returning student, locate the campus office that is designed to meet your specific needs. Check each chapter in this book for suggestions on "Where to Go for Help."
17. **Meet with your instructors and advisors.** This isn't high school. You should make it a point to meet with an instructor if you have something to discuss. Students who do tend to stay in college longer. Your instructors are required to have office hours; they expect you to visit. Also, find yourself a terrific academic advisor or counselor, someone you can go to for support and guidance.
18. **Enlist the support of your spouse, partner, or family.** As a returning student, you may need to adjust household routines and duties. Let others know when you need extra time to study. A supportive partner is a great ally, but a nonsupportive partner can threaten your success in college. If your partner feels threatened and tries to undermine what you are doing, sit down and talk it over, or seek counseling.
19. **Take your health seriously.** How much sleep you get, what you eat, whether you exercise, and what decisions you make about drugs, alcohol, and sex will all affect your well-being and how well you will do in classes. Find healthy ways to deal with stress. Avoid using legal prescription drugs "illegally." Your counseling center can help.
20. **Learn how to be assertive, yet tactful.** If you don't, others may walk all over you. If it's difficult for you to stand up for yourself, take assertiveness training. Be proud of your heritage. Stand tall and refuse to tolerate disrespect. Your counseling center probably offers workshops that can teach you to stand up for your rights in a way which respects the rights of others.

First-Year Commitment: Hangin' In

Why do so many students drop out of college in the first year?

For those fresh out of high school, a major problem involves newfound freedom in school. Your college teachers are not going to tell you how, or when to study. If you live on campus, your parents can't wake you in the morning, see that you eat properly and get enough sleep, monitor whether or how well you do your homework, or remind you to allow enough time to get to school. In almost every aspect of your life, getting it done suddenly depends on you.

For returning students, the opposite is true: a daunting lack of freedom. Working, caring for a family, and meeting other adult commitments and responsibilities compete for the time and attention it takes to do your best or even simply to survive in college. And the easiest thing to do is quit.

Whichever problem you are facing, what will motivate you to hang in? And what about the enormous investment of time and money that getting a college degree requires? Are you convinced that the investment will pay off? Or are you having thoughts such as these:

SEE EXERCISE 1.1: SOLVING A PROBLEM

- This is the first time someone has not been there to tell me I had to do something. Will I be able to handle all this freedom? Or will I just waste time?
- I've never been away from home before, and I don't know anybody. How am I going to make friends?
- I have responsibilities at home. Can I get through college and still manage to take care of my family? What will my family think about all the time I'll have to spend in classes and studying?
- As a minority on a primarily "white" campus, will I be in for some unpleasant surprises?
- Maybe college will be too difficult for me. I hear college professors are much more demanding than high school teachers.
- Not only do I miss being at home, but I hope I won't disappoint the people I care about and who expect so much of me.
- What if my children and spouse complain about all the time I spend studying?
- In high school, I got by without working too hard. Now I'll really have to study. Will I be tempted to cut corners, maybe even cheat?

Where to Go for Help

To find the college support services you need, ask your academic advisor or counselor; consult your college catalog, campus phone book, and home page on the Internet. Or call or visit student services (or student affairs). Most of these services are free. In subsequent chapters of this book, we will include a "Where to Go for Help" feature keyed to the chapter topic.

Academic Advisement Center. Help in choosing courses, information on degree requirements.
Academic Skills or Learning Center. Tutoring, help in study and memory skills, help in studying for exams.
Adult Reentry Center. Programs for returning students, supportive contacts with other adult students, information about services such as child care.
Career Center. Career library, interest assessments, counseling, help in finding a major, job and internship listings, co-op listings, interviews with prospective employers, help with résumés and interview skills.
Chaplains. Worship services, fellowship, personal counseling.
Commuter Services. List of off-campus housing, roommate lists, orientation to community. Maps, information on public transportation, child care, and so forth.
Computer Center. Minicourses, handouts on campus, and other computer resources.
Counseling Center. Confidential counseling on personal concerns. Stress management programs.
Disabled Student Services. Assistance in overcoming physical barriers or learning disabilities.
Financial Aid and Scholarship Office. Information on financial aid programs, scholarships, and grants.
Health Center. Help in personal nutrition, weight control, exercise, and sexuality. Information on substance abuse programs and other health issues. Often includes pharmacy.
Housing Office. Help in locating on- or off-campus housing.
Legal Services. Legal aid for students. If your campus has a law school, it may offer assistance by senior students.
Math Center. Help with math skills.
Physical Education Center. Facilities and equipment for exercise and recreational sports.
Writing Center. Help with writing assignments.

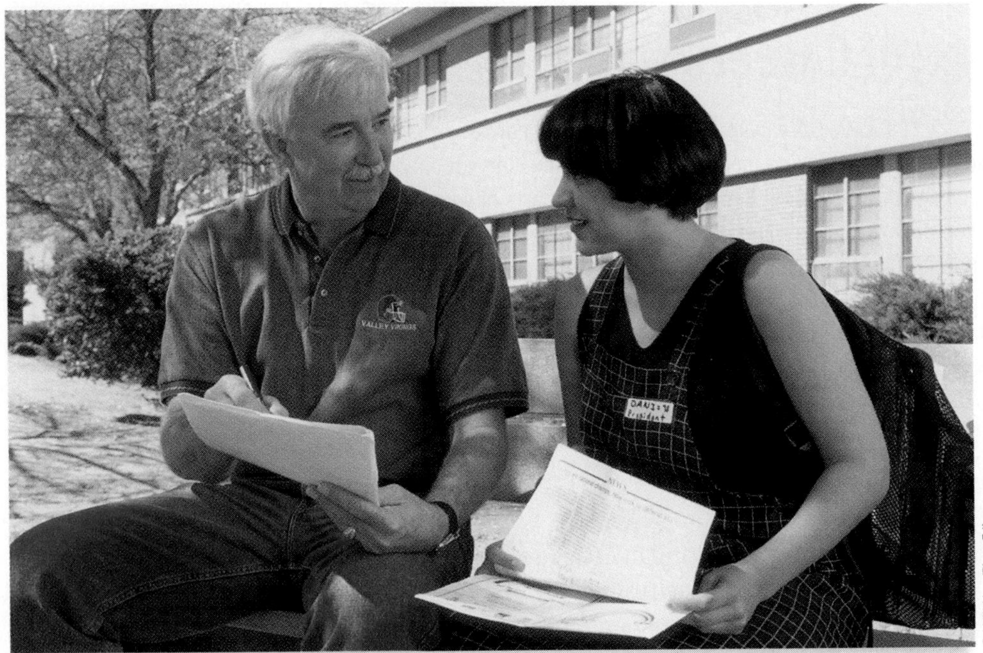

© Will Hart/PhotoEdit

- Will I like my roommate? What if he or she is from a different culture?
- What if I don't pick the right major? What if I don't know which major is right for me?
- Can I afford this? Can my parents afford this? I wouldn't want them to spend this much money only to see me fail.
- Maybe I'm the only one who's feeling like this. Maybe everyone else is just smarter than I am, and they know it.
- Looking around class makes me feel so old! Will I be able to keep up at my age?
- Will some teachers be biased because of my ethnic background?

SEE EXERCISE I.2: FOCUSING ON YOUR CONCERNS

High School versus College

Besides what we've already said, the mere differences between high school and college can threaten your survival—if you let them.

- College classes are larger and longer.
- College classes do not meet every day.
- College tests are given less frequently.

Examining Values

As you will discover later in this book, values form the basis of human behavior and lead either to compatibility or conflict between people.

Many students find that college life challenges their existing personal and moral values. First-year students are often startled at the diversity of personal moralities found on campus. For instance, in college you may discover even more alcohol, tobacco, and drug use than you saw in high school or in the working world. You may find yourself forming friendships with classmates whose personal values are politically different from yours. List three of the values you hold and several ways that those values have been challenged since you arrived on campus.

Speaking of Careers

Several decades ago, the majority of students attending college claimed they were there, first and foremost, to gain an education for life. Today, most students will tell you their reasons for choosing college have more to do with finding satisfactory careers that allow them to live comfortably for the rest of their lives. Bearing this in mind, think of college as "an investment in a fuller life." By *investment*, we mean the many years of hard work as well as the cost. And by *a fuller life*, we include not only your future career, but also the other parts of your life. College prepares you to be a more interesting person, whether at work or enjoying an evening of theater, music, ballet, and so forth. Or just being with someone you care about. Or having close friends over for dinner. Think about it. Isn't a "fuller life" what everyone ultimately wants?

- You will do more writing in college.
- You will have to choose from many more types of courses.
- Whereas peer pressure keeps many high school students from interacting with faculty, in college it's the norm to ask a teacher for counsel.
- You and your teachers will have more academic freedom—freedom to express different views, for example.
- College teachers usually have private offices and keep regular office hours.
- High school is more "textbook-focused," whereas college is more "lecture-focused."
- In high school you learn facts; there's little or no room for discussion or disagreement. In college you will be encouraged to do original research and to investigate differing points of view on a topic.
- College faculty are more likely to create and transmit original knowledge.
- College students have more work to do and more freedom and responsibility for getting it done.
- College students often live far from home.

Those Who Start and Those Who Finish

In 1900 fewer than 2 percent of Americans of traditional college age attended college. Today, new technologies and the information explosion are changing the workplace so drastically that few people can support themselves and their families adequately without some education beyond high school.

Today, more than 60 percent of high school graduates go on to college, with over 4,000 colleges serving more than 15 million students. Nearly half of those enrolling in college begin in two-year institutions. Adult students are also enrolling in record numbers. More than one-third of college students are over age 25.

Critical Thinking

From the list in this chapter, choose a strategy for success that is challenging for you. Brainstorm five reasons you find this strategy difficult to achieve. List five things you could do to master the strategy.

Table I.1 Unemployment and Earnings by Educational Attainment for Year-Round, Full-Time Workers Age 25+

2001 Unemployment Rate (%)	Education Attained 2000	Median Earnings ($)*
1.2	Professional degree	80,230
1.1	Doctorate	70,476
2.1	Master's degree	55,302
2.5	Bachelor's degree	46,276
2.9	Associate degree	35,389
3.5	Some college, no degree	32,400
4.2	High school graduate	28,807
7.3	Less than high school diploma	21,391

* These are *median* earnings, meaning half the group earned less and half the group earned more.

Source: Bureau of the Census, Bureau of Labor Statistics, 2002.

SEE WORKING TOGETHER EXERCISE: LIFE WITH AND WITHOUT COLLEGE

SEE EXERCISE I.3: SETTING LONG-TERM GOALS

In addition to higher earnings, according to the Carnegie Commission on Higher Education, as a college graduate, you will have a less erratic job history, will earn more promotions, and will likely be happier with your work. You will be less likely than a nongraduate to become unemployed. As the saying goes, "If you think education is expensive, try ignorance."

As the statistics in Table I.1 indicate, it pays to go to college in more ways than one. Not only does income go up, as a rule, with each degree earned, but the unemployment rate goes down as well. You not only stand to earn more with a college degree, you also stand to find it easier to get a job and hold on to it.

As for the strategies for success we described at the beginning of this chapter, review them periodically as you work through this book. You will find them listed on the opening page of every part of the book. As you revisit them, ask yourself if you feel you've developed skills in some of these areas. Which strategies have you mastered? Which do you still need to work on?

Reassess Yourself

Let's go back to the self-assessments that appear at the beginning of each chapter. These are opportunities for you to measure your progress. Each time you finish a chapter, we will ask you to return to the self-assessment for that chapter and see if you want to change any responses. Which of the items on page 5 did you check? Would you change any of your answers as a result of reading this chapter? If so, which ones, and why?

Exercises

The exercises at the end of each chapter will help you sharpen what we believe are the critical skills for college success: writing, critical thinking, learning in groups, planning, reflecting, and taking action. All these exercises, plus the Internet and InfoTrac® College Edition exercises, appear on the CD-ROM that accompanies this book.

EXERCISE I.1 Solving a Problem

What has been your biggest unresolved problem to date in college? What steps have you taken in attempting to solve it? Ask your instructor if you may write a note or e-mail to him or her about these two questions. Read your instructor's response and see if it's of any help to you. If you still have questions, ask to meet with your instructor.

Your Direct Access to InfoTrac® College Edition

If your instructor arranged for your purchase of this textbook to include a subscription, you can access InfoTrac® College Edition on the Internet. To set up your four-month InfoTrac® College Edition account, go to *<http://www.infotrac-college.com/wadsworth>* and submit the account number issued on the InfoTrac® College Edition insert that accompanies this book. The program will lead you through the enrollment process.

The InfoTrac® College Edition includes more than 10 million articles and abstracts from more than 5,000 periodicals. You'll find it easy to search for information using key words or the extensive Subject Guide. Many entries include the complete text of an article, which you can download to your computer. Each entry starts with an abstract to give you an idea of whether the article is likely to meet your needs.

Make InfoTrac® College Edition a regular part of your college success work. Use it to find information for writing papers and for broadening your learning in other courses, too.

Setting Goals for Success

College is an ideal time to begin setting and fulfilling short- and long-term goals. A short-term goal might be to set aside three hours this week to study chemistry, whereas a long-term goal might be to begin matching your career goals with the classes you plan to take while you're in college. It's okay if you don't yet know what you want to do with the rest of your life. It's even okay if you don't know what to major in. More than 60 percent of college students change majors at least once. The important thing is to always have a goal to work toward. In every chapter of this book, you'll find opportunities to set some short- and long-term goals. Regardless of what your goals are, the process is the same:

1. **Select a goal.** State it in measurable terms. Be specific about what you want to achieve and when (e.g., not "improve my study skills" but "master and use the recall column system of note taking by the end of October").
2. **Be sure that the goal is achievable.** Have you allowed enough time to pursue it? Do you have the necessary skills, strengths, and resources? If not, modify the goal to make it achievable.
3. **Be certain you genuinely want to achieve the goal.** Don't set out to work toward something only because you feel you should or because others tell you it's the thing to do. Be sure your goal will not have a negative impact on yourself or others and that it is consistent with your most important values.
4. **Know why the goal matters.** Be sure it has the potential to give you a sense of accomplishment.
5. **Identify and plan for difficulties you might encounter.** Find ways to overcome them.
6. **Devise strategies for achieving the goal.** How will you begin? What comes next? What should you avoid? Create steps for achieving your goal and set a timeline for the steps.[1]

Take a moment to set a goal for your first month in college.

My short-term goal is: ______________________________

I can achieve this goal by: ______________________________

I want to achieve this goal because: ______________________________

This goal matters because: ______________________________

I may encounter the following obstacles: ______________________________

My strategy for accomplishing this goal is: ______________________________

[1]Steps 1–6 are adapted from James D. McHolland and Roy W. Trueblood, *Human Potential Seminars*, Evanston, Illinois, 1972. Used by permission of the authors.

EXERCISE I.2 Focusing on Your Concerns

Browse the table of contents of this book. Find one or more chapters that address your most important concerns. Take a brief look at each chapter you have chosen. If a chapter appears to be helpful, read it before your instructor assigns it and try to follow its advice.

EXERCISE I.3 Setting Long-Term Goals

Use the six-step goal-setting process described on page 12 to identify one of your long-term goals and create a plan for achieving it. Make sure you can complete the following sentences:

My long-term goal is: ______________________________

I can achieve this goal by: ______________________________

I want to achieve this goal because: ______________________________

This goal matters because: ______________________________

I may encounter the following obstacles: ______________________________

My strategy for accomplishing this goal is: ______________________________

Working Together Exercise
Life with and without College

This chapter has stressed the differences between a high school and college education. Imagine you are still trying to decide whether or not to attend college. In a small group, make a list of reasons to earn a college degree. Then make a list of reasons to obtain a graduate degree. Then make a list of reasons not to go to college. For example, pipefitters earn impressive salaries, whereas librarians earn much less. How do you justify a college education on those terms?

See the CD-ROM for these additional exercises as well as all other exercises appearing in this chapter

Internet Exercise I.1	Using the *Digest of Education Statistics*
Internet Exercise I.2	How Other Colleges "Work"
Internet Exercise I.3	What's Changed in the Last Five Years?
InfoTrac® College Edition Exercise I.1	Researching the Value of College
Exercise I.4	Your Reasons for Attending College
Exercise I.5	The Many Reasons for College

1 Managing Your Time

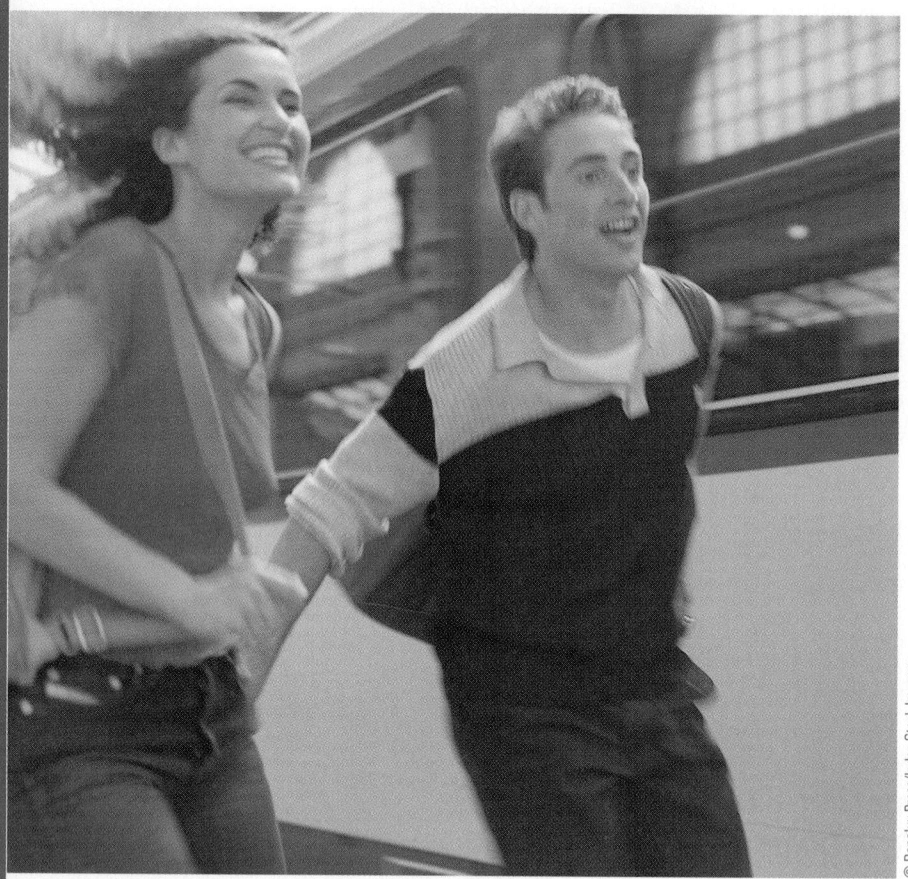

© Benelux Press/Index Stock Imagery

Jeanne L. Higbee of the University of Minnesota, Twin Cities, contributed her valuable and considerable expertise to the writing of this chapter.

Going Forward: Student Voices

My manager needs me to go to work tonight. I have a quiz in Spanish tomorrow, tests in math and psych on Thursday, and an English paper due on Friday. No way I can get all this done! I'm so stressed I can't even think. And I can't pull "all-nighters" three nights in a row!

Looking Back: Author Voices

Looking back on it now, I can't believe that I didn't start using a pocket calendar until after college when I was 25. Now, I never leave home without it. In all my years of college teaching my most successful students always have told me that time management was the key ingredient in their success. I believe them. So should you. **John Gardner**

In this chapter, YOU WILL LEARN

- How to take control of your time and your life
- How to use goals and objectives to guide your planning
- How to combat procrastination
- How to use a daily planner and other tools
- How to organize your day, your week, your school term
- The value of a "to do" list
- How to avoid distractions

ow do you approach time? Because people have different personalities and come from different cultures, they may also view time in different ways. Some of these differences may have to do with your preferred style of learning.

Time management involves

- Understanding when, how, and why you procrastinate
- Deciding where your priorities lie
- Anticipating future needs and possible changes
- Placing yourself in control of your time
- Making a commitment to being punctual
- Carrying out your plans

The first step to effective time management is recognizing that *you* can be in control.

How often do you find yourself saying, "I don't have time"? Once a week? Once a day? Several times per day? The next time you find yourself saying this, stop and think about that statement. Do you not have time, or have you made a choice, whether consciously or unconsciously, not to make time for that particular task or activity? When we say that we don't have time, we imply that we do not have a choice. But we *do* have a choice. We *do* have control over how we use our time. We *do* have control over many of the commitments we choose to make.

Being in control means that you make your own decisions. Two of the most often cited differences between high school and college are increased autonomy, or independence, and greater responsibility. If you are not a recent high school graduate, you have most likely already experienced a higher level of independence. But returning to school creates additional responsibilities above and beyond those you already have, whether those include employment, family, community service, or other activities. Whether you are beginning college immediately after high school, or are continuing your education after a hiatus, now is the time to establish new priorities for how you spend your time. To take control of your life and your time, and to guide your decisions, it is wise to begin by setting some goals for the future.

Setting Goals and Objectives

What are some of your goals for the coming decade? One goal may be to earn a two-year or four-year degree or technical certificate. Perhaps you plan to go on to gradu-

Self-Assessment
Time Management

Take a few moments to reflect on your past experiences with time management. Then respond to the following questions:

1. ________ How conscious am I of time passing? Do I always wear a watch?
2. ________ Do I procrastinate? Does whether I procrastinate depend on the task?
3. ________ How do my family, culture, lifestyle, commitments, gender, age, and other factors influence my views on time management?
4. ________ Do I consider myself a "morning person"? A "night person"? What are my most productive times of the day? How can I use those times of the day effectively?
5. ________ Am I punctual? Do I think it is important to be punctual? Am I early, prompt, or late to class, appointments, or meetings?
6. ________ Am I easily distracted?
7. ________ How do I prioritize my time? Do I value social activities more than being by myself? Goofing off more than studying?
8. ________ How does my use of time affect my stress level? Does my anxiety about getting work done on time (or not) affect the quality of my work?
9. ________ What are some specific things I do to manage my time? What tools do I use for time management (e.g., personal planner, hand-held PDA)?

ate or professional school. You already may have decided on the career that you want to pursue. As you look to the future, you may see yourself buying a new car, or owning a home. Maybe you want to own your own business someday, want time off to travel every year, or want to be able to retire early. Time management is one of the most effective tools to assist you in meeting these goals.

Your goals can be lofty, but they should also be attainable. You do not want to establish such high goals that you are setting yourself up for failure. Some goals may also be measurable, such as completing a degree program or earning a 3.0 or higher grade point average (GPA). But other goals, like "to be happy" or "to be successful," may mean different things to different people. No matter how you define success, you should be able to identify some specific steps you can take to achieve this goal. Perhaps one of the goals you will set is to find a good job upon completion of your degree. Now, at the beginning of your college experience, is an important time to think about what that means. A few of your objectives may be to determine what is a "good" job and to make yourself more competitive in the job market.

A college degree and good grades may not be enough. When setting goals and objectives and thinking about how you will allocate your time, you may want to consider the importance of:

- Having a well-rounded résumé when you graduate
- Setting aside time to participate in extracurricular activities
- Gaining leadership experience
- Engaging in community service
- Taking advantage of internship or co-op opportunities
- Developing job-related skills

- Participating in a study abroad program
- Pursuing relevant part- or full-time employment while you are also attending classes

When it is time to look for a permanent job, you want to be able to demonstrate that you have used your college years wisely, and that requires planning and effective time management, which in themselves are skills that employers value.

Beating Procrastination

SEE EXERCISE 1.1: UNDERSTANDING WHY YOU PROCRASTINATE

You've just begun to study for tomorrow's history test and a friend pops in and asks you to go to a concert. You drop the books, change clothes, and you're out the door.

That's procrastination. It can be an enemy for some and a friend for others. But generally, the more you procrastinate, the greater the danger of having tough times in college and throughout life.

Some of the smartest, most committed, and most creative people procrastinate. Being a procrastinator doesn't mean you are lazy or unmotivated. You shouldn't beat yourself up about it. Instead, use that energy to understand what is motivating you to procrastinate, even when you know you're sabotaging your success.

If the risks of procrastination are so high and the results so grim, why do we do it in the first place? Often, because as we anticipate meeting a particular obligation, we are struck by fear and its corollaries:

- **Performance anxiety.** Fear of doing a poor job. A lack of self-esteem may result in your believing that you cannot master a task no matter what you do, so you don't even try.
- **Dreading the outcome.** Fear of what will follow. If you do a poor job, you may be scolded by the teacher, or worse, fail the course.
- **Disliking the task.** Fear of specific steps. You may dread the early part of the project but may feel comfortable about what follows.
- **Boredom.** Fear of monotony. You've read the first two assigned articles and almost fell asleep. What's the point of continuing?

Overcoming procrastination takes self-discipline, self-control, and self-awareness. Schwartz and Dallett suggest:[1]

- Always anticipate the good that will come from finishing the task on time. Focus on your goal and its positive effects. Remind yourself that you can learn skills or gain knowledge that you need to accomplish a task. No one will think you are dumb; they will perceive you as someone who is willing to invest time and energy to improve your performance.
- Do the awkward or difficult task early in the day. You will then feel the exhilaration that comes with accomplishing a dreaded task.
- Give yourself credit for all that you do. Seek quality overall rather than perfection in everything. Rather than pressuring yourself too much, face your requirements and talents realistically.

Here are other ways to beat procrastination:

- Say to yourself, "I need to do this now, and I am going to do this now. I will pay a price if I do not do this now." Then get started.
- Use your "to do" list to focus on the things that aren't getting done. Working from a list will give you a feeling of accomplishment.

[1]Andrew Schwartz and Estelina Dallett, "Procrastinate." *The CPA Journal*, April 1993, *63*, no. 4:83 (3).

Examining Values

Discovering you procrastinate is actually an opportunity to reexamine your values and priorities. What is really important to you? Are these values important enough to forego some temporary fun or laziness in order to get down to work? Are they important enough to motivate you to seek help in overcoming procrastination?

- Break down big jobs into smaller steps. Tackle small tasks first.
- Promise yourself a reward for finishing the task. For more substantial tasks, give yourself bigger rewards.
- Eliminate distractions. Say "no" to friends and family who want your attention. Agree to meet them later. Let them be your reward for studying.
- Don't make or take phone calls during planned study sessions. Close your door.

A very different management view by Deep and Sussman[2] describe procrastinators as those who:

- Eagerly volunteer for impossible workloads. Want to take on more important tasks but seem to lack the ability to succeed.
- Agree to or suggest impossible deadlines.
- Often fail to deliver. His or her procrastination may be due to perfectionism, a fear of failure, or even a fear of success.
- Follow through only when constantly monitored.
- Spend more time on giving the appearance of progress than on actual progress.
- Blame bad luck or others when confronted with failure to deliver, or say, "I knew you'd want it done right."

Recent research indicates that college students who procrastinate in their studies also avoid confronting other tasks and problems and are more likely to develop unhealthy habits such as higher alcohol consumption, smoking, insomnia, poor diet, and lack of exercise. If you cannot get your procrastination under control, it is in your best interest to seek help at your campus counseling center before you begin to feel as if you are losing control over other aspects of your life as well.

SEE EXERCISE 1.2: THE IDEAL CLASS SCHEDULE

Setting Priorities

This book is full of suggestions for enhancing academic success. However, the bottom-line is keeping your eyes on the prize and taking control of your time and your life. Keeping your goals in mind, establish priorities in order to use your time effectively.

First, determine what your priorities are: attending classes, studying, working, spending time with the people who are important to you. Then think about the necessities of life: sleeping, eating, bathing, exercising, and relaxing. Leave time for fun activities like talking with friends, watching TV, going out for the evening, and so forth; you deserve them. But finish what *needs* to be done before you move from work to pleasure. And don't forget about personal time. Depending on your personality and cultural background, you may require more or less time to be alone.

If you live in a residence hall or share an apartment with other college students, communicate with your roommate(s) about how you can coordinate your class

[2]Sam Deep and Lyle Sussman, "When an Employee Says 'Can Do'—But Doesn't" (excerpt from "What to Say to Get What You Want"). *Executive Female*, May–June 1992, *15*, no. 3: 16(1).

schedules so that you each have some privacy. If you live at home with your family, particularly if you are a parent, work with your family to create special times as well as quiet study times.

Setting priorities is an important step. You are the only one who can decide what comes first, and you are the one who will need to accept the ramifications of your decisions.

You also must set priorities when you allocate your study time. You may have to prioritize the assignment that is due tomorrow over reading the chapters that will be covered in a test next week. Understandably, you do not want to procrastinate on all the reading until the night before the exam. Planning is critical or you will always find yourself struggling to meet each deadline.

Use a Daily Planner

In college, as in life, you will quickly learn that managing time is an important key not only to success, but to survival. A good way to start is to look at the big picture. Use the *term assignment preview* (Figure 1.1) on pages 20–21 to give yourself an idea of what's in store for you. Complete your term assignment preview by the beginning of the second week of classes so that you can continue to use your time effectively. Then purchase a week-at-a-glance organizer for the current year. Your campus bookstore may sell one designed just for your school, with important dates and deadlines already provided. If you prefer to use an electronic planner, go to the calendar link on your college's Web site and enter the key dates you need to know in your planner.

Regardless of the format you prefer (electronic or hard copy), enter the notes from your preview sheets into your planner, and continue to enter all due dates as soon as you know them. Write in meeting times and locations, scheduled social events (jot down phone numbers, too, in case something comes up and you need to cancel), study time for each class you're taking, and so forth. Carry your planner with you in a convenient place. *Now* is the time to get into the habit of using a planner to help you keep track of commitments and maintain control of your schedule.

This practice will become invaluable to you in the world of work. Check your notes daily for the current week and the coming week. Choose a specific time of day to do this, perhaps just before you begin studying, before you go to bed, or at a set time on weekends. But check it daily, and at the same time of day. It takes just a moment to be certain that you aren't forgetting something important, and it helps relieve stress!

Maintain a "To Do" List

Keeping a to do list can also help you avoid feeling stressed or out of control. Some people start a new list every day or once a week. Others keep a running list, and only throw a page away when everything on the list is done. Use your to do list to keep track of all the tasks you need to remember, not just academics. You might include errands you need to run, appointments you need to make, e-mail messages you need to send, and so on. Develop a system for prioritizing the items on your list—highlight them; use colored ink; or mark them with one, two, or three stars, or A, B, C. You can use your to do list in conjunction with your planner (see Figure 1.2).

As you complete each task, cross it off your list. You will be amazed at how much you have accomplished, and how good you feel about it.

Guidelines for Scheduling Week by Week

- Begin by entering all of your commitments for the week—classes, work hours, family commitments, and so on—on your schedule (see Figure 1.3).

	Monday	Tuesday	Wednesday	Thursday	Friday
Week 1					
Week 2					
Week 3					
Week 4					

	Monday	Tuesday	Wednesday	Thursday	Friday
Week 5					
Week 6					
Week 7					
Week 8					

Figure 1.1 **Term Assignment Preview**
Using the course syllabi provided by your instructors, enter all due dates on this term calendar. For longer assignments, such as term papers, divide the task into smaller parts and establish your own deadline for each part of the assignment. Give yourself deadlines for choosing a topic, completing your library research, developing an outline of the paper, writing a first draft, and so on.

	Monday	Tuesday	Wednesday	Thursday	Friday
Week 9					
Week 10					
Week 11					
Week 12					

	Monday	Tuesday	Wednesday	Thursday	Friday
Week 13					
Week 14					
Week 15					
Week 16					

Tuesday 9 am – History Class
10–11 am – Study history with Bruce
11–noon – free time. Study history notes
Lunch: Pizzarama with Jeff and Elaine
1:30 – Classes all afternoon till 4:30
Room at 5 and meet Luanne for dinner
7 pm – Start studying for Spanish and Math classes

Figure 1.2
Whatever chicken scratch it may be to someone else, a to do list is your guide to prioritizing the day.

SEE EXERCISE 1.3: TRACKING "ACTUAL TIME"

- Examine your toughest weeks on your term assignment preview sheet (see Figure 1.1). If paper deadlines and test dates fall during the same week, find time to finish some assignments early to free up study time for tests. Note this in your planner.
- Try to reserve two hours of study time for each hour spent in class. This "two-for-one" rule is widely accepted and reflects faculty members' expectations for how much work you should be doing to earn a good grade in their classes.
- Break large assignments such as term papers into smaller steps such as choosing a topic, doing research, creating a mind map or an outline, writing a first draft, and so on. Add deadlines in your schedule for each of the smaller portions of the project.
- All assignments are not equal. Estimate how much time you will need for each one and begin your work early. A good time manager frequently finishes assignments before actual due dates to allow for emergencies.
- Keep track of how much time it takes you to complete different kinds of tasks. For example, depending on your skills and interests, it may take longer to read a chapter in a biology text than in a literature text.
- Set aside time for research and other preparatory tasks. Most campuses have learning centers or computer centers that offer tutoring, walk-in assistance, or workshops to assist you with computer programs, databases, or the Internet.
- Schedule at least three aerobic workouts per week. (Walking to and from classes doesn't count!)

Use Figure 1.3 to tentatively plan how you will spend your hours in a typical week.

Organizing Your Day

Being a good student does not necessarily mean grinding away at studies and doing little else. Keep the following points in mind as you organize your day using a daily planner as shown in Figure 1.4:

SEE EXERCISE 1.4: YOUR DAILY PLAN

- Set realistic goals for your study time. Assess how long it takes to read a chapter in different types of texts and how long it takes you to review your notes from different instructors and schedule your time accordingly. Give yourself adequate time to review and then test your knowledge when preparing for exams.
- Use waiting time (on the bus, before class, waiting for appointments) to review.
- Prevent forgetting by allowing time to review as soon as reasonable after class.
- Know your best time of day to study.
- Don't study on an empty or full stomach.
- Pay attention to where you seem to study most effectively, and keep going back to that place. Keep all the supplies you need there and make sure you have ade-

	Sunday	Monday	Tuesday	Wednesday	Thursday	Friday	Saturday
6:00							
7:00							
8:00							
9:00							
10:00							
11:00							
12:00							
1:00							
2:00							
3:00							
4:00							
5:00							
6:00							
7:00							
8:00							
9:00							
10:00							
11:00							
12:00							

Figure 1.3 **Weekly Timetable**
A chart like this can help you organize your weekly schedule and keep track of how you're spending your time. Checking it at the end of each week is a good way to make yourself aware of ways that you may have misjudged how you use and manage your time.

DAILY PLANNER	
DATE MON TUE WED THU FRI SAT SUN	
APPOINTMENTS	
TIME	
8	
9	
10	
11	
12	
1	
2	
3	
4	
5	
6	
7	
8	

DAILY PLANNER	
DATE MON TUE WED THU FRI SAT SUN	
✔ TO DO	
PRIORITY	ESTIMATED TIME

Figure 1.4 Sample Daily Planner
List all of your classes and appointments for the day on the left side. Enter your to do list for the day on the opposite page. In the boxes provided, indicate A for top priority, B for a lower level of priority, and so on. Then return to the left-hand page to schedule times to complete your highest-priority tasks.

quate lighting, a chair with sufficient back support, and enough desk space to spread out everything you need.

- Study difficult or boring subjects first, when you are fresh. (*Exception:* If you are having trouble getting started, it might be easier to get started with your favorite subject.)
- Avoid studying similar subjects back to back if you might confuse the material presented in each.
- Divide study time into 50-minute blocks. Study for 50 minutes, take a 10- or 15-minute break, and then study for another 50-minute block. Try not to study for more than three 50-minute blocks in a row, or you will find that you are not accomplishing 50 minutes' worth of work. (In economics, this is known as the law of diminishing returns.)
- Break extended study sessions into a variety of activities, each with a specific objective. For example, begin by reading, then develop "flash cards" by writing key terms and their definitions or formulae on note cards, and finally test yourself on what you have read. You cannot expect yourself to concentrate on reading in the same text for three consecutive hours.
- Restrict repetitive, distracting, and time-consuming tasks such as checking your e-mail to a certain time, not every hour.

Where to Go for Help

ON CAMPUS

Academic Skills or Learning Center. Along with assistance on studying for exams, reading textbooks, and taking notes, these centers have specialists in time management who can offer advice for your specific problems.

Counseling Center. Another source to consider if your problems with time management involve emotional issues you are unable to resolve.

Your Academic Advisor/Counselor. If you have a good relationship with this person, he or she may be able to offer advice or refer you to another person on campus, including those in the offices above.

A Fellow Student. A friend and good student who is willing to help you with time management can be one of your most valuable resources in this area.

ONLINE

Go to **<http://www.dartmouth.edu/admin/acskills/success/time.html>** and review the contents of this page. Under "Time Management Resources," click to view the Time Management Video. You will need QuickTime® for this, which can be downloaded free from the QuickTime site.

ON INFOTRAC® COLLEGE EDITION

Using InfoTrac® College Edition, find the following article: "Time Management at Its Finest" (time management among business students), Amy Lamar, *Business Record (Des Moines)*, April 9, 2001, 17, no. i15:14. The article discusses how a single mother, a commuter, a stay-at-home dad, and a married couple cope with school and other responsibilities.

- Be flexible! You cannot anticipate every disruption to your plans. Build extra time into your schedule so that unexpected interruptions do not necessarily prevent you from meeting your goals.
- Reward yourself! Develop a system of short- and long-term study goals and rewards for meeting those goals.

Making Your Time Management Plan Work

With the best intentions, some students using a time management plan allow themselves to become overextended. If there is not enough time to carry your course load and meet your commitments, drop any courses before the drop date so you won't have a low grade on your permanent record. If you are on financial aid, keep in mind that you must be registered for a certain number of credit hours to be considered a full-time student and thereby maintain your current level of financial aid.

Don't Overextend Yourself

Learn to say no. Do not take on more than you can handle. Do not feel obligated to provide a reason; you have the right to decline requests that will prevent you from getting your own work done. If you're a commuter student, or if you must carry a heavy workload in order to afford going to school, you may prefer scheduling your classes together in blocks without breaks.

Although block scheduling allows you to cut travel time by attending school one or two days a week, and may provide more flexibility for scheduling employment or

Speaking of Careers

Writing in "Progressive Grocer," May 2001, Gerald Nilsson-Weiskott reminds us that the advent of the computer in the early 1980s was expected to increase leisure time, reduce the workweek to 32 hours, and enable people to achieve greater balance in their lives. In reality, people are working harder and longer, he explains, because of computers, e-mail, cell phones, and fax machines. Technology has caused us all to expect immediate responses to our questions, with little time left for thinking.

"We come in earlier, work later and on weekends. We are good at keeping busy, but not at getting the important things resolved. We are all experiencing 'hurry sickness,' and it's getting worse," Nilsson-Weiskott warns.

Two strategies that may help workers: Have a "no internal interruptions" policy—phone calls or drop-ins—for 2 hours each day. Then batch your phone calls. In addition, spend 15 minutes planning your day. Prioritize effectively so you are making good decisions about the use of your time.

Gerald Nilsson-Weiskott, Ph.D., is founder of the Leadership Development Group, Columbus, Ohio, specializing in stress and change management, and a lecturer at Ohio State University's School of Public Policy and Management.

family commitments, it can also have significant drawbacks. There is little time to process information or to study between classes. If you become ill on a class day, you could fall behind in all your classes. You may become fatigued sitting in class after class. Finally, you might become stressed when exams are held in several classes on the same day.

Block scheduling may work better if you can attend lectures at an alternative time in case you are absent, if you alternate classes with free periods, and if you seek out instructors who allow you flexibility in completing assignments.

Reduce Distractions

Where should you study? Avoid places associated with leisure—the kitchen table, the living room, or in front of the TV—they lend themselves to interruptions by others. It's not usually a good idea to study in bed. Either you will drift off when you need to study, or you will learn to associate your bed with studying and not be able to go to sleep when you need to. Instead, find quiet places to do your work.

Try to stick to a routine as you study. The more firmly you have established a specific time and a quiet place to study, the more effective you will be in keeping up with your schedule. If you have larger blocks of time available on the weekend, for example, take advantage of that time to review or catch up on major projects, such as term papers, that can't be completed effectively in 50-minute blocks. Break down large tasks and take one thing at a time; then you will make more progress toward your ultimate academic goals.

Here are some more tips to help you deal with distractions:

- Don't snack while you study. Ever wonder where that whole bag of chips went? However, it's fine to take your textbook with you to lunch or dinner, if you're dining alone. With a healthy meal in front of you, you can multitask: feeding your mind while you're feeding your body.
- Leave the TV, CD player, tape deck, and radio off, unless the background noise or music really helps you concentrate on your studies or drowns out more distracting noises (people laughing or talking in other rooms or down the hallway, for instance).
- Don't let personal concerns interfere with studying. If necessary, call a friend or write in a journal before you start to study, and then put your worries away. You

Setting Goals for Success

Brainstorm some goals for prioritizing your time in college. What's most important to you? Academics? Being on a sports team? Keeping a job? Your children? Using the goal-setting steps you read about in the Introduction, determine how you will achieve academic success without having to disrupt your priorities.

My priorities are:

1. ____________________

2. ____________________

3. ____________________

My time management goal is: ____________________

I can achieve this goal by: ____________________

I want to achieve this goal because: ____________________

It's important because: ____________________

I may encounter these obstacles: ____________________

My strategy for accomplishing this goal is to: ____________________

might actually put your journal in a drawer and consider that synonymous with putting your problems away.

- Develop an agreement with the people you live with about "quiet" hours.

Time and Critical Thinking

Few important questions in higher education have a right or wrong answer. Good critical thinkers have a high tolerance for ambiguity. Confronted by a difficult question, they suspend judgment until they can gather information and weigh the merits of different arguments. Thus, effective time management does not always mean making decisions or finishing projects hastily. Effective critical thinkers resist finalizing their thoughts on important questions until they believe that they have developed the best answers possible.

Critical Thinking

Twenty years ago, some people predicted that computers and the Internet would reduce the amount of time it takes to get things done. It may be true that we can get some things done faster, but the result is usually that we expect—or others expect us—to do more than ever before. As a society, we're exposed to a lot more distractions than our parents were, because we are constantly available via e-mail, cell phones, and instant messaging. How can we manage our time, instead of letting technology manage us? Brainstorm some strategies for preserving blocks of quality time for reading and studying. Also, list some ideas for how you can use technology to help you manage your time.

This is not an argument in favor of ignoring deadlines, but it does suggest the value of beginning your research, reading, and even the writing phases of a project early, so that you will have time to change direction if necessary as you gather new insights. Give your thoughts time to incubate. Allow time to visit the library more than once. Talking about your ideas with other students or your teacher can also be helpful. Sometimes, insights come unexpectedly, when you are not consciously thinking about a problem. If you begin a project as early as you can, you will have time to give it the level of thought it deserves.

Reassess Yourself

We placed the chapter on time management at the front of the book because we believe it is the key to all the other skills you will develop during your college years. Also, as we have said, using a good time management system the rest of your life can free you from some of the stress and confusion you are bound to face from time to time. Time can be our greatest resource or our worst enemy. Choose the former. Now go back and review your answers to the self-assessment. Are there any responses you now want to change? And take a time out before your next chapter assignment. Which of the items on page 16 did you check? Would you change any of your answers as a result of reading this chapter? If so, which ones, and why?

Exercises

Each of these exercises will let you further explore the topic of each chapter. You'll find all these exercises, plus Internet and InfoTrac® College Edition exercises, on the CD-ROM that accompanies this book.

EXERCISE 1.1 Understanding Why You Procrastinate

Check the items that may explain why it's difficult for you to do things on time:

____I'm afraid I won't do a good job.

____I believe everyone else in class will do a better job.

____I'm afraid of what my teacher will say about my work

____I just don't like the assignment. If I did, I'd have no problem.

____I know I'll get bored if I start working on this.

____I always volunteer to do too much and then can't get started on anything.

Next, review your choices and come up with one suggestion for combating every one of them:

1. ______________________________

2. ______________________________

3. ______________________________

4. ______________________________

5. ______________________________

EXERCISE 1.2 The Ideal Class Schedule

Using the weekly timetable (see Figure 1.3), create your ideal class schedule. Then look in your school's schedule of courses for next term and see if you can find courses you need that fit your ideal schedule. Complete this activity before you meet with your advisor to talk about registration for next term.

EXERCISE 1.3 Tracking Actual Time

Using the weekly timetable (see Figure 1.3) or your planner or electronic organizer, keep track of how you spend your time every hour for an entire week. Fill in every time slot. Then count how many hours you spent on various activities. How many hours did you spend studying? With family? Socializing? By yourself/personal time? Exercising? Relaxing? Working? Sleeping? Doing household chores such as laundry or dishes? Watching television? Eating? Shopping? Reading for pleasure? Talking on the phone? What activities merit more time? On which activities should you be spending less time? In what ways did you waste time?

EXERCISE 1.4 Your Daily Plan

Using one day from this week's schedule, make a daily plan by filling in the daily planner in Figure 1.4. Circle the day of the week. List the day's appointments on the page with hours of the day. On the opposite page, list your to do activities. Using a simple priority system, label them with an A, B, or C, with A's deserving the most attention. By tackling these first, you may not finish your list but you probably will be more satisfied with your accomplishments.

Working Together Exercise
Predicting Time Usage

Predict your time usage. Interview another student in your class about how he or she believes they spend the hours of one week on particular activities—sleeping, attending class, studying, and working, for instance. In turn, have the student interview you. Carry that student's notes about you around for a week and compare it to how you actually spent the time. How accurately did you predict your week?

See the CD-ROM for these additional exercises as well as all other exercises appearing in this chapter

Exercise 1.5	Reward Yourself
Internet Exercise 1.1	Only 168 Hours in a Week
Internet Exercise 1.2	Limiting Your Time Online
Internet Exercise 1.3	Accessing Your Institution's Academic Calendar
Internet Exercise 1.4	Procrastination Resources
InfoTrac® College Edition Exercise 1.1	Getting It Together
InfoTrac® College Edition Exercise 1.2	Balancing Work and School
InfoTrac® College Edition Exercise 1.3	Biorhythms and Time

2 Discovering How You Learn

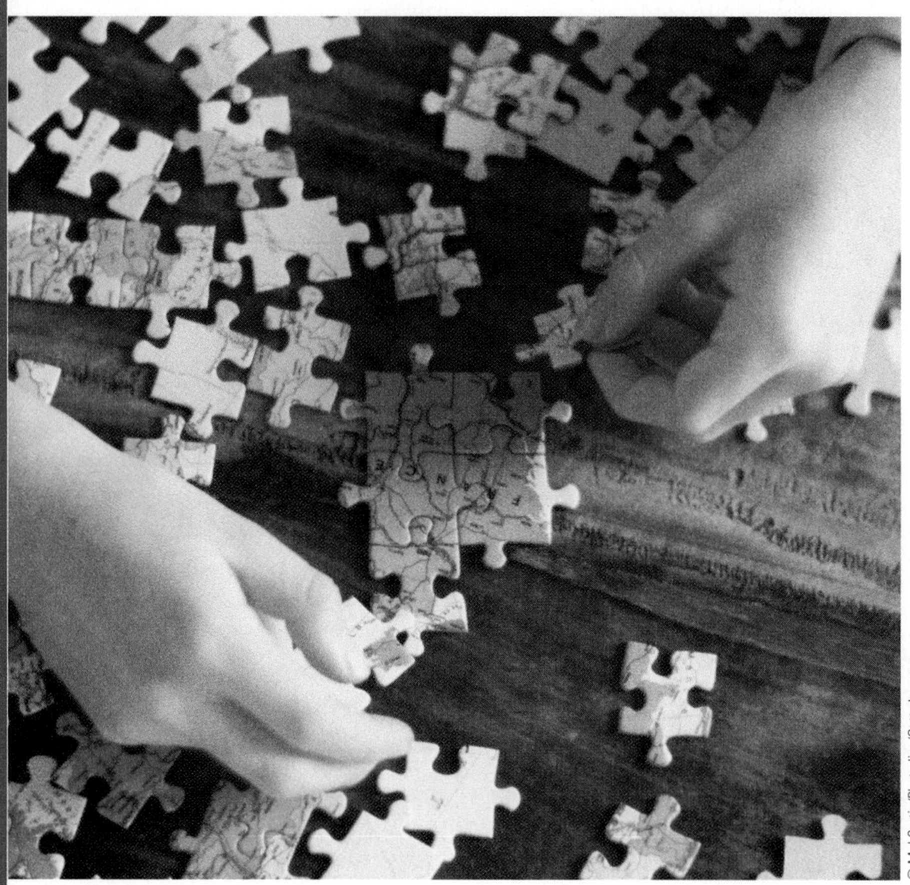

© Mel Curtis/Photodisc/Getty Images

Tom Carskadon of Mississippi State University contributed his valuable and considerable expertise to the writing of this chapter.

Going Forward: Student Voices

I studied like crazy for my big test, but the professor's questions were totally out of left field. I knew everything important, but I failed it.

Looking Back: Author Voices

My family did not own a TV while I was growing up. They wanted us to become readers. I listened to a lot of radio, and read a great deal, too. I was an "auditory" learner and did well in lecture courses. But today most of my students aren't auditory learners and don't like lecture courses. Too bad, because they are going to get a lot of them! **John Gardner**

In this chapter, YOU WILL LEARN

- How to determine your learning preferences
- How your learning style can affect your classroom behavior
- How a mix of learning styles can enhance study groups
- How to adapt to your instructors' teaching styles

Perhaps you find history easier than mathematics or biology easier than English. Part of the explanation has to do with what is called your learning preferences—the way you prefer to acquire knowledge, which is a part of your overall personality.

Learning preferences affect not only how you absorb material as you study, but also how you draw conclusions from it. Some students learn more effectively through visual means, others by listening to lectures, and still others through class discussion, hands-on experience, memorization, or a combination of these.

Visual learners have to "see it to believe it." They may have artistic abilities, may find some sounds irritating, and may have trouble following lectures. They may do better using graphics as a learning aid. They tend to remember notes by visualizing precisely where on their notebook page they wrote the information they seek.

Auditory learners remember best what they hear. They may have difficulty following written directions and may find reading and writing exhausting. They may do better by supplementing written notes with a tape of the lecture (with the instructor's permission), summarizing on tape what they read, and participating actively in discussions.

Tactile learners tend to remember what they touch. They like hands-on learning, may have difficulty sitting still, and learn better through physical activity. They may do better in active settings such as lab work and role playing, or using a computer and taking frequent study breaks.

Some people learn better by studying alone, and others prefer study groups. Although no one learning style is inherently better than another, you will need to adapt to the style required in a course.

Learning about Your Personality and Psychological Type

Personality is a general term referring to your characteristic ways of thinking, feeling, and behaving. *Psychological type* refers specifically to the personality theory of Carl Gustav Jung, the great twentieth-century psychoanalyst. Jung described the different personality types, but it was Isabel Briggs Myers and her mother Katharine Cook Briggs who developed a reliable test for identifying and measuring the psychological types described by Jung. This test is called the Myers–Briggs Type Indicator® (MBTI®). Although there are many different theories and tests of personality, in this chapter we will be using the work of Jung, Myers, and Briggs.

We have a good reason for choosing this approach: The MBTI® is the most widely used personality test designed for normal individuals, and it is given to

Self-Assessment

Personality and Learning Styles

Take a moment to reflect on these statements about personality and learning styles. Check those statements that are true:

1. ______ Some personality types are a lot better than others.

2. ______ It's best to avoid being an introvert.

3. ______ The help of a trained professional is required to determine your personality type.

4. ______ Personality tests are mostly bunk (unproven and useless).

5. ______ People will do better if they concentrate on their own favorite learning styles rather than try to use those that work better for other people.

6. ______ Each learning style has its own particular traps.

7. ______ If you can figure out your instructor's learning preferences, you can study for the kind of test you think your instructor is most likely to give.

8. ______ It's better to work where most of your coworkers match your personality type.

9. ______ When it comes to dating and mating, opposites attract.

10. ______ If you want to learn the most in college, surround yourself with people whose personality types are different from yours.

several million people worldwide each year. Thousands of research studies have been carried out to support the validity of this test.

Note that all the psychological types we will describe are normal and healthy; there is no good or bad, or right or wrong—people are simply different. Various strengths and weaknesses are commonly associated with each preference that makes up a psychological type. This is why Myers entitled her only book *Gifts Differing* (a phrase taken from the Book of Romans in the Christian Bible).

Also note that we will be talking about *preferences*, not abilities. What's the difference between preferences and abilities? A preference is a naturally occurring inborn physical inclination for something—like being right-handed or left-handed. In almost any complex task, you use both your hands, even though one is your favorite or preferred hand. However, just because you are right-handed doesn't mean that you can't learn to do a lot of important things with your left hand, too. Much of this chapter will help you remember not to go through college—or life—"one-handed."

Identifying Your Psychological Type

By reading the descriptions included in this chapter, you will probably get a preliminary idea of what your psychological type may be. This is no substitute, however, for taking the MBTI® personality inventory (or any similar acceptable inventory). If you are enrolled in a college success course, your teacher may give it to you. If not, someone in your college or counseling center, career/placement center, or psychology department most likely will let you take the MBTI®.

© SW Productions/Photodisc/Getty Images

© Pixtal Age Fotostock

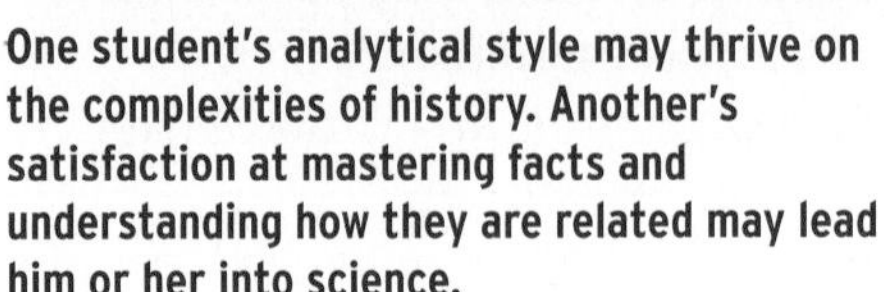

One student's analytical style may thrive on the complexities of history. Another's satisfaction at mastering facts and understanding how they are related may lead him or her into science.

The results that you will receive are only an indicator of your actual personality type, not the final word. Ultimately, you are the best judge of your own personality type. For various reasons, the way you respond at the time you take the test may not turn out to be an accurate indicator of your actual type. Therefore, it is important to go over your results with someone who is well trained in interpreting this instrument in order to figure out what your true type is. For this reason, we cannot recommend online tests that give you instant feedback but no professional consultation to verify your actual type.

The Preferences

Your psychological type is the combination of your preferences on four different scales of the MBTI®. These scales measure how you take in information and how you then make decisions or come to conclusions about that information. They also measure your orientation toward the outer and inner worlds. Like being left-handed or right-handed, these preferences are of an "either-or" nature. But like your hands, you actually use both possible preferences—it's just that one is your natural favorite.

Each preference has a one-letter abbreviation. The four letters together make up your "type." Myers, for instance, was an INFP: someone preferring Introversion, iNtuition, Feeling, and Perceiving. Now here are all the preferences and what they mean.

Extraversion (E) versus Introversion (I): The Inner or Outer World

The E-I preference indicates whether you direct your energy and attention primarily toward the outer world of people, events, and things or the inner world of thoughts, feelings, and reflections.

Extraverts tend to be outgoing, gregarious, and talkative. They often "think with the volume on," saying out loud what is going through their minds. They are energized by people and activity, and they seek this in both work and play. They are people of action, who like to spend more time doing things than thinking about them. At their best, they are good communicators who are quick to act and lead. At their worst, they talk too much and too loudly, drowning out others, they put their feet in their mouths, and they act before they think.

Introverts prefer to reflect carefully on things and think them through before taking action. They think a lot, but they tend to "think with the volume off"; if you want to know what's on their minds, you may have to ask them. They are refreshed by quiet and privacy. At their best, introverts are good, careful listeners whose thoughts are deep and whose actions are well considered. At their worst, they may be too shy and not aware enough of the people and situations around them, and they may think about things so long that they neglect to actually start doing them.

Sensing (S) versus Intuition (N): Facts or Ideas

The S-N preference indicates how you perceive the world and take in information: directly, through your five senses; or indirectly, using your intuition.

Sensing types are interested above all in the facts, what is known and what they can be sure of. Typically, they are practical, factual, realistic, and down to earth. They can be very accurate, steady, precise, and patient and effective with routine and details. They are often relatively traditional and conventional. They dislike unnecessary complication, and they prefer to practice skills they already know. At their best, sensing types can be counted on to do things right and keep doing things right, with every detail well taken care of. At their worst, they can plod along while missing the point of why they are doing what they do, not seeing the forest (the whole picture) through the trees (the details).

Intuitive types are fascinated by possibilities: not so much the facts themselves, but what those facts mean, what concepts might describe those facts, how those might relate to other concepts, what the implications of the facts would be, and so on. Intuitive types are less tied to the here and now and tend to look further into the future and the past. They need inspiration and meaning for what they do, and they tend to work in bursts of energy and enthusiasm. Often, they are original, creative, and nontraditional. They may have trouble with routine and details, however, and they would rather learn a new skill than keep practicing the one they have already mastered. They can be bad at facts and may exaggerate without realizing it. At their best, intuitive types are bright, innovative people who thrive in academic settings and the world of invention and ideas. At their worst, they can be impractical dreamers whose visions fall short because of inattention to practical detail.

Thinking (T) versus Feeling (F): Logic or Values

The T-F preference indicates how you prefer to make your decisions: through logical, rational analysis or through your subjective values, likes, and dislikes.

Thinking types are usually logical, rational, analytical, and critical. They pride themselves on reasoning their way to the best possible decisions. They tend to decide things relatively impersonally and objectively, and they are less swayed by feelings and emotions—both their own and other people's. Other people's feelings sometimes puzzle or surprise them. They can deal with interpersonal disharmony and can be firm and assertive when they need to be. In all their dealings, they need and value fairness. At their best, thinking types are firm, fair, logical, and just. At their worst, they may be cold, insensitive to other people's feelings, and overly blunt and hurtful in their criticisms.

Feeling types are typically warm, empathic, sympathetic, and interested in the happiness of others as well as themselves. They need and value harmony, and they may be distressed and distracted by argument and conflict. They sometimes have trouble being assertive when it would be appropriate to do so. Above all, they need and value kindness. At their best, feeling types are warm and affirming and facilitate cooperation and goodwill among those around them while pursuing the best human values. At their worst, feeling types can be illogical, emotionally demanding, reluctant to tackle unpleasant tasks, and unperturbed by objective reason and evidence.

Judging (J) versus Perceiving (P): Organization or Adaptability

The fourth pair of preferences was devised by Myers and Briggs to enhance and clarify some of Jung's ideas. The J-P preference indicates how you characteristically approach the outside world: making decisions and judgments, or observing and perceiving instead.

Judging types approach the world in a planned, orderly, organized way; as much as possible, they try to order and control their part of it. They make their decisions relatively quickly and easily. They like to make and follow plans. They begin at the beginning, end at the end, and try to finish one thing before starting the next. They are usually punctual and tidy, and they appreciate those traits in others. At their best, judging types are natural organizers who get things done and done on time. At their worst, judging types may jump to conclusions prematurely, be too judgmental of people, make decisions too hastily without enough information, and have trouble changing their plans even when those plans are not working.

Perceiving types don't try to control the world, as much as adapt to it. Theirs is a flexible, wait-and-see approach. They deal comfortably and well with changes, unexpected developments, and emergencies, adjusting their plans and behaviors as needed. They tend to delay decisions so that they can keep their options open and gather more information. They may procrastinate to a serious degree, however, and they may try to carry on too many things at once, without finishing any of them. At their best, perceiving types are spontaneous, flexible individuals who roll with the punches and find ways to take the proverbial lemons in life and turn them into lemonade. At their worst, perceiving types may become messy, disorganized procrastinators who cannot be relied on.

Because there are two possible choices for each of four different preferences, there are sixteen possible psychological types. The four preferences that make up one of the sixteen types may interact in a unique way. You can find out more about this if you take the MBTI® at your counseling center and have it interpreted there. For simplicity, we will deal mainly with the four main preference choices rather than the sixteen individual types.

Using Your Personality for Better Learning

SEE EXERCISE 2.1: A TYPE MAP

Remember we said that no preference is right or wrong, and no type is better or worse than another. No matter which one you have, if it's yours, it's the right one! The basis for healthy type development consists of two things: (1) developing your favorite preferences and getting really good at them; but also (2) developing the flexibility to switch to the other choices when that is what the situation calls for, and learning how to use those nonfavorites well, too.

Examining Values

Can learning preferences have an influence on your value system? Certainly, those who value time and organization may do so because of their J learning preference. Conversely, those who value the freedom to be on "their own" schedules may do so as a result of their P learning preference. If you decide to take the MBTI®, review your learning preferences when you get the results and speculate, in writing, on how those preferences may help determine what you value most and least.

The key to using psychological type to succeed in college is to use all the attitudes and functions (E, I, S, N, T, F, J, and P) effectively in a logical sequence. As you go about your studies, here is the system we recommend:

1. **Sensing.** Get the facts. Use Sensing to find and learn the facts. What are the facts? How do we know them? What is the factual evidence for what is being said?
2. **Intuition.** Get the ideas. Now use Intuition to consider what those facts mean. Why are those facts being presented? What concepts and ideas are being supported by those facts? What are the implications? What is the "big picture"?
3. **Thinking.** Critically analyze. Use Thinking to analyze the pros and cons of what is being presented. Are there gaps in the evidence? What more do we need to know? Do the facts really support the conclusions? Are there alternative explanations? How well does what is presented hang together logically? How could our knowledge of it be improved?
4. **Feeling.** Make informed value judgments. Why is this material important? What does it contribute to people's good? Why might it be important to you personally? What is your personal opinion about it?
5. **Introversion.** Think it through. Before you take any action, carefully go over in your mind everything you have encountered so far.
6. **Judging.** Organize and plan. Don't just dive in! Now is the time to organize and plan your studying so you will learn and remember everything you need to. Don't just plan in your head, either; write down your plan, in detail.
7. **Extraversion.** Take action. Now that you have a plan, act on it. Do whatever it takes. Create note cards, study outlines, study groups, and so on. If you are working on a paper instead of a test, then now is the time to start writing.
8. **Perceiving.** Change your plan as needed. Be flexible enough to change your plan if it isn't working. Expect the unexpected and deal with the unforeseen. Don't give up the whole effort the minute your original plan stops working; figure out what's wrong, and come up with another, better plan and start following that.

Coping with Your Instructors' Teaching Styles

If you and your instructor share common learning preferences, you will probably have little trouble following him or her. In most of your classes, however, that won't be the case. Although the majority of undergraduates prefer sensing (S), the majority of faculty prefer intuition (N).

Introverted students prefer to come away from class with "the big picture," while the teacher may present information in chunks. One thing introverts can do is to review these bits of information and come up with the big picture on their own. This works especially well in groups of introverts.

Extraverted students learn best by explaining to others and while working in groups. If this isn't the case in class, a simple remedy is to discuss the material in small groups outside of class, focusing on explaining each fact to other students.

Sensing students learn best when the lectures are well organized. If your instructor tends to pause regularly to ask questions of students, or goes into detail on one point instead of moving on to the topic, remember that he or she is not trying to bamboozle you. One way to tolerate this is to use a double-column system of note taking. Take notes in one column that are part of the structure of the lecture. Take notes on peripheral material in the other column, including questions and answers. Later, focus on reviewing the main points, but be sure to go over the material in the other column as well.

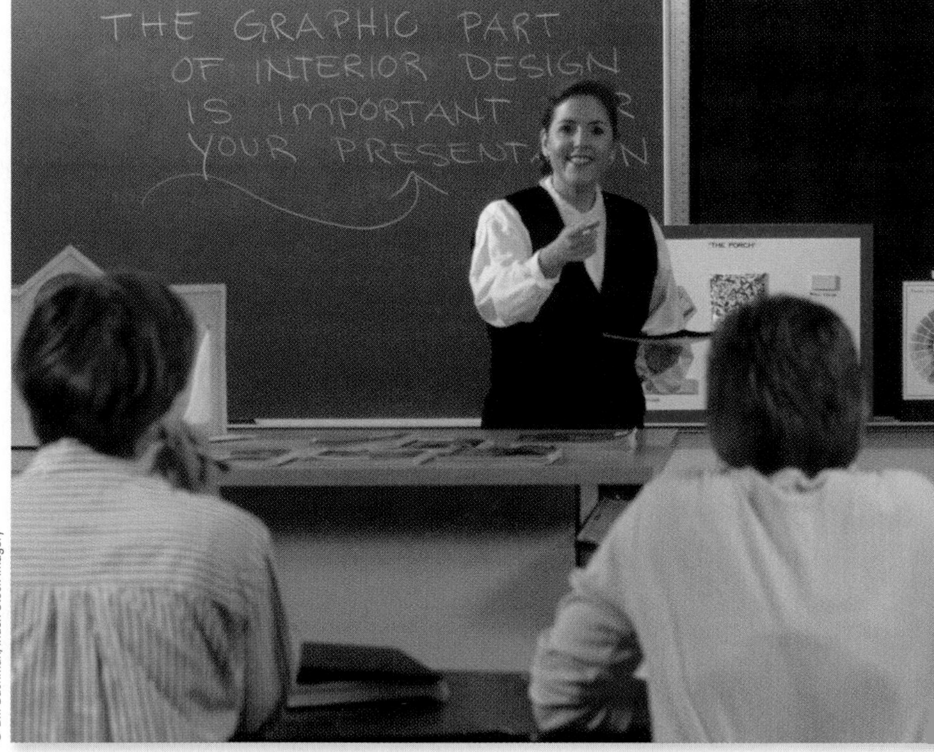

© Bill Bachman/Index Stock Imagery

Instructors, like students, bring their own personality types to the learning environment.

Intuitive students prefer to "discover" knowledge rather than hear it explained and want to understand the big picture rather than the little details that sensing people generally prefer. In a class taught by a nonintuitive teacher, intuitive students should gather the main points in class, then review and organize them into one or more big pictures. This is another instance where study groups can be most effective.

Thinking students value fairness and the use of objective criteria in decision making, whereas feeling students value harmony. The majority of college faculty are thinking types. They write objectives for the course to provide a distinct path for their students. Feeling students may be uninterested in such objectives because they believe that not all stated objectives will be completed. If you're a feeling student, write down the course goals, take lecture notes, and—later—react to the notes in a separate column.

Perceptive students like to postpone action while seeking more data, whereas judging people focus on completing the task as soon as possible. The majority of college faculty *and* undergraduate students are judging. A judging type should use the double-column method of taking notes, leaving one column for comments and questions later. In answering an essay question, first analyze the question and jot down key ideas, organize the ideas logically, and then write the essay.

SEE EXERCISE 2.2: "COVERING THE BASES" FOR A TEST

If you're a perceptive student, try breaking a complex assignment or project into a series of smaller steps, providing deadlines for each of those steps. This may help keep you on target.[1]

SEE EXERCISE 2.3: ADAPTING TO DIFFERING TEACHING STYLES

[1]Adapted from Harvey J. Brightman, "Myers-Briggs Type Indicator Applied to Learning Styles. Master Teacher Programs: Improving University-Level Teaching and Learning," University of Georgia. Athens, 2004.

Helpful Hints for Each Type

Much of the following advice might help any personality type, but because each type tends to have characteristic strengths and weaknesses, some suggestions are particularly apt for certain types. For each of the main preferences, here is some specific advice:

Tips for Extraverts

1. Studying is your most important activity, so don't let your other activities take up all your study time. Also, don't try to multitask: You can't study effectively while you are simultaneously instant-messaging your buddies, visiting with your friends, eating a meal, watching TV, and so on.
2. Study in groups, put the material into words, and talk about it out loud; but prepare for group study sessions by working carefully with the material beforehand.
3. Participate in class by asking questions or making comments—but think these through before you say them out loud.
4. Get involved in as many class demonstrations, projects, lab exercises, field trips, interest groups, and other course-related activities as you can.

Tips for Introverts

1. Find a quiet, comfortable place where you can study on your own without being disturbed. Don't try to study in your room, unless yours is uncommonly quiet and free of interruptions.
2. Put what you are studying and want to remember into written words.
3. Don't be afraid to ask questions in class; if you have a question, others are probably wondering the same thing, and they will silently bless you for asking. Also feel free to go to your instructor's office hours and ask questions or make comments one on one.
4. Don't get "lost in space" with your own thoughts. Be sure to pay attention at all times to what is going on in class, and stay "on task" as you study.

Tips for Sensing Types

1. Some students give broad, sweeping generalizations without supporting facts—but you are more likely to give lots of facts without tying them together. When studying the facts, take time to consider why you are studying them, what concepts they illustrate, and why they are important.
2. Don't accept everything just as it is given to you; think about it, work with it, and make it your own.
3. Ask for the time you need to do your best on tests—it never hurts to ask. (The worst your instructor can do is say, "No, I'm sorry, I can't.") If you don't have enough time, do everything that is relatively quick and easy for you first, even if that means taking things out of order; then do as much as you can with as many things as possible that are left. Move fast and skip around.
4. Go beyond the obvious on test questions, and watch out for subtle traps. On papers and other assignments, go beyond the minimum; top grades usually go to students who do more than was required, but still stick to the point.

Tips for Intuitive Types

1. Always be able to cite facts, evidence, and examples. Don't skip over the details, whether in studying, writing papers, or taking tests. In math and science courses, show all your work.
2. Don't exaggerate or overstate your case; make sure what you're saying is accurate and well justified.
3. Follow instructions. Often, you may want to do things your own way, but get your instructor's approval to do so first. The safest bet is to do everything as instructed, and then if you'd like to add something more creative afterwards, fine. Just explain to your instructor what you added and why.
4. Try to work on things steadily, not in fits and starts; find less important parts you can work on when you are not especially enthused or inspired. Realize that you may greatly underestimate how much time you will need to study or write papers, so as a rule of thumb, plan for at least twice as much time as you think you will need.

Tips for Thinking Types

1. College should be fair, but it isn't always; be prepared for that, and after a certain point, accept it.
2. Don't over-argue your points, just because you feel certain you are right. After a certain point, you can't simply "logic" people into submission. If it's not a major point, simply express yourself and then let it go.
3. Don't neglect the human side of things. People's likes and values do matter and must be taken into consideration.
4. Remember to praise as well as criticize.

Tips for Feeling Types

1. Don't expect special favors because you are a nice person. Your teachers fail lots of nice people every year. They don't enjoy doing it, but if you don't meet the same expectations as everyone else, you aren't going to pass the course.
2. Work as hard on things that you find disagreeable as you work on things you like. It's best to start with what you don't want to do, and then reward yourself by doing work that you like.
3. Stand up for yourself and your point of view, but learn to use and accept logical arguments.
4. Remember to constructively criticize as well as praise.

Tips for Judging Types

1. Avoid absolute statements, those with drastic and extreme opposites.
2. Keep an open mind. Get all the facts and considerations before you make up your mind, and don't jump to conclusions—about ideas or people—too quickly.
3. Don't be afraid to change you mind—that's a big part of what college is about.
4. Don't panic if your plans don't work; just change them and try again. It's not good if you can't meet a deadline, but no student has ever been executed for it. Explain your situation to your instructor, and do the best you can.

Tips for Perceiving Types

1. Procrastination is your worst enemy! Beware of it and learn to defeat it. Dr. Judy Provost's book, *Procrastination—Using Psychological Type Concepts*

Speaking of Careers

WHAT IF YOUR TYPE DOESN'T MATCH YOUR MAJOR OR CAREER CHOICE?

You may find yourself in a major and career path in which your psychological type is unusual. Should you change your major? Not necessarily, if you are happy with it. Consider these questions, suggested by renowned psychologist type expert Dr. Mary McCaulley:

1. Do you know what people in this field actually *do* day to day? Research this, talk to people in the field, visit job sites, and take advantage of any cooperative learning program placements available in this field.
2. Can you be comfortable being a "psychological minority," working in a setting where most people have personalities very different from your own?
3. Can and will you shift your communication style to match that used by the majority of people in your field? For instance, if you are motivated by human values, can you shift to talking the language of facts and figures if that is how the people in authority think?

If the answer to all three questions is yes, then go for it! People who go into a field with their eyes open, even though they are unusual types in that field, are just as likely as other types to succeed in it. Often, they bring to the job a viewpoint that may be overlooked by most people in that field, and therefore can be all the more valuable.

If you cannot honestly answer yes to each of the three questions above, you may wish to use that information to look at other fields, perhaps those where your type is more prevalent.

to Help Students (Center for Application of Psychological Types, 1988), may be of particular help to you. If you don't know where to start, start anywhere—just start.

2. Don't present all sides of something and then leave it hanging; come to conclusions, even if tentative.
3. Don't abandon all your plans just because you fail to live up to some of them. You will get better at it. Just modify your plans, then resume following some of it.
4. Don't assume your teachers will cut you a break and accept things late. Poor planning on your part may not constitute an emergency on theirs; if they let everyone turn things in late, they couldn't do their jobs. If it's unavoidable that you'll be late, talk to your instructor beforehand and explain. Also remember that repeatedly coming to class late makes a poor impression and may lower your grade.

SEE WORKING TOGETHER EXERCISE: A GROUP CAMPUS RECRUITING BROCHURE PROJECT

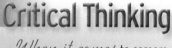

Critical Thinking

When it comes to careers, psychological type doesn't answer the question, "Could I do this job?" but it does help with the question, "Would I like this job?" There are lots of jobs you could do, but would hate. Make a list of three to five jobs that you think you would love to do, that would play to your natural strengths and preferences. Why did you choose those particular jobs? Because of prior work experience? Because of research you've done on careers? Or on a hunch? If you've completed a psychological type of inventory, jot down some thoughts on how your type does—or does not—match your career interests.

Where to Go for Help

ON CAMPUS

By reading the descriptions included in this chapter, you will probably get a preliminary idea of what your psychological type may be. This is no substitute, however, for taking the MBTI® personality test. Quite possibly, your teacher in this course will give it to you. If not, someone in your college or university counseling center, career center, learning assistance/support center, or psychology department can probably administer the MBTI®. You might also talk to your instructors about how you perceive their teaching styles and how this relates to your learning style. They could confirm your analysis and give you some helpful hints on how to do better in their courses.

ONLINE

We cannot recommend online tests that give you instant feedback but no professional consultation to verify your actual type. The test results that you receive are only an indicator of your actual personality type, not the final word.

Beware of home-made tests of psychological type that abound on the Internet. Many of these tests are inaccurate and poorly constructed. The MBTI® does not appear online without professional consultation.

Ultimately, *you* are the best judge of your own personality type. For various reasons, the way you respond at the time you take the test may not always turn out to be an accurate indicator of your actual type. Therefore, it is important to go over your results with someone who is well trained in interpreting this instrument in order to figure out what your true type is.

You can take the MBTI® online *and* get professional interpretation by phone from the Center for Applications of Psychological Type **<http://www.capt.org>.** This will cost you about $100. Odds are that you can get the MBTI® from someone in person right on your own campus for free or at nominal cost (see above).

The Web site of the Myers & Briggs Foundation, **<http://www.myersbriggs.org>,** provides concise and helpful information. You can find more references at **<http://www.mbti.com>** and **<http://www.capt.org>.**

Reassess Yourself

Let's go back to the self-assessment that appears at the beginning of this chapter. This is an opportunity for you to measure your progress, to check in with yourself and see how your approach to college, relationships, and life may have changed upon learning more about psychological types and learning styles. Which of the items on page 32 did you check? Would you change any of your answers as a result of reading this chapter? If so, which ones, and why?

Exercises

Each of these exercises will let you further explore personality types and learning styles. You'll find all these exercises, plus Internet and InfoTrac College Edition exercises, on the CD-ROM that accompanies this book.

EXERCISE 2.1 A Type Map

Write down the following headings: Myself; close friend #1; close friend #2; best boyfriend or girlfriend for dating; favorite teacher in high school or college; person I cannot stand #1; person I cannot stand #2; worst boyfriend or girlfriend for dating;

Setting Goals for Success

Having read about the various preferences, you should now be able to apply your preference to college success. Brainstorm some goals for using the strengths of your particular preference to learn more effectively in class and out of it. Use the goal-setting steps you read about in the Introduction to determine how you can make your type work for you.

My psychological preference is: ____________________
The strengths of this preference are:

1. ____________________
2. ____________________
3. ____________________

My goal is to apply these strengths to achieve college success. I can do this by:

1. ____________________
2. ____________________
3. ____________________

I want to achieve this goal because: ____________________

It's important because: ____________________

I may encounter these obstacles: ____________________

My strategy for accomplishing this goal is to: ____________________

and worst teacher in high school or college. Think about people from your life who would fall into each category. You do not have to name these people; just write down the categories, and have someone specific in mind for each. Now write down your best guess as to your own psychological type and those of each of the other people. Do you notice any patterns? How could you use type to gain a comfortable understanding of the "worst" people in your life?

EXERCISE 2.2 "Covering the Bases" for a Test

Give everyone in your group a short passage of material to study. Now, instead of *taking* a test on it, put yourself in your instructor's shoes and make up test questions on it. First, make up questions that would draw on Sensing (facts, evidence, details); next Intuition (concepts, implications, possibilities, the big picture); then Thinking (logical analysis, pros and cons, critical thinking); and finally Feeling (explicit and implicit values, opinions, impact on people). Do you see why you have to cover all the bases in order to study effectively for a test?

EXERCISE 2.3 Adapting to Differing Teaching Styles

Choose the instructor whose class you find most difficult. Then choose another whose class you look forward to attending each day. Then choose a third instructor who's somewhere in between. For each instructor, jot down signal words that suggest what the teacher's learning preferences might be. Later, review your lists of words and write down what strategies you might use to overcome a "learning preference barrier." After two weeks, reassess. Is the difficult instructor as difficult? What about any changed perceptions on the other two instructors?

Working Together Exercise
A Group Campus Recruiting Brochure Project

After all class members learn or guess their own types, form three groups of 3–5 students each. All members of Group 1 should be Extraverted Sensing types; all members of Group 2 should be Introverted Intuitive types; for Group 3, get as many of the different preferences represented as possible. Have each group outline or write a brief recruiting brochure aimed at convincing prospective students to come to your college or university. Think of several pictures you could include to illustrate your brochure. You don't need to take them; just note what sort of pictures you would use. After the groups are done, have all three groups share their results with the rest of the class. Do you notice any differences in the approach of each group? Which group do you think produced the best plan for a brochure, and why?

See the CD-ROM for these additional exercises as well as all other exercises appearing in this chapter

Internet Exercise 2.1	**Serendipity**
Internet Exercise 2.2	**Type Descriptions**
InfoTrac® College Edition Exercise 2.1	**A Great Mind in Psychology**
InfoTrac® College Edition Exercise 2.2	**Research Studies**

Part 2

Get Set

(Study, Study, Stud

©Jeff Greenberg/Index Stock Imager

3

Thinking Critically, Learning Actively

©Mike Mesgleski/Index Stock Imagery

Going Forward: Student Voices

On my history quiz I had to choose two possible causes of the Civil War and then provide evidence that these causes were true or false. Give me a break. I could recite the dates of battles and the names of generals. That's what a lot of high school quizzes were like. But now I've really got to think.

Looking Back: Author Voices

Looking back I think college was more interesting than high school because we were made to figure out most things by ourselves. No pat answers from the teacher. More like, "How can you explain this?" and "You'll need to do some reading to come up with some possible answers." The more I read, the more I realized the many possible answers I could offer. Before too long, it got to be fun. Jerry Jewler

In this chapter, YOU WILL LEARN

- Why there are no "right" and "wrong" answers to many important questions
- Four aspects of critical thinking
- How critical arguments differ from emotional arguments
- The big difference between high school and college
- The importance of critical thinking beyond college
- What active learning means and how it can help you learn more easily
- The value of studying with other students
- How to choose "active" teachers and be comfortable in their classes

In college, one of the most important lessons has less to do with what you're learning and more to do with *how* you're learning. You can be a passive learner or an active learner. You can memorize and regurgitate facts, or you can think critically and creatively about the content of your courses. Whether you participate fully in learning or sit back and listen is up to you. Imagine that your instructor tells you on the first day of class:

> *I'm going to fill your minds with lots of important facts, and I expect you to take extensive notes and to know those facts in detail when you take your quizzes. The important thing in my class is how well you learn the material and how frequently you choose the right answers.*

Or imagine the instructor introducing the course like this:

> *Although I've taught this course many times, it's never quite the same. Each time a new group of students begins the course, they bring their own values, ideas, and past knowledge to the material. The important thing in my class is that you use your heads. You certainly will need to read the assignments and take notes on the material in class. But that's only the beginning. In this class, you'll learn to analyze facts, decide which facts are supportable by evidence, and work to convince others of your beliefs. And remember, while there are lots of wrong conclusions, there also may be more than one right conclusion.*

When you earn your college degree and land a job, chances are your employer is going to be more interested in how well you can think than in how well you can memorize minute bits of information. The second instructor seems to be moving in that direction. She admits that many possibilities may exist. The first instructor will *tell you what you should know*; the second instructor wants you—through class discussion, small group sessions, problem solving, research, and other methods—*to discover the truths yourself.* If you do, you will probably have more faith in your conclusions, remember the information much more easily, and feel more positive about your college experience.

Self-Assessment
Critical Thinking

Check all the items that apply to you:

1. _______ I frequently allow my emotions to get in the way of making the right decision.
2. _______ I find it hard to appreciate the achievements of a person if I find that person irritating.
3. _______ I am quick to reject ideas that I come up with. As a result, I don't come up with many good ideas.
4. _______ An answer is either right or it isn't.
5. _______ I am usually uncomfortable asking a question or making comments in class.
6. _______ I have never participated in a study team.
7. _______ If I can't tolerate an instructor, I try to get out of that class as soon as possible rather than work on my relationship with that instructor.
8. _______ Most college teachers prefer that students not bother them during or outside of class.

Note: The more items you checked, the more you need to read this chapter to learn how to modify these behaviors.

What Is Critical Thinking?

If you have just completed high school, you may be experiencing an awakening as you enter college. (Even if you're an older returning student, discovering that your instructor trusts you to find valid answers may be somewhat stressful.) In high school you may have been conditioned to believe that things are either right or wrong. If your high school teacher asked, "What are the three branches of the U.S. government?" you had only one choice: "legislative, executive, and judicial." What you might have learned were the names of the three branches, but knowing names doesn't necessarily help you understand what the branches do, or how they do it, even though these three names suggest certain basic functions.

It's not enough just to hear the words; it's more important to understand the ideas behind the words.

A college instructor might ask instead, "Under what circumstances might conflicts arise among the three branches of government, and what does this

©Sonda Dawes/The Image Works

reveal about the democratic process?" Certainly, there is no simple—or single—answer. Most likely, your instructor is attempting not to embarrass you for giving a wrong answer but to engage you in the process of critical thinking.

A Higher-Order Thinking Process

Critical thinking is a process of choosing alternatives, weighing them, and considering what they suggest. Critical thinking involves understanding why some people believe one thing rather than another—whether you agree with those reasons or not. Critical thinking is learning to ask pertinent questions and testing your assumptions against hard evidence.

If you lack critical thinking capabilities, you might exhibit behaviors similar to these:

- You try to reach a classmate on the phone to ask a question about tomorrow's quiz. When you can't reach him, you become so anxious that you can't study or sleep.
- You are asked to read two news articles about the 2004 presidential election. One claims the electoral college system is outdated; the other defends that system. After reading them, you can't see how both sides might be right. You don't even know which one is wrong.
- On the day an important paper is due, a heavy snowstorm rolls in. You brave the cold to get to class. When you arrive, no one—including the teacher—is there. You take a seat and wait for class to begin.
- You are assigned a short research paper on vaccine safety. You decide to begin your search on the World Wide Web. When you type the key words "vaccines" and "danger" into Google, you get 75,000 hits and don't know how to begin sorting through them, so you just read the first four or five.

Now let's transform you into a critical thinker and look at what the outcomes might be:

SEE EXERCISE 3.1: REFLECTING ON ARGUMENTS

- When you can't reach a classmate on the phone to ask a question about tomorrow's quiz, you review the material once more, then call one or more other classmates. Then you consider their views against your textbook and class. Instead of deciding on one point of view for each important topic, you decide to keep in mind all those that make sense, leaving your final decision until you have the quiz in your hand.
- You compare the representation afforded by the electoral college system with the representation afforded by the popular vote, using InfoTrac College Edition

Examining Values

You and your friends are discussing whether war is often the only answer when a threat is posed somewhere in the world. In your heart, you know that it is never justifiable to kill other human beings. You don't even believe in the death penalty, no matter how heinous the crime. But others in the group think differently. They say war is the ultimate solution when nothing else works–and in this situation, nothing else seems to have worked. Using your critical thinking skills, gather some articles about war as a solution. Also look for one or two articles supporting your position. After reading the articles, answer the following questions:

1. What were the key points of each article?
2. Did the articles–pro and con–alter your perspective on war?
3. Is there a right answer to the question of whether war is ever the solution?

Speaking of Careers

Employers hiring college graduates often say they want an individual who can find information, analyze it, organize it, draw conclusions from it, and present it convincingly to others. One executive said she looked for superior communication skills "because they are in such short supply these days." These skills are the basic ingredients of critical thinking, which include the ability to:

- Manage and interpret information in a reliable way.
- Examine existing ideas and develop new ones.
- Pose logical arguments, arguments that further the absorption of knowledge. In college, the term *argument* refers not to an emotional confrontation but to reasons and information brought together in the logical support of some idea.
- Recognize reliable evidence and form well-reasoned arguments.

Search the classified ads, either in the newspaper or online. Look for two or three job listings in the field that interests you. What critical thinking key words do these listings include? Why do these employers want these skills?

to find at least three articles defending each side of the issue. You look further to see if any article supports the system as it now stands. Now you have a number of things to write about. You find there isn't a clear-cut answer. That's okay. It's what you learned that counts.

- On the day an important paper is due, a heavy snowstorm rolls in. You check the college Web site first thing that morning and discover that classes have been cancelled. You stay at home and submit your paper on time by sending it to your instructor by e-mail.
- You are assigned to research vaccine safety. You type your key words into Google, and then you refine your search using the advanced search function. By applying critical thinking skills, you quickly eliminate obviously biased sources and sources that lack scientific authority. You choose six credible sources as the basis for your paper.

Walking through the Process

When thinking about an argument, a good critical thinker considers questions such as the following:

- *Is the information given in support of the argument true?* For example, could it be possible that both the electoral college system and the popular vote system might be equally representative?
- *Does the information really support the conclusion?* If you determine that each system has its merits (the electoral college gives more voting power to the less populated states, whereas the popular vote represents how the majority of voters feel), can you conclude that there may be a more judicious way to employ both systems in presidential elections?
- *Should I withhold judgment until better evidence is available?* Maybe you haven't any proof that a system which counted both the electoral vote and the popular vote would be more equitable because it has never been tried. Maybe it's time to set up a trial using a small sample.
- *Is the argument really based on good reasoning, or does it appeal mainly to my emotions?* You may think the electoral vote can alter the results of elections in a way that undermines the intentions of the voters, as evidenced in the 2000

presidential election when winner George W. Bush won the electoral college vote and Al Gore won the popular vote. But you need to come to terms with your emotions and ask if they are guiding you to this conclusion instead of relevant information that supports the argument.

- *Based on the available evidence, are other conclusions equally likely (or even more likely)?* Is there more than one right or possible answer? Perhaps there is a third or fourth way to count the vote by replacing the electoral college concept with something else.
- *What more should I do in order to reach a good conclusion?* You may need to do more reading about the election process and find some evidence that the system didn't work as planned in earlier presidential elections. Then you might try to find out how people felt about the voting system. Since you are far from an expert on this, perhaps you should hold a forum with local voters to gain more views on the pros and cons of the electoral college system. This is creative as well as critical thinking.

When communicating an argument or idea to others, a good critical thinker knows how to organize it in an understandable, convincing way in speech or in writing.

Four Aspects of Critical Thinking

Critical thinking cannot be learned overnight nor always accomplished in a neat set of steps. Yet as interpreted by William T. Daly, teacher of political science at the Richard Stockton College of New Jersey, the critical thinking process can be divided into four basic steps. Practicing these basic ideas can help you become a more effective thinker.

SEE EXERCISE 3.2: THE CHALLENGE OF CLASSROOM THINKING

SEE EXERCISE 3.3: HARD OR EASY?

SEE WORKING TOGETHER EXERCISE: GATHERING INFORMATION FOR DECISION MAKING

1. Abstract Thinking: Using Details to Discover the Big Ideas

From large numbers of facts, seek the bigger ideas or the abstractions behind the facts. What are the key ideas? Even fields like medicine, which involve countless facts, culminate in general ideas such as the principles of circulation or the basic mechanisms of cell division. Ask yourself what larger concepts the details suggest. For example, you read an article that describes how many people are using the Internet now, how much consumer information it provides, what kinds of goods you can buy cheaply over the Internet, and also that many low-income families are still without computers. Think carefully about these facts, and you might arrive at several different important generalizations.

One might be that as the Internet becomes more important for shopping, the lack of computers in low-income households will put poor families at an even greater disadvantage. Or your general idea might be that because the Internet is becoming important for selling things, companies will probably find a way to put a computer in every home.

2. Creative Thinking: Seeking Connections, Finding New Possibilities, Rejecting Nothing

Use the general idea you have found to see what further ideas it suggests. The important thing at this stage is not to reject any of your ideas. Write them all down. You'll narrow this list in the next step.

This phase of thinking can lead in many directions. It might involve searching for ways to make the Internet more available to low-income households. Or it might involve searching out more detailed information on how much interest big companies really have in marketing various goods to low-income families. In essence, the creative thinking stage involves extending the general idea—finding new ways it might apply or further ideas it might suggest.

3. Systematic Thinking: Organizing the Possibilities, Tossing Out the Rubbish

Systematic thinking involves looking at the outcome of the second phase in a more demanding, critical way. Which of your solutions seems the most promising after you have conducted an exhaustive search for materials? Do some answers conflict with others? Which ones can be achieved? If you have found new evidence to refine or further test your generalization, what does that new evidence show? Does your original generalization still hold up? Does it need to be modified? What further conclusions do good reasoning and evidence support? Which notions should be abandoned?

4. Precise Communication: Being Prepared to Present Your Ideas Convincingly to Others

Intelligent conclusions aren't very useful if you cannot share them with others. Consider what your audience will need to know to follow your reasoning and be persuaded. Remember to have "facts in hand." Don't be defensive; instead, just be logical.

Critical Thinking and the Internet

Evaluating sources is a crucial part of the critical thinking process. You cannot determine whether the evidence you uncover is true unless you know the credibility of its source. But how do you judge a source's credibility? If your source is a printed publication, you can usually find the name of the author or sponsoring organization on the document. A little further investigating will reveal more information about the perspective of the people behind it.

But on the Internet, anyone can publish what looks like an authoritative document. Many of those who post Web sites on the Internet are determined to deceive, not to inform. What's more, the search engines themselves are not designed to evaluate accuracy, the basis for credibility. What comes up first in the search is often more inflammatory than informative.

For instance, if you type "gun control AND politics" into a search engine, you will get hits from gun collectors, gun control advocates, news organizations, and academic journals. You may be able to discern quickly that some of these sources are not using reliable data and that some are simply spouting opinion. How quickly—and effectively—you are able to separate the wheat from the chaff depends on your critical thinking skills.

Critical Thinking in College

Critical thinking depends on your ability to evaluate different perspectives and to challenge assumptions made by you or others. To challenge how you think, a good

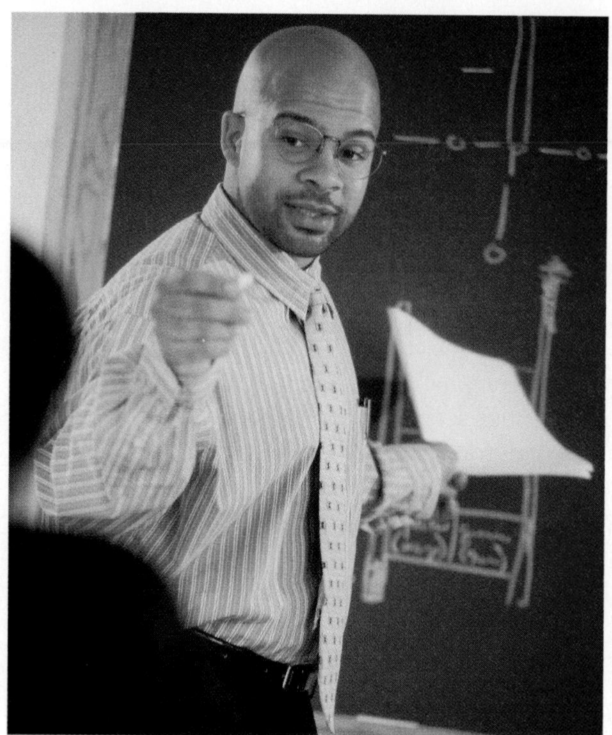
©Comstock Images/Alamy

A good class becomes a critical thinking experience. Asking a sensible question may be more important than trying to find the elusive "right" answer.

college teacher may insist that how you solve a problem is as important as the solution, and even may ask you to describe that problem-solving process.

Because critical thinking depends on discovering and testing connections between ideas, your instructor may ask open-ended questions that have no clear-cut answers, questions of "Why?" "How?" or "What if?" For example: "In these essays we have two conflicting ideas about whether bilingual education is effective in helping children learn English. What now?" Your instructor may ask you to break a larger question into smaller ones: "Let's take the first point. What evidence does the author offer for his idea that language immersion programs get better results?" She or he may insist that more than one valid point of view exists: "So, for some types of students, you agree that bilingual education might be best? What other types of students should we consider?"

Your instructor may require you to explain concretely the reason for any point you reject: "You think this essay is wrong. Well, what are your reasons?" Or he or she may challenge the authority of experts: "Dr. Fleming's theory sounds impressive. But here are some facts he doesn't account for. . . ." You may discover that often your instructor reinforces the legitimacy of your personal views and experiences: "So something like this happened to you once, and you felt exactly the same way. Can you tell us why?" And you also will discover that it's okay to change your mind.

It is natural for new college students to find this mode of thinking difficult and to discover that answers are seldom entirely wrong or right but more often somewhere in between. Yet the questions that lack simple answers usually are the ones most worthy of study.

Using logic to figure things out instead of depending purely on how you feel about something makes college more interesting and also more challenging. This higher-order thinking process should also lead to higher grades.

Active Learning

Because most college teachers emphasize critical thinking, they offer you the chance to move from a pattern of being taught *passively* to one of learning *actively*.

Active learning is simply a method that involves students actively. It happens whenever your teacher asks you a question in class, puts you in groups to solve a problem, requires you to make an oral presentation to the class, or does anything else that gives you and other students a voice in the learning process.

The Many Benefits of Active Learning

In addition to placing you "in the center" of learning, active learning teaches you a variety of skills employers want most: thinking, writing, oral communication, goal setting, time management, relationship building, problem solving, ethical reasoning, and more. All these skills are an important part of leadership as well.

A teacher who urges students to collaborate on an assignment is aware that two or more heads may be far more productive than one. Each student turns in an original piece of work but is free to seek advice and suggestions from another student. More than likely, this is how you will be working after college, so it makes sense to learn how to collaborate—rather than compete—now.

Students who embrace active learning not only learn better but also enjoy their learning experiences more. Even if you have an instructor who lectures for an entire period and leaves little or no time for questions, you might form a study group with three or four other students, so that each of you can benefit from what the others have learned. Or you might ask the teacher for an appointment to discuss unanswered questions from the lecture. By doing so, you can transform a passive learning situation into an active one. In a passive classroom, where you listen and take notes, you are less likely to retain information or put it to use.

Active learners are willing to try new ideas and discover new knowledge by exploring the world around them instead of just memorizing facts. Here are some things you can do to practice learning actively:

- Choose teachers who will actively engage you in learning. Ask friends for recommendations.
- Even in a class of 50 or more, sit as close to the front as you can and never hesitate to raise your hand if you don't understand something. Chances are, the other 49 didn't understand it either.
- Put notes into your own words instead of just memorizing the book or the lecture.
- Study with other students. Talking about assignments and getting other points of view will help you learn the material faster and more thoroughly.
- Follow the suggestions in this book about managing your time, optimizing your learning preferences, taking class notes, reading texts, and studying for exams.
- If you disagree with what your instructor says, politely challenge him or her. Good teachers will listen and may still disagree with you, but they may think more of you for showing you can think and that you care enough to challenge them.
- Stay in touch with teachers, other students, and your academic advisor. One great way is through e-mail. Or call and leave a voice mail if the person is out.

Why Active Learners Can Learn More than Passive Learners

Active learning puts students in charge of their own education. Although you may acquire knowledge listening to a lecture, you may not be motivated to think about what that knowledge means. Through active learning, you will learn not only the material in your notes and textbooks, but also how to:

- Work with others
- Improve your critical thinking, listening, writing, and speaking skills

- Function independently and teach yourself
- Manage your time
- Gain sensitivity to cultural differences

Becoming an Active Learner

Active learning requires preparation before and after every class, not just before exams. This includes browsing in the library, making appointments to talk to faculty members, making outlines from your class notes, going to appropriate cultural events, working on a committee, asking someone to read something you've written to see if it's clear, or having a serious discussion with students whose personal values are different from yours.

Yet with all its benefits, some students resist active learning out of fear of trying something new and challenging. One student described an active learning class as "scary" and a more traditional class as "safe." The traditional class was safe because the teacher did not make students sit in a semicircle, and he used a textbook and lectures to explain ideas. On the other hand, discussions were scary because of the process, the uncertainty, and the openness.[1]

Studies have indicated that the larger the class, the less most students want to speak out. As one student explains, "If I give the wrong answer in a class of 50, 49 students will see me as a dunce." Yet when the instructor creates an atmosphere where such participation is comfortable and makes it clear that even reasonable "wrong" answers are better than no answers at all, you probably will want to participate more often.

According to student development theory, an active approach to learning and living has the potential to produce individuals who are well rounded in all aspects of life. The hexagon in Figure 3.1 depicts seven aspects of development, with intellectual development at its center. Optimal personal development depends on each area's supporting every other area. For example, with good active learning skills, you likely will feel more comfortable socially, gain a greater appreciation for diversity and education, and be better able to clarify your major and future career. Staying physically active can reduce stress and keep your mind alert while you study. Developing a sense of values (see Chapter 7) can help you choose your friends more carefully and decide how you manage your time.

The One-Minute Paper

One way to practice active learning daily is through a process called the *one-minute paper*. In a major study of teaching at Harvard University, one of many suggestions for improving learning was a simple feedback exercise. At the end of each class, students were asked to write what they thought was the main issue of that class and what their unanswered questions were for the next class. Gradually, this became a habit.

Even if your instructors don't require it, try writing your one-minute paper each day at the end of class. Use it to think about the main issues discussed that day, and save it so that you can ask good questions at the next class meeting.

SEE WORKING TOGETHER EXERCISE: DIFFERENCES BETWEEN HIGH SCHOOL AND COLLEGE

Teachers and Active Learning

Teachers who promote active learning go the extra mile to make classes interesting. So should you. Instead of blending in with your peers—as many new students seem

[1]Adapted from Russell A. Warren, "Engaging Students in Active Learning," *About Campus*, March–April 1997.

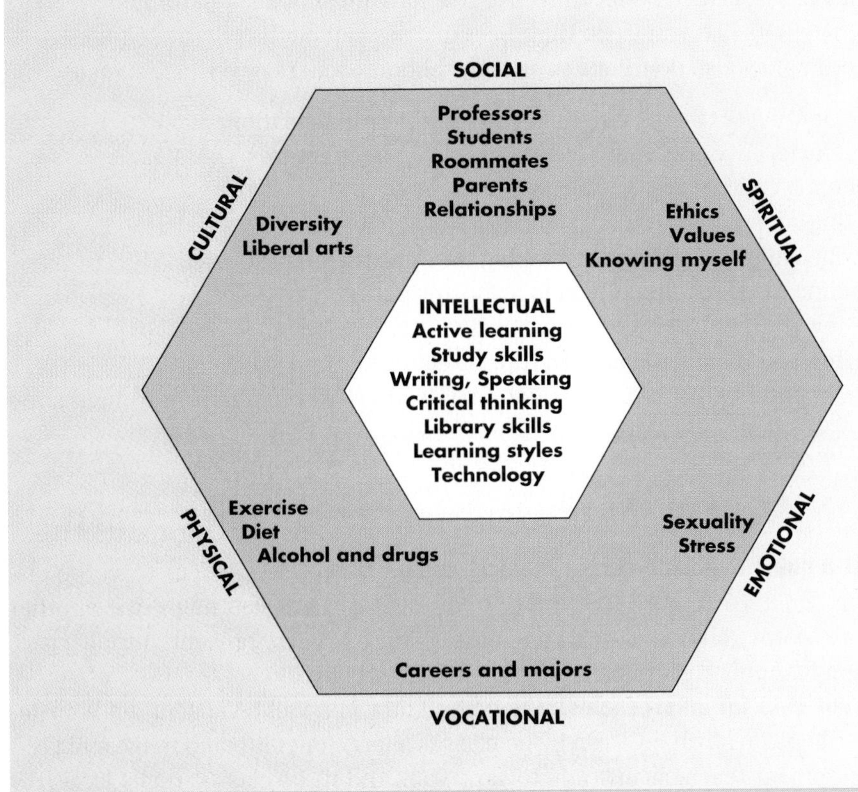

Figure 3.1 Aspects of Student Development

to do—ask questions in class. Try to do something innovative with every paper and project. Sure, you'll make some mistakes, but your instructor probably will appreciate your inventiveness, reward you for it, and be more willing to help you improve your work.

Just as good teachers invite you to speak out in class, they also keep lines of communication open. They not only grade your work but also may ask you how you're learning, what you're learning, and how well you believe they are teaching. In fact, some of the best learning may take place one on one in the instructor's office. Research shows that students who have conferences with their teachers outside of class have a greater chance of returning to college for their second year. In high school, this wasn't cool. In college it's hot.

Your college instructors will encourage you to develop new ways of thinking, to realize there may be many acceptable answers as opposed to only one, to question existing knowledge, to take issue with something they might say, to ask questions in class, and to offer possible solutions to problems. You may be surprised to find that most college teachers do not fit the stereotype of the ivory tower scholar. Though many college instructors spend some of their time doing scholarship and performing

Critical Thinking

Look back over the differences between high school and college teachers. List five to ten qualities and behaviors you believe college teachers want in their students. Why did you choose these behaviors? How many of your choices have a direct relationship to your learning preferences and value system?

service, a majority of them admit they love teaching most of all, and for good reason: Motivating students like you to do their best in class can be deeply satisfying.

Instructors may also do things your high school teachers never did, such as:

- Supplementing textbook assignments with other information
- Giving exams covering both assigned readings and lectures
- Questioning conclusions of other scholars
- Accepting several different student opinions on a question
- Never checking to see if you are taking notes or reading the text
- Demanding more reading of you in a shorter period of time
- Giving fewer quizzes or many more quizzes
- Expecting you to be familiar with topics related to their field
- Being sympathetic to difficulties you may have while holding firm to high standards of grading

Making the Most of the Student-Instructor Relationship

1. **Make it a point to attend class regularly and on time.** And participate in the discussion; you'll learn more if you do. If you miss a class, you might get another student's notes, but that isn't the same thing as being present during class. Learning is simply easier when you're there every day.
2. **Save your cuts for emergencies.** When you know you will be absent, let your instructor know in advance, even if the class is a large one. It could make a big difference in your teacher's attitude toward you. And if the class is really large, it's one way of introducing yourself.
3. **Sit near the front.** Studies indicate that students who do so tend to earn better grades.
4. **Speak up.** Ask questions when you don't understand something or need clarification, and voice your opinion when you disagree.
5. **See your instructor outside class when you need help.** Instructors are required to keep office hours for student appointments. Make an appointment by phone, e-mail, or at the end of class. You will likely be pleasantly surprised at how much your instructor is willing to work with you. Get your instructor's e-mail address and use it.
6. **Share one or more one-minute papers with your instructor.** You can do this either in writing or through e-mail. It could be the start of an interesting dialogue.

Teachers, Students, and Academic Freedom

College instructors believe in the freedom to speak out, whether it be in a classroom discussion about economic policy or at a public rally on abortion or gay rights. What matters more than what instructors believe is their right to proclaim that belief to others without fear. Colleges and universities have promoted the advancement of knowledge by granting scholars virtually unlimited freedom of inquiry, as long as human lives, rights, and privacy are not violated.

Some teachers may speak sarcastically about a politician you admire. Although you need not accept such ideas, you must learn to evaluate them for yourself.

Academic freedom also extends to college students. You will have the right to disagree with the instructor if you feel differently about an issue, but be certain you can support your argument with reliable published or personal evidence. And remember: The instructor has final authority where your grades are concerned.

Above all, discuss—never attack. Cite something you read or heard, and ask what the instructor thinks about your approach to the issue.

Where to Go for Help

ON CAMPUS

Learning (Assistance/Support) Center. Most every campus has one or more of these. Sometimes, they provide help for students in all subjects at all levels; sometimes, they are specific to one discipline, especially math or English. The staff will know many if not all of your instructors and can provide good coping advice to use with active learning strategies.

Counseling Center. Maybe your relationships with teachers and courses are putting you under excessive stress. This is a fairly common issue among new college students and there's help right on campus at the Counseling Center, which provides free and confidential support for students. At the Counseling Center, you can get confidential feedback on the sources of your stress and learn some healthy coping mechanisms.

Faculty Members. Talk with your instructors about your learning style and any problems you are having in their courses. Most of them will work with you to incorporate critical thinking and active learning into your classroom and study process.

Academic Advisor/Counselor. They usually can help you learn how to make your relationships with college teachers a success. Find out how your advisor also can help you find courses where you can think critically and learn actively.

ONLINE

- Go to **<http://www.ntlf.com/html/lib/bib/91-9dig.htm>** and read the article "Active Learning: Creating Excitement in the Classroom." Comment on the authors' interpretation of the active learning process.
- Go to **<http://teaching.berkeley.edu/bgd/collaborative.html>** and read the information designed for teachers on collaborative learning. According to the author, collaborative learning forces one to learn actively. Do you agree?

ON INFOTRAC® COLLEGE EDITION

- Gregory, Roper. "Teachers' Guilt (problems of liberal pedagogy)," *First Things: A Monthly Journal of Religion and Public Life,* November 2002,: 21(2).
- For a different perspective on how learning groups work, read "Using Cooperative Learning Groups to Develop Health-Related Cultural Awareness." Eva I. Doyle, Chris French Beatty, and Mary Walker Shaw, *Journal of School Health,* February 1999, 69, no. 2: 73(1).

Collaborative Learning Teams

Besides "teaming" with your teachers to enhance your learning, you can also team with your fellow students as a collaborative learning team.

How does such collaboration improve learning? Joseph Cuseo of Marymount College, an expert on collaborative learning, points to these factors:

- Learners learn from one another as well as from the instructor.
- Collaborative learning is by its very nature active learning, and so tends to increase learning by involving you more actively.
- "Two heads are better than one." Collaboration can lead to more ideas, alternative approaches, new perspectives, and better solutions.

- If you're not comfortable speaking out in larger classes, you will tend to be more comfortable speaking in smaller groups, resulting in better communication and better ideas.
- You will develop stronger bonds with other students in the class, which may increase everyone's interest in attending.
- An environment of "positive competition" among groups is developed when several groups are asked to solve the same problem—as long as the instructor clarifies that the purpose is for the good of all.
- The group experience helps you to develop leadership skills.
- You will learn to work with others, a fact of life in the work world.

If two heads are better than one, four heads may be even better at examining course content.

© Mark Richards/PhotoEdit

When students work effectively in a supportive group, the experience can be a highly powerful way to enhance academic achievement and meaningful learning. Interviews with college students at Harvard University revealed that nearly every senior who had been part of a study group considered this experience to be crucial to his or her academic progress and success.

Making Learning Teams Productive

Not all learning groups are equally effective. Sometimes, teamwork is unsuccessful or fails to reach its potential because no one thought through how the group should be formed or how it should function. Use the following strategies to develop high-quality learning teams that maximize the power of peer collaboration:

SEE EXERCISE 3.4: TO COLLABORATE OR NOT?

SEE EXERCISE 3.5: FORMING YOUR IDEAL LEARNING TEAM

1. Remember that learning teams are more than study groups. Don't think that collaborative learning simply involves study groups that meet the night before major exams. Effective student learning teams collaborate regularly for other academic tasks besides test review sessions.
2. In forming teams, seek students who will contribute quality and diversity to the group. Look for fellow students who are motivated, attend class regularly, are attentive and participate actively while in class, and complete assignments. Include teammates from different ethnic, racial, or cultural backgrounds, different age groups, and different personality types and learning styles. Include males and females. Resist the urge to include people who are exactly like you. Choosing only your friends can often result in a learning group that is more likely to get off track.
3. Keep the group small (four to six teammates). Smaller groups allow for more face-to-face interaction and eye contact and less opportunity for any one individual to shirk his or her responsibility to the team. Also, it's much easier for small groups to meet outside class. Consider choosing an even number of teammates (four or six), so you can work in pairs in case the team decides to divide its work into separate parts.

Setting Goals for Success

FINDING A MENTOR

A *mentor* is someone you trust to guide and advise you. This person may be an academic advisor, instructor, department chair, older student, or anyone else who appears to offer interest, wisdom, and support. Most important, a mentor is someone who will deal with you confidentially and who is genuinely interested in your well-being but asks little or nothing in return. A mentor is also a person who represents many of the attributes you hope to have in the future—a role model.

Brainstorm some goals for finding a college mentor. Using the goal-setting steps you read about in the Introduction, determine what qualities you seek in a mentor and how to go about finding one.

My mentor would have the following qualities:

1. ____________________

2. ____________________

3. ____________________

I can achieve this goal of finding a mentor by: ____________________

I want to achieve this goal because: ____________________

(OR)

I have no interest in finding a mentor because: ____________________

4. Hold individual team members personally accountable for their own learning and for contributing to the learning of their teammates. Research on study groups at Harvard indicates that they are effective only if each member has done the required work in advance of the group meeting (e.g., completing required readings and other assignments). One way to ensure accountability is to have each member come to group meetings with specific information or answers to share with teammates as well as questions to ask the group. Or have individual members take on different roles or responsibilities, such as mastering a particular topic, section, or skill to be taught to others.

The Many Types of Learning Teams

1. **Note-taking teams.** Team up with other students immediately after class to share and compare notes. One of your teammates may have picked up something you missed, or vice versa. By meeting immediately after class, your group may still have a chance to consult with the instructor about any missing or confusing information.
2. **Reading teams.** After completing reading assignments, team with other students to compare your highlighting and margin notes. See if all agree on what the author's major points were and what information you should study for exams.
3. **Library research teams.** Forming library research teams is an effective way to develop a support group for reducing "library anxiety" and for locating and sharing sources of information. (*Note:* Locating and sharing sources of information isn't cheating or plagiarizing as long as the final product you turn in represents your own work.)

4. **Team/instructor conferences.** Have your learning team visit the instructor during office hours to seek additional assistance in study or completing work.

   You may find it easier to see an instructor in the company of other students. And the feedback from your instructor is also received by your teammates, so that useful information is less likely to be forgotten. Your team visit also tells your instructor that you are serious about learning.
5. **Team test results review.** After receiving test results, the members of a learning team can review their individual tests together to help one another identify the sources of their mistakes and to identify any answers that received high scores. This provides each team member with a clearer idea of what the instructor expects. You can use this information for subsequent tests and assignments. Returning students may wish to form their own groups and discuss the differences between their lives before college and now; or they may prefer to join a group of recent high school graduates to hear and provide a different point of view.

Reassess Yourself

Now that you've read about critical thinking, active learning, and collaborating with other students, go back to the self-assessment that appears at the beginning of this chapter. This is an opportunity for you to measure your progress, to check in with yourself and see how reading this chapter may have changed your approach to learning. Which of the items on page 49 did you check? Would you change any of your answers as a result of reading this chapter? If so, which ones, and why?

Exercises

Each of these exercises will let you further explore the topic of each chapter. You'll find all these exercises, plus Internet and InfoTrac College Edition exercises, on the CD-ROM that accompanies this book.

EXERCISE 3.1 Reflecting on Arguments

Review the list of questions on pages 51–52 of this chapter, in the section titled "Walking through the Process." Are they the kinds of questions that you tend to ask when you read, listen to, or take part in discussions? For an entire day, keep this list with you and try to apply the questions to a lecture and discussion. Note whether other people are stating their assumptions or conclusions.

EXERCISE 3.2 The Challenge of Classroom Thinking

Think about your experiences in each of your classes so far this term:

- Have your instructors pointed out any conflicts or contradictions in the ideas they have presented? Or have you noted any contradictions that they have not acknowledged?
- Have they asked questions for which they sometimes don't seem to have the answers?
- Have they challenged you or other members of the class to explain yourselves more fully?
- Have they challenged the arguments of other experts? Have they called on students in the class to question or challenge certain ideas?
- How have you reacted to their words? Do your responses reflect critical thinking?

Write down your thoughts for possible discussion in class. Consider sharing them with your instructors.

EXERCISE 3.3 Hard or Easy?

In your opinion, is it harder to think critically than to base your arguments on how you feel about a topic? What are the advantages of finding answers based on your feelings? Based on critical thinking? How might you use both approaches in seeking an answer?

EXERCISE 3.4 To Collaborate or Not?

Some people may prefer to work alone. This chapter has already listed many benefits of working together. What are some of the benefits of working by yourself? What might influence your decision to work alone as opposed to collaborating? What might influence you to prefer collaboration?

EXERCISE 3.5 Forming Your Ideal Learning Team

If you were to form a group with two or three other students in this class, whom would you choose, and for what characteristics? Write a paper describing your group. Don't reveal their names. Instead, name your collaborators A, B, and so forth. If you had to choose one more person, who would that be and why? In what ways do members of this group complement one another's strengths and weaknesses, including yours?

Working Together Exercise
Gathering Information for Decision Making

In groups of four to six, choose a major problem on campus, such as binge drinking, cheating, date rape, parking, safety, class size, or lack of student participation in organizations. Between this class and the next, seek information about this problem, and possible solutions, by interviewing a campus authority on the topic, searching for articles on InfoTrac College Edition, searching campus library holdings, and/or conducting a survey of students. When you regroup during the next class, share your findings, citing your sources, with other members of the group. Try to reach consensus in the group on the best way to solve the problem. If any members of the group are using emotional rather than logical arguments, point it out to them.

Working Together Exercise
The Differences between High School and College

This chapter lists just a few of the differences between high school and college that you may encounter. With a small group of other students, brainstorm other differences. Appoint one person in the group to list which differences seem beneficial and which do not. Explain your choices to the rest of the class.

See the CD-ROM for these additional exercises as well as all other exercises appearing in this chapter

Internet Exercise 3.1	Your Teachers'—and Your Own—Responsibilities
Internet Exercise 3.2	Finding Faculty E-Mail Addresses
Internet Exercise 3.3	Critical Thinking Resources
InfoTrac® College Edition Exercise 3.1	Researching Teachers, Collaboration, and Active Learning
InfoTrac® College Edition Exercise 3.2	Researching Critical Thinking

4

Listening, Note Taking, and Participating

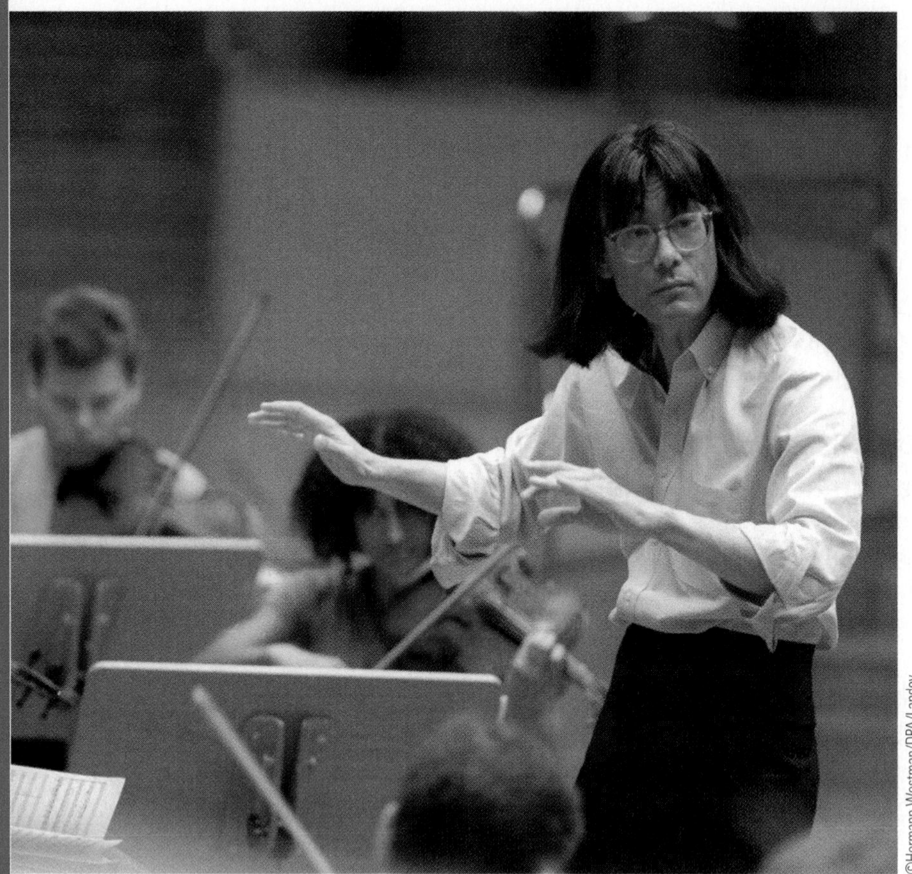
©Hermann Wostman/DPA/Landov

Jeanne L. Higbee of the University of Minnesota, Twin Cities, contributed her valuable and considerable expertise to the writing of this chapter.

Going Forward: Student Voices

I can't believe it! I got a 65 on my first history test, and I thought I knew my lecture notes backward and forward. I was in class every day, but maybe I just wasn't listening hard enough. Guess I'll have to write faster and take down everything the instructor says, or I'll never pass this course.

Looking Back: Author Voices

In my first term of college, I was flunking everything except English and PE, until an older and outstanding student showed me how he took lecture notes and urged me to imitate his strategy. He was my savior! Once I did as he did, my grades skyrocketed and the rest is history—a history of very good grades, a great deal of learning, and a fulfilling career. **John Gardner**

In this chapter, YOU WILL LEARN

- How to assess your note-taking skills and how to improve them
- Why it's important to review your notes as soon as reasonable after class
- How to prepare to remember before class
- How to listen critically and take good notes in class
- Why you should speak up in class
- How to review class and textbook materials after class

In virtually every college class you take, you'll need to master two skills to earn high grades: listening and note taking. Taking an active role in your classes—asking questions, contributing to discussions, or providing answers—will help you listen better and take more meaningful notes. That in turn will enhance your ability to learn: to understand abstract ideas, find new possibilities, organize those ideas, and recall the material once the class is over.

Listening and note taking are critical to your academic success because your college instructors are likely to introduce new material in class that your texts don't cover, and chances are that much of this material will resurface on quizzes and exams. By the way, none of the statements in the self-assessment inventory is considered good practice for the classroom. Instead, keep these suggestions in mind as you read the rest of this chapter:

1. Since writing down everything the instructor says is probably not possible and you are not sure what is important to remember, ask questions in class, go over your notes with a tutor or someone from your campus learning center, or compare your notes with a friend's.
2. Don't record a lecture unless you can concentrate on listening to the tape while commuting. Instead, consider asking the instructor to speak more slowly or to repeat key points, or meet with a study group to compare notes. If there is a reason you do need to tape-record a lecture, be sure to ask the instructor's permission first. But keep in mind that it will be difficult to make a high-quality recording in an environment with so much extraneous noise. And even though you're recording, take notes.
3. Don't copy an outline from the board until the instructor covers each point in sequence. Write down the first point and listen. Take notes. When the next point is covered, do the same, and so on.
4. Take notes on the discussion. Your instructors may be taking notes on what is said and could use them on exams. You should be participating as well as taking notes.
5. Choose the system that works for you. If a formal outline works for you, fine. If it doesn't, consider other suggestions provided in this chapter for organizing your notes so you can come back to them later and understand them.
6. If something is not clear, ask the instructor in class or after class. Your friend may not have "gotten it" either or may have misunderstood the point the instructor was making.

Self-Assessment

Listening, Note Taking, and Participating

Read each of the following statements and put a check mark in front of those that come close to describing you:

1. _______ If I can't tell what's important in a lecture, I write down everything the instructor says.
2. _______ If an instructor moves through the material very fast, it might be a good idea to tape-record the lecture and not worry about paying attention in class.
3. _______ If the instructor puts an outline on the board, I usually copy it right away.
4. _______ Listening in a class that is mainly discussion is better than trying to take notes.
5. _______ Most of my friends take notes in outline form; I guess I should do the same.
6. _______ When the instructor says something I don't understand, I figure I'll get it from a friend later.
7. _______ If I arrive early, I spend the time before class talking to my friends.
8. _______ I rarely or never compare my notes with those of another student or a study group.
9. _______ Whatever I miss in class, I'll catch up on in the textbook.
10. _______ It's better to sit and take notes than to raise my hand and ask a question.

7. Instead of chatting with friends before class begins, review your study notes for the previous class.
8. Make it a habit to review notes with one or two other students.
9. Be aware that what the instructor says in class may not always be in the textbook. And vice versa.
10. Speak up! People tend to remember what they have said more than what others are saying to them.

SEE EXERCISE 4.1: YOU WILL FORGET. REMEMBER?

Pay attention to the suggestions in this chapter, decide which ones work best for you, and practice them regularly until they become part of your study routine.

Short-Term Memory: Listening and Forgetting

Many instructors draw a significant proportion of their test items from their lectures; remembering what is presented in class is crucial to doing well on exams.

Ever notice how easy it is to learn the words of a song? We remember songs and poetry more easily in part because they follow a rhythm and a beat, because we may repeat them—sometimes unconsciously—over and over in our heads, and because they often have a personal meaning for us—we relate them to something in our everyday lives. We remember prose less easily unless we make an effort to relate it to

3. **Keep an open mind.** Every class holds the promise of discovering new information and uncovering different perspectives. Some teachers may intentionally present information that challenges your value system. One of the purposes of college is to teach you to think in new and different ways and to provide support for your own beliefs. Instructors want you to think for yourself, and do not necessarily expect you to agree with everything they or your classmates say, but if you want people to respect your values, you must show respect for them as well by listening to what they have to say with an open mind.
4. **Get organized.** Develop an organizational system. Decide what type of notebook will work best for you. Many study skills experts suggest using three-ring binders because you can punch holes in syllabi and other course handouts and keep them with your class notes. If you prefer using spiral notebooks, consider buying multisubject notebooks that have pocket dividers for handouts, or be sure to maintain a folder for each course. Create a recording system to keep track of grades on all assignments, quizzes, and tests. Retain any papers that are returned to you until the term is over and your grades are posted on your transcript. That way, if you need to appeal a grade because an error occurs, you will have the documentation you need to support your appeal. If you keep your notes and other course materials organized throughout the term, you will be aware of where you stand going into final exams and prepared to review efficiently.

During Class: Listen Critically

Listening in class is not like listening to a TV program, listening to a friend, or even listening to a speaker at a meeting. Knowing how to listen in class can help you get more out of what you hear, understand better what you have heard, and save time. Here are some suggestions:

1. **Be ready for the message.** Prepare yourself to hear, listen, and receive the message. If you have done the assigned reading, you will know what details are already in the text so that you can focus your notes on key concepts during the lecture. You will also know what information is not covered in the text, and will be prepared to pay closer attention when the instructor is presenting unfamiliar material.
2. **Listen to the main concepts and central ideas, not just to fragmented facts and figures.** Although facts are important, they will be easier to remember and make more sense when you can place them in a context of concepts, themes, and ideas. You want to understand the material, and simply memorizing it won't help you understand it.
3. **Listen for new ideas.** Even if you are an expert on the topic, you can still learn something new. Do not

Listen with a pencil in your hand. It will help you be an active listener.

© Design Pics Inc./Alamy

assume that college instructors will present the same information you learned in a similar course in high school.

4. **Really hear what is said.** Hearing sounds is not the same as hearing the intended message. Listening involves hearing what the speaker wants you to understand. Don't give in to distractions and try not to pass quick judgment on what is being said. As a critical thinker, make a note of questions that come to mind as you listen but save the judgments for later.
5. **Repeat mentally.** Words can go in one ear and out the other unless you make an effort to retain them. Think about what you hear and restate it silently in your own words. If you cannot translate the information into your own words, ask for further clarification.
6. **Decide whether what you have heard is not important, somewhat important, or very important.** If it's really not important, let it go. If it's very important, make it a major point in your notes by highlighting or underscoring it, or use it as a major topic in your outline if that is the method you use for note taking. If it's somewhat important, try to relate it to a very important topic by writing it down as a subset of that topic.
7. **Ask questions.** Early in the term, determine whether the instructor is open to responding to questions during lecture. Some teachers prefer to save questions for the end, or to have students ask questions during separate discussion sections or office hours. To some extent, this may depend on the nature of the class, such as a large lecture versus a small seminar. If your teacher is open to answering questions as they arise, do not hesitate to ask if you did not hear or understand what was said. It is best to clarify things immediately, if possible, and other students are likely to have the same questions. If you can't hear another student's question, ask that the question be repeated.
8. **Listen to the entire message.** Concentrate on "the big picture," but also pay attention to specific details and examples that can assist you in understanding and retaining information.
9. **Respect your own ideas and those of others.** You already know a lot of things. Your own thoughts and ideas are valuable, and you need not throw them out just because someone else's views conflict with your own. At the same time, don't reject new ideas too casually.
10. **Sort, organize, and categorize.** When you listen, try to match what you are hearing with what you already know. Take an active role in deciding how best to recall what you are learning.

During Class: Take Effective Notes

You can make class time more productive by using your listening skills to take effective notes. Here's how:

1. **Decide on a system.** One method for organizing notes is called the Cornell format, in which you create a "recall" column on each page of your notebook by drawing a vertical line about 2–3 inches from the left border. As you take notes during lecture, write only in the wider column on the right and leave the recall column on the left blank. (If you have large handwriting and this method seems unwieldy, consider using the back of the previous notebook page for your recall column.) We'll return to the recall column later (see Figure 4.2, page 76).

   You may also want to develop your own system of abbreviations. For example, you might write "inst" instead of "institution" or "eval" instead of "evaluation." Just make sure you will be able to understand your abbreviations when it's time to review.

Setting Goals for Success

BEING A BETTER LISTENER

Being a better listener is a worthy goal in all aspects of your life. Think of some ways to improve your listening skills. For instance, do you tend to interrupt your friends when they are speaking? Do you daydream during lectures? Do you tune out your parents? Choose a goal for becoming a better listener in a specific situation, like one of those we just described.

My goal for better listening is: ______________________________

I can achieve this goal by: ______________________________

I want to achieve this goal because: ______________________________

It's important because: ______________________________

I may encounter these obstacles: ______________________________

My strategy for accomplishing this goal is to: ______________________________

2. **Identify the main ideas.** Good lectures always contain key points. The first principle of effective note taking is to identify and write down the most important ideas around which the lecture is built. Although supporting details are important as well, focus your note taking on the main ideas. Such ideas may be buried in details, statistics, anecdotes, or problems, but you will need to locate and record them for further study.

   Some instructors announce the purpose of a lecture or offer an outline, thus providing you with the skeleton of main ideas, followed by the details. Others develop overhead transparencies or PowerPoint presentations, and may make these materials available on a class Web site before lecture. If so, you can enlarge them, print them out, and take notes right on the teacher's outline.

   Some lecturers change their tone of voice or repeat themselves for each key idea. Some ask questions or promote discussion. If a lecturer says something more than once, chances are it's important. Ask yourself, "What does my instructor want me to know at the end of today's session?"
3. **Don't try to write down everything.** Some first-year students try to do just that. They stop being thinkers and become stenographers. Learn to avoid that trap. If you're an active listener, you will ultimately have shorter but more useful notes.

   As you take notes, leave spaces so that you can fill in additional details later that you might have missed during class. But remember to do it as soon after class as possible; remember the forgetting curve.
4. **Don't be thrown by a disorganized lecturer.** When a lecture is disorganized, it's your job to try to organize what is said into general and specific frameworks. When the order is not apparent, you'll need to indicate in your notes where the gaps lie. After the lecture, you will need to consult your reading material or classmates to fill in these gaps.

   You might also consult your instructor. Most instructors have regular office hours for student appointments, yet it is amazing how few students use these opportunities for one-on-one instruction. You can also raise questions in class.

   Asking such questions may help your instructor discover which parts of his or her presentation need more attention and clarification.

Examining Values

You overhear students making the following statements:

> The lecture for this course is so boring. I usually doodle or work on homework for more important classes while the teacher drones on.
>
> I don't really know why I come to class, since the tests are based more on the book than the lecture. I should stay home and read the textbook so I can get an A in the class.
>
> I came to college to learn, and that means soaking up as much knowledge as I can. Sure my teachers can get longwinded at times, but I always leave class feeling like I learned at least one new thing.

What do these statements tell you about the values of each of these students? What does each student value most?

5. **Return to your recall column.** The recall column is essentially the place where you write down the main ideas and important details for tests and examinations as you sift through your notes as soon after class as feasible, preferably within an hour or two. It can be a critical part of effective note taking and becomes an important study device for tests and examinations. In anticipation of using your notes later, treat each page of your notes as part of an exam-preparation system.

   If you are a visual learner, dividing the page creates a visual image that makes it easier to picture key concepts. If you are an interactive learner, study in pairs or with a group. Test one another on the key words or phrases you have jotted down in the recall column to see how much you can remember of the material presented in the lecture.

   If you are an aural learner, look at the recall column while you cover the rest of the page, and recite what you remember from your notes in your own words out loud. Keep in mind that you want to use as many of your five senses as possible to enhance memory. The recall column is a powerful study device that reduces forgetting, helps you warm up for class, and promotes understanding during class.

SEE EXERCISE 4.2: MEMORY: USING A RECALL COLUMN

Taking Notes in Nonlecture Courses

Always be ready to adapt your note-taking methods to match the situation. Group discussion is becoming a popular way to teach in college because it involves active learning. On your campus you may also have Supplemental Instruction (SI) classes that provide further opportunity to discuss the information presented in lectures.

How do you keep a record of what's happening in such classes? Assume you are taking notes in a problem-solving group assignment. You would begin your notes by asking yourself "What is the problem?" and writing down the answer. As the discussion progresses, you would list the solutions offered. These would be your main ideas. The important details might include the positive and negative aspects of each view or solution.

The important thing to remember when taking notes in nonlecture courses is that you need to record the information presented by your classmates as well as from the instructor and to consider all reasonable ideas, even though they may differ from your own.

When a course has separate lecture and discussion sessions, you will need to understand how the discussion sessions augment and correlate with the lectures. If different material is covered in a lecture or discussion, you may need to ask for guidance in organizing your notes. When similar topics are covered, you can combine your notes so that you have comprehensive, unified coverage of each topic.

How to organize the notes you take in a class discussion depends on the purpose or form of the discussion. But it usually makes good sense to begin with a list of issues or topics that the discussion leader announces. Another approach is to list the questions that the participants raise for discussion. If the discussion is exploring reasons for and against a particular argument, it makes sense to divide your notes into columns or sections for pros and cons. When conflicting views are presented in discussion, it is important to record different perspectives and the rationales behind them.

Your teacher may ask you to defend your own opinions in light of those of others.

Comparing and Recopying Notes

You may be able to improve your notes by comparing notes with another student or in a study group or learning community, if one is available to you. Knowing that your notes will be seen by someone else will prompt you to make your notes well organized, clear, and accurate. See whether your notes are as clear and concise as the other person's and whether you agree on the important points that should be included in the recall column. Share how you take and organize your notes with each other and see if you get new ideas for using abbreviations. Take turns testing each other on what you have learned. By doing this, you are predicting exam questions and determining whether you can answer them.

Incidentally, comparing notes is not the same as copying somebody else's notes. You simply cannot learn as well from someone else's notes, no matter how good they are, if you have not attended class.

If your campus has a note-taking service, check with your instructor about making use of this service, but keep in mind that the notes are intended to supplement the ones you take, not to substitute for them. You may have to pay for this service. Some students choose to copy their own notes as a means of review, or because they think their notes are too messy and that they will not be able to understand them later. Unless you are a tactile learner, copying or typing your notes may not help you learn the material. A more profitable approach might be to summarize your notes in your own words.

SEE WORKING TOGETHER EXERCISE: COMPARING NOTES

Finally, have a backup plan in case you do need to be absent due to illness or a family emergency. Exchange phone numbers and e-mail addresses with other students so that you can contact one of them to learn what you missed and get a copy of their notes. Also contact your instructor to explain your absence and set up an appointment during office hours to make sure you understand the work you missed.

Other Kinds of Notes

- *Outline notes* are widely used. If you use this approach, try to determine the instructor's outline and recreate it in your notes. Add details, definitions, examples, applications, and explanations.
- *Definitional notes* work in some courses. Using this method, you would enter the major terms on the left edge of the page, then place all material for a particular term—definitions, explanations, examples, and supporting evidence—beside that term.
- *Paragraph notes* work in some situations. Write detailed paragraphs, with each containing a summary of a topic. This may work better for summarizing what you have read than for class notes, because it may be difficult to summarize the

topic until your teacher has covered it completely. By that time, it may be too late to recall critical information.

- *Fact notes* include only the critical points from the lecture or discussion. The major problem with this method is trying to organize the facts into meaningful groups.

Class Notes and Homework

Good class notes can help you complete homework assignments. Follow these steps:

1. **Take 10 minutes to review your notes.** Skim the notes and put a question mark next to anything you do not understand at first reading. Draw stars next to topics that warrant special emphasis. Try to place the material in context: What has been going on in the course for the past few weeks? How does today's class fit in?
2. **Do a warm-up for your homework.** Before doing the assignment, look through your notes again. Use a separate sheet of paper to rework examples, problems, or exercises. If there is related assigned material in the textbook, review it. Go back to the examples. Cover the solution and attempt to answer each question or complete each problem. Look at the author's work only after you have made a serious personal effort to remember it.

   Keep in mind that it can help to go back through your course notes, reorganize them, highlight the essential items, and thus create new notes that let you connect with the material one more time and are better than the originals.
3. **Do any assigned problems and answer any assigned questions.** Now you are actually starting your homework. As you read each question or problem, ask: What am I supposed to find or find out? What is essential and what is extraneous? Read the problem several times and state it in your own words. Work the problem without referring to your notes or the text, as though you were taking a test. In this way, you'll test your knowledge and will know when you are prepared for exams.
4. **Persevere.** Don't give up too soon. When you encounter a problem or question that you cannot readily handle, move on only after a reasonable effort. After you have completed the entire assignment, come back to those items that stumped you. Try once more, then take a break. You may need to mull over a particularly difficult problem for several days. Let your unconscious mind have a chance. Inspiration may come when you are waiting for a stoplight or just before you fall asleep.
5. **Complete your work.** When you finish an assignment, talk to yourself about what you learned from this particular assignment. Think about how the problems and questions were different from one another, which strategies were successful, and what form the answers took. Be sure to review any material you have not mastered. Seek assistance from the teacher, a classmate, study group, learning center, or tutor to learn how to answer any questions that stumped you.

You may be thinking, this all sounds good, but who has the time to do extra work? In reality, this approach does work and can actually save you time. Try it for a few weeks. You will find that you can diminish the frustration that sometimes comes when you tackle your homework cold, and that you will be more confident going into exams.

Computer Notes in Class?

Laptops are often poor tools for taking notes. Computer screens are not conducive to making marginal notes, circling important items, or copying diagrams. And

Where to Go for Help

ON CAMPUS

Learning Assistance Support Center. Every campus has one of these and this chapter's topic is one of their specialties. More and more we are finding that the best students, and good students who want to be the best students, use learning centers as much as students who are having academic difficulties. These services are offered by both full-time professionals and highly skilled student tutors, many of whom are available at times convenient for you.

Fellow College Students. Often, the best help we can get is the closest to us: from fellow students. But, of course, not just any student. Keep an eye out in your classes, residence hall, co-curricular groups, and other places for the most serious, purposeful, and directed students. Those are the ones to seek out. Find a tutor. Join a study group. Students who do these things are much more likely to stay in college and be successful. It does not diminish you in any way to seek assistance from your peers.

ONLINE

See guidelines for speaking in class and ideas for grading class participation at **<http://trc.virginia.edu/tc/1996/Grading.htm>.**

ON INFOTRAC® COLLEGE EDITION

"What Was Your Name Again? Some Tips for Remembering Names (and Avoiding This Question)," Marilyn S. Nyman, *American Salesman*, August 1996, 41, no. 8: p27(3).

although most students can scribble coherently without watching their hands, few are really good keyboarders. Entering notes on a computer after class for review purposes may be helpful, especially if you are a tactile learner. Then you can print out your notes and highlight or annotate just as you would handwritten notes.

After Class: Respond, Recite, Review

Don't let the forgetting curve take its toll on you. As soon after class as possible, review your notes and fill in the details you still remember, but missed writing down, in those spaces you left in the right-hand column.

Critical Thinking

Divide a piece of loose-leaf paper as shown in Figure 4.2. In one of your classes other than this one, take notes on the right side of the paper, leaving the recall column and the last few lines on the page blank. As soon after class as possible, use the critical thinking process to abstract the main ideas and write them in the recall column. Use the blank lines at the bottom to write a summary sentence or two for that page of notes. Also use the recall column to jot down any thoughts or possibilities that occur to you. Examples might be "I wonder what I can connect this information to so I can recall it later?" or "Maybe if I break my American lit notes into small chunks, they'll be easier to remember." Finally, check at least two sources related to the topic to see whether you can gain further insight. Apply that knowledge to your existing notes and identify it as "Other Sources." It may give you the edge you need to raise your grade.

Relate new information to other things you already know. Organize your information. Make a conscious effort to remember. One way is to recite important data to yourself every few minutes; if you are an aural learner, repeat it out loud. Another is to tie one idea to another idea, concept, or name, so that thinking of one will prompt recall of the other. Or you may want to create your own poem, song, or slogan using the information.

For interactive learners, the best way to learn something may be to teach it to someone else. You will understand something better and remember it longer if you try

Sept. 21 How to take notes

Problems with lectures	Lecture not best way to teach. Problems: Short attention span (may be only 15 minutes!). Teacher dominates. Most info is forgotten. "Stenographer" role interferes with thinking, understanding, learning.
Forgetting curves	Forgetting curves critical period: over ½ of lecture forgotten in 24 hours.
Solution: Active listening	Answer: Active listening, really understanding during lecture. Aims— (1) immediate understanding (2) longer attention (3) better retention (4) notes for study later
Before: Read Warm up	BEFORE: Always prepare. Read: Readings parallel lectures & make them meaningful. Warm up: Review last lecture notes & readings right before class.
During: main ideas	DURING: Write main ideas & some detail. No stenos. What clues does prof. give about what's most important? Ask. Ask other questions. Leave blank column about 2½" on left of page. Use only front side of paper.
After: Review Recall Recite	AFTER: Left column for key recall words, "tags." Cover right side & recite what tags mean. Review/Recall/Recite

Figure 4.2 **Sample Lecture Notes.**

Speaking of Careers

It should be pretty obvious that the skills of listening, note taking, and participating apply to the world of work as well as to the world of the classroom. To prepare for a meeting, you probably will have a memo, a recommendation, or other materials to read. Marking the major issues and writing questions in the margins will help prepare you to participate. Even though someone may be assigned to take notes for the group, you may want to jot down a few relevant reminders for yourself, too.

Think about the line of work you are interested in pursuing after college. Make a short list of the ways you will likely have to use the skills covered in this chapter in that job. This is just another example of how college prepares you for life!

to explain it. This helps you discover your own reactions and uncover gaps in your comprehension of the material. (Asking and answering questions in class also provides you with the feedback you need to make certain your understanding is accurate.) Now you're ready to embed the major points from your notes into your memory. Use these three important steps for remembering the key points in the lecture:

1. **Write the main ideas in the recall column.** For 5 or 10 minutes, quickly review your notes and select key words or phrases that will act as labels or tags for main ideas and key information in the notes. Highlight the main ideas and write them in the recall column next to the material they represent.
2. **Use the recall column to recite your ideas.** Cover the notes on the right and use the prompts from the recall column to help you recite *out loud* a brief version of what you understand from the class in which you have just participated.

   If you don't have a few minutes after class when you can concentrate on reviewing your notes, find some other time during that same day to review what you have written. You might also want to ask your teacher to glance at your recall column to determine whether you have noted the proper major ideas.
3. **Review the previous day's notes just before the next class session.** As you sit in class the next day waiting for the lecture to begin, use the time to quickly review the notes from the previous day. This will put you in tune with the lecture that is about to begin and also prompt you to ask questions about material from the previous lecture that may not have been clear to you.

These three engagements with the material will pay off later, when you begin to study for your exams.

What if you have three classes in a row and no time for recall columns or recitations between them? Recall and recite as soon after class as possible. Review the most recent class first. Never delay recall and recitation longer than one day; if you do, it will take you longer to review, make a recall column, and recite. With practice, you can complete your recall column quickly, perhaps between classes, during lunch, or while riding a bus.

Participating in Class: Speak Up!

Learning is not a spectator sport. To really learn, you must talk about what you are learning, write about it, relate it to past experiences, and make what you learn part of yourself.

Participation is the heart of active learning. We know that when we say something in class, we are more likely to remember it than when someone else does. So when a teacher tosses a question your way, or when you have a question to ask, you're actually making it easier to remember the day's lesson.

Naturally, you will be more likely to participate in a class where the teacher emphasizes discussion, calls on students by name, shows students signs of approval and interest, and avoids shooting you down for an incorrect answer. Often, answers you and others offer that are not quite correct can lead to new perspectives on a topic.

Unfortunately, large classes basically force instructors to use the lecture method. And large classes can be intimidating. If you speak up in a large class and feel you've made a fool of yourself, everyone else in the class will know it. Of course, that's somewhat unrealistic, since you've probably asked a question that they were too timid to ask, and they'll silently thank you for doing so. If you're lucky, you might even find that the instructor of such a class takes time out to ask or answer questions. To take full advantage of these opportunities in all classes, try using these techniques:

1. **Take a seat as close to the front as possible.** If you're seated by name and your name is Zoch, plead bad eyesight or hearing—anything to get moved up front.
2. **Keep your eyes trained on the teacher.** Sitting up front will make this easier for you to do.
3. **Raise your hand when you don't understand something.** But don't overdo it. The instructor may answer you immediately, ask you to wait until later in the class, or throw your question to the rest of the class. In each case, you benefit in several ways. The instructor gets to know you, other students get to know you, and you learn from both the instructor and your classmates.
4. **Never feel that you're asking a "stupid" question.** If you don't understand something, you have a right to ask for an explanation.
5. **When the instructor calls on you to answer a question, don't bluff.** If you know the answer, give it. If you're not certain, begin with, "I think . . . , but I'm not sure I have it all correct." If you don't know, just say so.
6. **If you've recently read a book or article that is relevant to the class topic, bring it in.** Use it either to ask questions about the piece or to provide information from it that was not covered in class. Next time you have the opportunity, speak up. Class will go by faster, you and your fellow students will get to know one another, your instructor will get to know you, and he or she will in all likelihood be grateful to have your participation.

SEE EXERCISE 4.3: WHEN SPEAKING UP IN CLASS IS A REAL PAIN

Reassess Yourself

Now that you've read about listening, note taking, and participating, go back to the self-assessment that appears at the beginning of this chapter. This is an opportunity for you to measure your progress, to check in with yourself and see how reading this chapter may have changed your approach to learning. Which of the items on page 66 did you check? Would you change any of your answers as a result of reading this chapter? If so, which ones, and why?

Exercises

Each of these exercises will let you further explore the topic of this chapter. You'll find all these exercises, plus Internet and InfoTrac® College Edition exercises, on the CD-ROM that accompanies this book.

EXERCISE 4.1 You Will Forget. Remember?

To underscore that memory is a short-term thing, ask your teacher to begin this experiment by whispering a sentence into the ear of one student. Then that student does the same with another student, and so forth until each student has participated. The last student then recites what he or she heard. Then the teacher recites what he or she originally said. It is rare to have the two statements even remotely resemble one another. What does this suggest?

EXERCISE 4.2 Memory: Using a Recall Column

Suppose the information in this chapter had been presented to you as a lecture rather than a reading. Using the system described previously, you produce lecture notes that might look like those in Figure 4.2. Cover the right-hand column. Using the recall column, try reciting in your own words the main ideas from this chapter. Uncover the right-hand column when you need to refer to it. If you can phrase the main ideas from the recall column in your own words, you are well on your way to mastering this note-taking system for dealing with lectures. Does this system seem to work? If not, why not?

EXERCISE 4.3 When Speaking Up in Class Is a Real Pain

If you're uncomfortable speaking up in class, you're not alone. Use this plan to prepare yourself for participating in the class of your choosing:

1. After completing the assigned reading, review the chapter(s) again and choose three or four points that are not entirely clear to you.
2. Write practice questions based on these points, such as: "I was wondering how it would change things if . . .?", "I didn't understand what the textbook author meant by . . .", "I find it interesting that your explanation of . . . is like that. Could there be other explanations?"

Write any sensible questions that come to mind. Guess how the instructor might answer each one. Once you are familiar with the phrasing you will be using, you should be more at ease, and able to participate more freely in class.

If appropriate, e-mail, write, or thank the instructor in person for helping you understand the points you asked about.

Working Together
Comparing Notes

Pair up with another student and compare your class notes for this course. Are your notes clear? Do you agree on what is important? Take a few minutes to explain to each other your note-taking systems. Agree to use a recall column during the next class meeting. Afterward, share your notes again and check on how each of you used the recall column. Again, compare your notes and what each of you deemed important.

See the CD-ROM for these additional exercises as well as all other exercises appearing in this chapter

Exercise 4.4	Listening and Memory
Exercise 4.5	Applying an Active Listening and Learning System
Internet Exercise 4.1	Study Skills Guides on the Internet
Internet Exercise 4.2	Assessing Participation
InfoTrac® College Edition Exercise 4.1	Researching Listening and Learning

5

Reading and Remembering

©Royalty-Free/ CORBIS

Jeanne L. Higbee of the University of Minnesota, Twin Cities, contributed her valuable and considerable expertise to the writing of this chapter.

Going Forward: Student Voices

Five pages down, thirty to go! This stuff is so boring! I have no idea what I just read. Oh well, at a page a minute I should be done in half an hour.

Looking Back: Author Voices

Half the time I couldn't make sense of what the textbook said. Even when I tried hard, something always distracted me. I'd daydream about things I'd rather be doing and then doing those things instead of studying. I finally learned how to read a textbook, but my ignorance certainly lowered my first-year grades. **Jerry Jewler**

In this chapter, YOU WILL LEARN

- What it means to "prepare to read"
- How to preview reading material
- Strategies for reading your textbooks efficiently
- How to mark your textbooks
- Why you should review your reading
- How to adjust your reading style to the material
- Ways to develop a more extensive vocabulary
- Techniques you can use to better remember what you read and hear

hy is reading college textbooks more challenging than reading high school texts or reading for pleasure? College texts are loaded with concepts, terms, and complex information that you are expected to learn on your own in a short period of time. To do this, you will need to learn and use a reading method such as the one in this chapter.

With effort, you can improve your reading dramatically, but remember to be flexible. How you read should depend on the material. Assess the relative importance and difficulty of the assigned readings, and adjust your reading style and the time you allot accordingly. Connect one important idea to another by asking yourself, "Why am I reading this? Where does this fit in?" When the textbook material is virtually identical to the lecture material, you can save time by concentrating mainly on one or the other. It takes a planned approach to read textbook materials and other assigned readings with good understanding and recall.

The following plan for textbook reading can pay off. It is designed to increase your focus and concentration, promote greater understanding of what you read, and prepare you to study for tests and exams. This system is based on four steps: previewing, reading, marking, and reviewing.

Previewing

The purpose of previewing is to get the "big picture," to understand how what you are about to read is connected to what you already know and to the material the instructor is covering in class.

Begin by reading the title of the chapter. Ask yourself, "What do I already know about this subject?" Next, quickly read through the introductory paragraphs, then read the summary at the beginning or end of the chapter (if one is there). Finally, take a few minutes to page through the chapter headings and subheadings. Note any study exercises at the end of the chapter.

As part of your preview, note how many pages the chapter contains. It's a good idea to decide in advance how many pages you can reasonably expect to cover in your first 50-minute study period. This can help build your concentration as you

Self-Assessment

Evaluating Your Reading Habits

Read each of the following statements and put a check mark in front of those that come close to describing you:

1. ______ I skim or "preview" a chapter before I begin to read.
2. ______ I use strategies to keep myself from losing concentration while reading.
3. ______ I wait to underline, highlight, or annotate the text until *after* I read a page or section.
4. ______ I take notes after I read.
5. ______ I pause at the end of each section or page to review what I have read.
6. ______ After reading, I recite key ideas to myself or with a partner.
7. ______ I review everything I have read for a class at least once a week.
8. ______ I write down unfamiliar words as I read and then look up their definitions.
9. ______ I use memory aids to help myself remember what I've read.

work toward your goal of reading a specific number of pages. Before long, you'll know how many pages is practical for you.

Keep in mind that different types of textbooks may require more or less time to read. For example, depending on your interests and previous knowledge, you may be able to read a psychology text more quickly than a logic text that presents a whole new system of symbols.

Mapping

Mapping the chapter as you preview it provides a visual guide to how different chapter ideas fit together. Because about 75 percent of students identify themselves as visual learners, visual mapping is an excellent learning tool for test preparation as well as reading (see Chapter 2: Discovering How You Learn).

How do you map a chapter? While you are previewing, use either a wheel or branching structure (Figure 5.1). In the wheel structure, place the central idea of the chapter in the circle, place secondary ideas on the spokes emanating from the circle, and place offshoots of those ideas on the lines attached to the spokes. In the branching map, the main idea goes at the top, followed by supporting ideas on the second tier, and so forth. Fill in the title first. Then, as you skim through the rest of the chapter, use the headings and subheadings to fill in the key ideas.

Alternatives to Mapping

Perhaps you prefer a more linear visual image. Then consider making an outline of the headings and subheadings in the chapter. You can fill in the outline after you read. Or make a list. Making a list can be particularly effective when dealing with a text that introduces lots of new terms and their definitions. Set up the list with the terms in the left column and fill in definitions, descriptions, and examples on the right after you read. Divide the terms on your list into groups of five, seven, or nine,

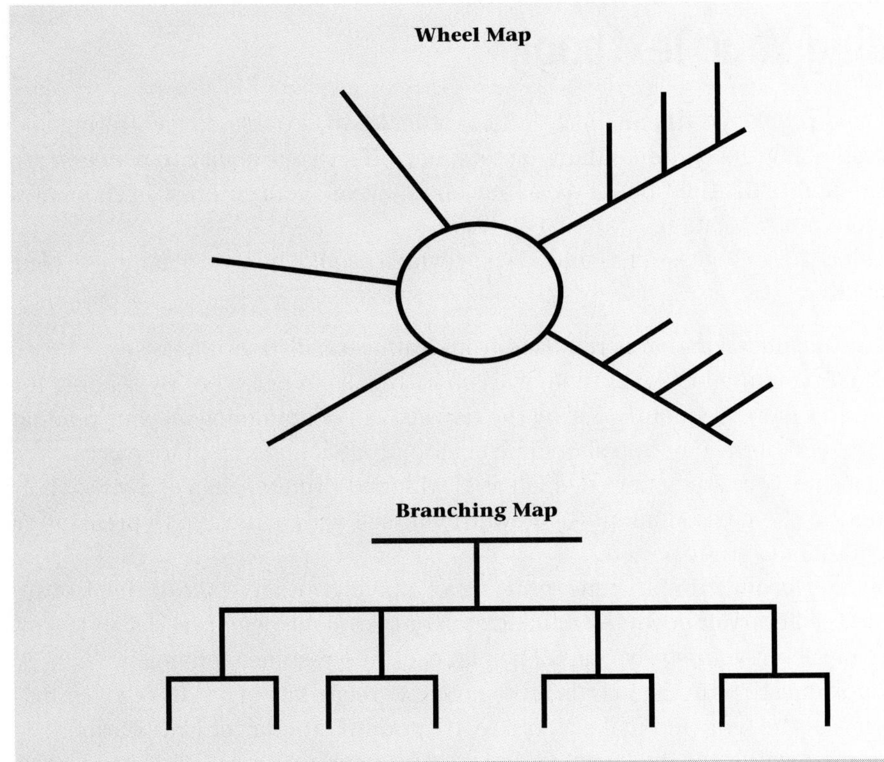

Figure 5.1 Wheel and Branching Maps.

and leave white space between the clusters so that you can visualize each group in your mind. This practice is known as *chunking.* Research indicates that we learn material better in chunks of five, seven, or nine.

SEE EXERCISE 5.1: PREVIEWING AND CREATING A VISUAL MAP

If you are an interactive learner, make lists or create a flash card for each heading and subheading. Then fill in the back of each card after reading each section in the text. Use the lists or flash cards to review with a partner, or to recite the material to yourself.

Previewing, combined with mapping, outlining, or flash cards, may require more time up front, but it will save you time later because you have created an excellent review tool for quizzes and tests. You will be using your visual learning skills as you create "advance organizers" to help you associate details of the chapter with the larger ideas. Such associations will come in handy later.

SEE EXERCISE 5.2: DOING WHAT IT TAKES TO UNDERSTAND

As you preview the text material, look for connections between the text and the related lecture material. Call to mind the related terms and concepts that you recorded in lecture. Use these strategies to warm up. Ask yourself, "Why am I reading this? What do I want to know?"

Critical Thinking

Turn one statement in this chapter into a question. For instance, you might select a sentence from the section on Reading Your Textbook on page 84 and ask the question, "Why should I read in 50-minute blocks of time, with short breaks in between?" Use the critical thinking process to find an answer to that question. Brainstorm some ideas, sift through them, and choose one or two that seem to work. Share your process and results with other students in your group.

Reading Your Textbook

Two common problems students have with textbooks are trouble concentrating and not understanding the content. Many factors may affect your ability to concentrate and understand texts: the time of day, your energy level, your interest in the material, and your study location.

Consider these suggestions, and decide which would help you improve your reading ability:

- Find a study location that is removed from traffic and distracting noises.
- Read in 50-minute blocks of time, with short breaks in between. By reading for 50 minutes more frequently during the day instead of cramming all your reading in at the end of the day, you should be able to process material more easily.
- Set goals for your study period, such as "I will read twenty pages of my psychology text in the next 50 minutes." Reward yourself with a 10-minute break after each 50-minute study period.
- If you are having trouble concentrating or staying awake, take a quick walk around the library or down the hall. Stretch or take some deep breaths and think positively about your study goals. Then go back and resume studying.
- Jot study questions in the margin, take notes, or recite key ideas. Reread confusing parts of the text, and make a note to ask your instructor for clarification.
- Experiment with your reading rate. Try to move your eyes more quickly over the material by focusing on phrases, not individual words. If that doesn't work, go back to the method that does.
- Focus on the important portions of the text. Pay attention to the first and last sentences of paragraphs and to words in italics or bold print.
- Use the glossary in the text to define unfamiliar terms.

Setting Goals for Success

DEVELOPING YOUR MEMORY

The benefits of having a good memory are probably obvious to you. In school, your memory will help you retain information and ace tests. After college, the ability to recall names, procedures, and appointments readily will save you energy and time. What do you find hardest to remember in the courses you are taking? Names and dates in history? How to perform particular mathematical calculations? Certain rules of grammar and syntax? Select a goal for improving your memory in that area and devise a plan to implement your goal.

I want to be able to remember the following things better: __________

I can achieve this goal by: __________

I want to achieve this goal because: __________

It's important because: __________

I may encounter these obstacles: __________

My strategy for accomplishing this goal is to: __________

Reading to Question, to Interpret, to Understand

An important step in textbook reading is to monitor your comprehension. As you read, ask yourself, "Do I understand this?" If not, stop and reread the material. Look up words that are not clear. Try to clarify the main points and how they relate to one another.

Another way to check comprehension is to try to recite the material out loud to yourself or your study partner. Using a study group to monitor your comprehension gives you immediate feedback and is highly motivating. One way that group members can work together is to divide up a chapter for previewing and studying and get together later to teach the material to one another.

After you have read and marked or taken notes on key ideas from the first section of the chapter, proceed to each subsequent section until you have finished the chapter. After you have completed each section—and *before* you move on to the next section—ask again, "What are the key ideas? What will I see on the test?" At the end of each section, try to guess what information the author will present in the next section.

Good reading should lead you from one section to the next, with each new section adding to your understanding.

Marking Your Textbook

Think a moment about your goals for marking in your texts. Some students report that marking is an active reading strategy that helps them focus and concentrate on the material as they read. In addition, most students expect to use their text notations when studying for tests. To meet these goals, some students like to underline, some prefer to highlight, and others use margin notes or annotations. Look at Figure 5.2 on pages 86–87 for examples of different methods of marking. You can also combine methods.

No matter what method you prefer, remember the following important guidelines.

Read Before You Highlight

After completing your preview, you are ready to read the text actively. With your wheel or branching map or outline, you should be able to read more quickly and with greater comprehension.

To avoid marking too much or marking the wrong information, read first without using your pencil or highlighter. Newspaper editors say you should "sit on your hands" the first time you read something, to avoid getting caught up in the details before you grasp the big ideas. When you have reached the end of a section, stop and ask yourself, "What are the key ideas in this section? What do I think I'll see on the test?" Then, and only then, decide what to underline or highlight.

Annotate

You may want to try a strategy known as annotating the text. In your own words, write key ideas in the margins of the text. This involves two strategies, taking notes and paraphrasing what you've read.

Take Notes

If you just mark pages, you are committing yourself to at least one more viewing of all the pages that you have already read—all 400 pages of your anatomy or art history textbook. A more productive use of your time might be taking notes, creating flash cards, making lists, or outlining textbook chapters. These methods are also more practical if you intend to review with a friend or study group.

CONCEPT CHECKS

7. Some students who read a chapter slowly get very good grades; others get poor grades. Why?

8. Most actors and public speakers who have to memorize lengthy passages spend little time simply repeating the words and more time thinking about them. Why? (Check your answers on page 288.)

People need to monitor their understanding of a text to decide whether to keep studying or whether they already understand it well enough. Most readers have trouble making that judgment correctly.

Self-Monitoring of Understanding

Whenever you are studying a text, you periodically have to decide, "Should I keep on studying this section, or do I already understand it well enough?" Most students have trouble monitoring their own understanding. In one study, psychology instructors asked their students before each test to guess whether they would do better or worse on that test than they usually do. Students also guessed after each test whether they had done better or worse than usual. Most students' guesses were no more accurate than chance (Sjostrom & Marks, 1994). Such inaccuracy represents a problem: Students who do not know how well they understand the material will make bad judgments about when to keep on studying and when to quit.

why

Even when you are reading a single sentence, you have to decide whether you understand the sentence or whether you should stop and reread it. Here is a sentence once published in the student newspaper at North Carolina State University:

> He said Harris told him she and Brothers told French that grades had been changed.

How

Ordinarily, when good readers come to such a confusing sentence, they notice their own confusion and reread the sentence or, if necessary, the whole paragraph. Poor readers tend to read at their same speed for both easy and difficult materials; they are less likely than good readers to slow down when they come to difficult sentences.

Although monitoring one's own understanding is difficult and often inaccurate, it is not impossible. For example, suppose I tell you that you are to read three chapters dealing with, say, thermodynamics, the history of volleyball, and the Japanese stock market. Later you will take tests on each chapter. Before you start reading, predict your approximate scores on the three tests. Most people make a guess based on how much they already know about the three topics. If we let them read the three chapters and again make a guess about their test performances, they do in fact make more accurate predictions than they did before reading (Maki & Serra, 1992). That improvement indicates some ability to monitor one's own understanding of a text.

A systematic way to monitor your own understanding of a text is the **SPAR method:** **S**urvey, **P**rocess meaningfully, **A**sk questions, and **R**eview and test yourself. Start with an overview of what a passage is about, read it carefully, and then see whether you can answer questions about the passage or explain it to others. If not, go back and reread.

SPAR
Survey
Process
Ask
Review

Also decide about larger units?

The Timing of Study

Other things being equal, people tend to remember recent experiences better than earlier experiences. For example, suppose someone reads you a list of 20 words and asks you to recall as many of them as possible. The list is far too long for you to recite from your phonological loop; however, you should be able to remember at least a few. Typically, people remember items at the beginning and end of the list better than they remember those in the middle.

That tendency, known as the **serial-order effect,** includes two aspects: The *primacy effect* is the tendency to remember the first items; the *recency effect* refers to the tendency to remember the last items. One explanation for the primacy effect is that the listener gets to rehearse the first few items for a few moments alone with no interference from the others. One explanation for the recency effect is that the last items are still in

Cause of primacy effect

Memory Improvement

283

Figure 5.2 Sample Marked Pages.

Source: Pages adapted with permission from James W. Kalat, *Introduction to Psychology*, 4th ed., Pacific Grove, CA: Brooks/Cole, 1996.

the listener's phonological loop at the time of the test.

Cause of recency effect

The phonological loop cannot be the whole explanation for the recency effect, however. In one study, British rugby players were asked to name the teams they had played against in the current season. Players were most likely to remember the last couple of teams they had played against, thus showing a clear recency effect even though they were recalling events that occurred weeks apart (Baddeley & Hitch, 1977). (The phonological loop holds information only for a matter of seconds.)

So, studying material—or, rather, *reviewing* material—shortly before a test is likely to improve recall. Now let's consider the opposite: Suppose you studied something years ago and have not reviewed it since then. For example, suppose you studied a foreign language in high school several years ago. Now you are considering taking a college course in the language, but you are hesitant because you are sure you have forgotten it all. Have you?

Harry Bahrick (1984) tested people who had studied Spanish in school 1 to 50 years previously. Nearly all agreed that they had rarely used Spanish and had not refreshed their memories at all since their school days. (That is a disturbing comment, but beside the point.) Their retention of Spanish dropped noticeably in the first 3 to 6 years, but remained fairly stable from then on (Figure 7.18). In other words, we do not completely forget even very old memories that we seldom use.

In a later study, Bahrick and members of his family studied foreign-language vocabulary either on a moderately frequent basis (practicing once every 2 weeks) or on a less frequent basis (as seldom as once every 8 weeks), and tested their knowledge years later. The result: More frequent study led to faster learning; however, less frequent study led to better long-term retention, measured years later (Bahrick, Bahrick, Bahrick, & Bahrick, 1993).

The principle here is far more general than just the study of foreign languages. *If you want to remember something well for a test,* your best strategy is to study it as close as possible to the time of the test, in order to take advantage of the recency effect and decrease the effects of retroactive interference. Obviously, I do not mean that you should wait until the night before the test to start studying, but you might rely on an extensive review at that time. You should also, ideally, study under conditions similar to the conditions of the test. For example, you might study in the same room where the test will be given, or at the same time of day.

However, *if you want to remember something long after the test is over,* then the advice I have just given you is all wrong. To be able to remember something whenever you want, wherever you are, and whatever you are doing, you should study it under as varied circumstances as possible. Study and review at various times and places with long, irregular intervals between study sessions. Studying under such inconsistent conditions will slow down your original learning, but it will improve your ability to recall it long afterwards (Schmidt & Bjork, 1992).

studying for test vs. studying for long term

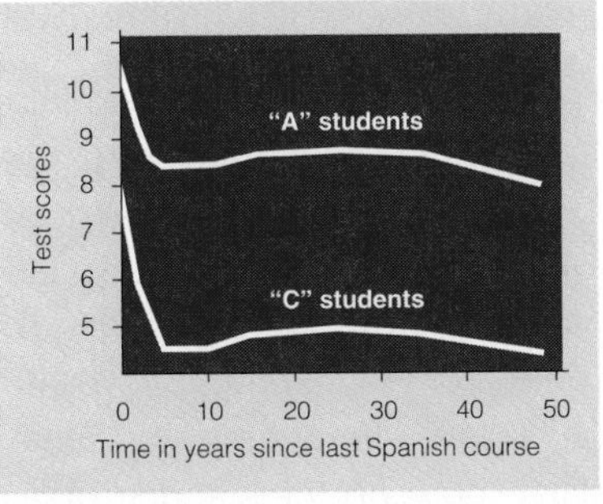

FIGURE 7.18
(Left) Spanish vocabulary as measured by a recognition test shows a rapid decline in the first few years but then long-term stability. (From Bahrick, 1984.) (Right) Within a few years after taking your last foreign-language course, you may think you have forgotten it all. You have not, and even the part you have forgotten will come back (through relearning) if you visit a country where you can practice the language.

CHAPTER 7
MEMORY
284

Say It Your Own Way

Sometimes, highlighting or underlining can provide you with a false sense of security. You may have determined what is most important, but you have not necessarily tested yourself on your understanding of the material. When you force yourself to put something in your own words when taking notes, you are not only predicting exam questions but also assessing whether you can answer them.

SEE EXERCISE 5.3: PREPARING TO READ, THINK, AND MARK

Although these active reading strategies take more time initially, they can save you time in the long run because they not only promote concentration as you read but also make it easy to review. So you probably won't have to pull an all-nighter before an exam.

Reviewing

The final step in effective textbook reading is reviewing. Many students expect the improbable—that they will read through their text material one time and be able to remember the ideas 4, 6, or even 12 weeks later at test time. More realistically, you will need to include regular reviews in your study process. Here is where your notes, study questions, annotations, flash cards, visual maps, or outlines will be most useful. Your study goal is to review the material from each chapter every week.

Consider ways to use your many senses to review. Recite out loud. Tick off each item in a list on each of your fingertips. Post diagrams, maps, or outlines around your living space so that you will see them often and will likely be able to visualize them while taking the test.

Developing Your Vocabulary

Textbooks are full of new terminology. In fact, one could argue that learning chemistry is largely a matter of learning the language of chemists and that mastering philosophy or history or sociology requires a mastery of the terminology of each particular discipline.

If words are such a basic and essential component of our knowledge, what is the best way to learn them? Follow these basic vocabulary strategies:

- During your overview of the chapter, notice and jot down unfamiliar terms.
- Consider making a flash card for each term, or making a list.
- When you encounter challenging words, consider the context. See if you can predict the meaning of an unfamiliar term using the surrounding words.
- If context is not enough, try analyzing the term to discover the root or other meaningful parts of the word. For example, the word *emissary* has the root "to emit" or "to send forth," so we can guess that an emissary is someone sent forth with a message. Similarly, note prefixes and suffixes. For example, *anti-* means "against" and *pro-* means "for."

Examining Values

The four-step reading process described in this chapter requires a commitment to active learning. It means working through a reading process rather than lazily scanning the pages of your textbooks.

How much time do you allot to reading for your courses? Is it sufficient time to follow the four-step method? Are you willing to devote more time to reading? If not, why not?

Where to Go for Help

ON CAMPUS

Learning Assistance Support Center. Every campus has one of these and reading assistance is one of their specialties. The best students, good students who want to be the best students, and students with academic difficulties all use learning centers. These services are offered by both full-time professionals and highly skilled student tutors.

Fellow College Students. Often, the best help we can get is the closest to us. Keep an eye out in your classes, residence hall, co-curricular groups, and so forth for the best students, those who appear to be the most serious, purposeful, and directed. Find a tutor, whether or not you have to pay for one. Join a study group. Students who do these things are much more likely to be successful.

ONLINE

Go to **<http://www.mtsu.edu/~studskl/Txtbook.html>** for additional material on reading textbooks. Visit **<http://www.lcc.ctc.edu/faculty/kdemarest/INDV96/TextbkLinks.htm>** for more reading assistance from a number of different colleges and universities.

ON INFOTRAC® COLLEGE EDITION

Reading key to classroom success. Lucia Herndon, *Knight Ridder/Tribune News Service*, October 14, 1997, p. 1014K0456 (originated from Knight-Ridder Newspapers). Although this InfoTrac® College Edition article discusses reading skills for children, we believe much of it applies to college students. Do you agree?

Can your PC help you read faster? *Bill Machrone, PC Magazine*, March 12, 1996, 15, no. 5:83(1). This unusual InfoTrac® College Edition article is about an experiment using a computer to help people read faster. What's your take on it?

Memorizing comes easy for O'Brien. *New Straits Times*, June 5, 2001, p. NSTP17052121. Read about a man who was dyslexic as a child and not only learned to memorize, but also set a world record for it.

- Use the glossary/index of this text, a dictionary, or *<www.m-w.com/netdict.htm>* (*The Merriam-Webster Dictionary Online*) to locate the definition. Note any multiple definitions and search for the meaning that fits this usage.
- Take every opportunity to use these new terms in your writing and speaking. If you use a new term, then you'll know it! In addition, studying new terms on flash cards or study sheets can be handy at exam time.

Improving Your Memory

Forty years after he had heard a song, a man thought about it one day, hummed the tune, and began singing the lyrics. He had no idea what had triggered this memory and was astounded when he found he knew all the words.

Of course, this was a rather unusual song. Music and rhymes are known aids to memory, but the lyrics of this rather daffy song offered another aid: They were based on the alphabet. "A, you're adorable; B, you're so beautiful: C, you're a cutie full of charms. . . ." Rhymes, music, and lyrics pegged to letters all made it easier to remember the song. But you aren't trying to remember a song. What you are trying to remember are thoughts, concepts, reasons, and ideas.

Anecdotal evidence suggests that elephants, which possess the largest brains of any land animal, are intelligent creatures with impressive memories. The animals can learn up to 100 commands. After mastering tricks, circus elephants seem able to recall them indefinitely. Other animals, including the domesticated dog, have the capacity to associate human words with actions. When you say, "Gracie, sit!" Gracie usually sits.[1]

Cal Fussman tells of discovering a simple way to remember things:

> *My eureka came at the library when I stumbled onto a book called* Total Recall *by Joan Minninger. I fixed on a phrase on the jacket that read, "How to Remember 20 Things in Less Than Two Minutes." The book suggests associating the first ten things you want to remember with body parts, starting at the top of your head and going down to your forehead, nose, mouth, throat, chest, belly button, hips, thighs, and feet.*
>
> *I was determined to memorize a list of twelve white wines, going roughly from lightest to weightiest. I tapped the top of my head. That would be the two lightest whites, Soave and Orvieto. Then my forehead—that'd be Riesling. Nose: Muscadet. Mouth: Champagne. Throat: Chenin blanc. . . . I tapped each corresponding body part, saying the name of the wine aloud. By the fifth time, without even trying, crazy associations began to invade my mind. As I tapped the top of my head, I thought, Start Out, and the S made me think of Soave and the O of Orvieto. I touched my forehead, thought, Reeeemember, and the Reeee brought Riesling off my tongue. I tapped my nose and smelled musk cologne, which triggered Muscadet, then tapped my lips and blew a kiss as if I'd just tasted Dom Perignon champagne. . . . Took me less than three minutes—and it solved my problems.*[2]

Another way to "peg" words goes like this: As you're driving to campus, choose some landmarks along the way. The next day, as you pass those landmarks, relate them to something from your class notes or readings. The white picket fence might remind you of "work 20 hours or less a week," whereas the tall oak tree on the next block reminds you to "work on campus if at all possible."

Remember How You Remember Best

Have you ever had to memorize a speech, or lines from a play? One actor records her lines as well as the lines of others on a cassette and listens to them in her car when driving to and from work each day. Another actor records only others' lines and leaves blank time on the tape so that he can recite his lines at the proper moments. Another remembers lines by visualizing where they appear in the script: left-hand page, top; right-hand page, middle; and so forth. And another simply reads and rereads the script over and over until it becomes second nature.

Can you apply similar approaches to remembering material for exams? To some degree, perhaps. But though knowing certain words will help, remembering concepts and ideas may be much more important. To embed such ideas in you mind, ask yourself as you review your notes and textbooks:

1. What is the essence, or main point, of the idea?
2. Why does this idea make sense? (What is the logic behind it?)
3. What arguments against the idea could there be?
4. How does this idea connect to other ideas in the material?

[1]Steve Nadis, "Who You Calling Dumbo? (Memory in Elephants)," *Omni*, June 1993, 15, no. 8: 20.
[2]Cal Fussman, "Thanks for the Memory," *Esquire*, February 1999, 131, 12:142(1).

Speaking of Careers

Think about some successful people that you know, have read about, or have seen on television. Many of them rose to the top of their professions by developing a knack for remembering crucial information: the politician who seems to never forget a person's name; your family physician, who seems to be able to remember entire manuals of diagnostic and pharmaceutical information without having to look it up; the teacher who has a wealth of knowledge at his or her fingertips. What types of information will you need to remember in your future career? And how will you remember it?

More Aids to Memory

The human mind has discovered ingenious ways to remember information. Here are some additional methods that may be useful to you when you're nailing down the causes of the Civil War, trying to remember the steps in a physics problem, or absorbing a mathematical formula.

1. **Overlearn.** Even after you know the material, go over it again to make sure you'll retain it for a long time. Test yourself—make sure you really know it as well as you think you do. Recite it out loud in your own words.
2. **Use multiple senses.** Read it, discuss it, draw, write, or type it.
3. **Categorize.** If the information seems to lack an inherent organization, impose one. Most information can be organized in some way, even if only by the look or sound of the words. For example, if you are trying to remember the names of the first ten presidents of the United States, you might remember that there are 2 A's, 2 J's, and 2 M's, and then memorize W-HVT (the initials for Washington, Harrison, Van Buren, and Tyler). Or that six of them have names ending in "n."
4. **Use mnemonics.** Create rhymes, jingles, sayings, or nonsense phrases that repeat or codify information. "Homes" is a mnemonic for remembering the five Great Lakes: Huron, Ontario, Michigan, Erie, and Superior. How can you forget this state capital when you know that "Arkan saw a little rock"? Or ask yourself, "D'you know (Juneau) the capital of Alaska?" "Spring forward, fall back" tells many Americans how to reset their clocks twice a year. Setting a rhyme to music is one of the most powerful ways to make words memorable.
5. **Associate.** Relate the idea to something you already know. Make the association as personal as possible. If you're reading a chapter on laws regarding free speech, pretend that your right to speak out on a subject that's important to you

©Walter Bibikow/Index Stock Imagery

Symbols are often used as memory joggers.

may be affected by those laws. In remembering the spelling difference between *through* and *threw,* think of walking through something "rough," and that *threw* comes from *throw.*

6. **Visualize.** Make yourself see the things that you've associated with important concepts. To recall an important point regarding free speech, imagine yourself in a colonial court imploring the assembled crowd to understand your reasoning. To remember what caused the *Titanic* to sink, visualize the ocean water bursting through the small tears in the hull, popping rivets that held the hull together. Concentrate on the images so they'll become firmly planted in your memory.
7. **Use flash cards.** Write the word or information to be learned on one side and the definition or explanation on the other. Review the cards in groups of five, seven, or nine. After you have mastered a group, go on to the next. Prepare them early and spend more time on the hard ones. Review often.

SEE EXERCISE 5.4: SHARPENING YOUR MEMORY

Reassess Yourself

Now that you've read about reading and memory, go back to the self-assessment that appears at the beginning of this chapter. This is an opportunity for you to measure your progress, to check in with yourself and see how reading this chapter may have changed your approach to learning. Which of the items on page 82 did you check? Would you change any of your answers as a result of reading this chapter? If so, which ones, and why?

Exercises

Each of these exercises will let you further explore the topic of this chapter. You'll find all these exercises, plus Internet and InfoTrac® College Edition exercises, on the CD-ROM that accompanies this book.

EXERCISE 5.1 Previewing and Creating a Visual Map

Preview this chapter and create a visual map, noting the following information: title, key points from the introduction, any graphics (maps, charts, tables, diagrams), study questions, or exercises built into or at the end of the chapter, introduction and summary paragraphs. Create either a wheel or branching map as shown in Figure 5.1. Add spokes or tiers as necessary.

Working Together Exercise
Comparing Visual Maps

After completing Exercise 5.1, gather in a small group and compare your work. Now, arrange the same information from your visual maps in outline form. Which seems to work better for you? Why?

EXERCISE 5.2 Doing What It Takes to Understand

How far must you go to understand the material in a textbook? Here is one way to find out. If you need to go through all the steps, don't panic. Most people would probably have to do the same.

- Read a brief chapter in your book as if you were reading for pleasure.

- Read it a second time, but pause at the end of each section to mentally review what you just read.
- Read it a third time, pause at the end of each section for review, then go back and highlight important words or sentences.
- Read it a fourth time and do all of the above. This time ask a friend to read with you and discuss each passage in the chapter before going on to the next. Also stop and take notes, write in the margins, highlight, and so forth.

EXERCISE 5.3 Preparing to Read, Think, and Mark

Choose a reading assignment for one of your classes. After previewing the material as described earlier in this chapter, begin reading until you reach a major heading or until you have read at least a page or two. Now, stop and write down what you remember from the material. Then go back to the same material and mark what you believe are the main ideas. Don't fall into the trap of marking too much. Now, list four of the main ideas from the reading:

1. ______________________________
2. ______________________________
3. ______________________________
4. ______________________________

EXERCISE 5.4 Sharpening Your Memory

Practice using association, visualization, and flash cards to improve your memory. Try this with a week's lessons from one of your courses.

1. **Visualization.** Close your eyes and "see" your notes or textbook assignments in action. Break your notes into chunks and create a visual image for each chunk.
2. **Association.** Associate a chunk of information to something familiar. If you want to remember that *always* usually signifies a wrong answer on multiple choice or true/false quizzes, associate the word *always* with a concept such as "always wrong."
3. **Flash cards.** Write a key word from the material on one side and put the details on the reverse. Review often, looking at only five to nine cards at a time. An example might be: Write the words "Ways to Remember" on one side, and on the other write "Go over it again. Use all senses. Organize it. Mnemonics. Association. Visualization. Flash cards." Which of the methods worked best for you? Why?

Working Together Exercise
The Memory Game

This exercise should demonstrate how difficult it can be to remember things accurately. One student whispers the name of an object (lamp, bike, hamburger, etc.) to the other. Then the second student whispers the word(s) to the third student and adds a second word or phrase. The third student whispers both words, adding still another word, and so forth. Each student who adds a word should write it down. When the final student recites the list, students whose words were left out or changed should speak up. The class should then discuss what strategies they were using to remember the list and why they forgot certain items.

See the CD-ROM for these additional exercises as well as all other exercises appearing in this chapter

Exercise 5.5	Expanding Your Vocabulary
Exercise 5.6	How to Read Fifteen Pages of a Textbook in an Hour or Less
Internet Exercise 5.1	Reading Web Pages Critically
InfoTrac® College Edition Exercise 5.1	Researching How to Read Texts
InfoTrac® College Edition Exercise 5.2	Learning More about Memory

6 Taking Tests

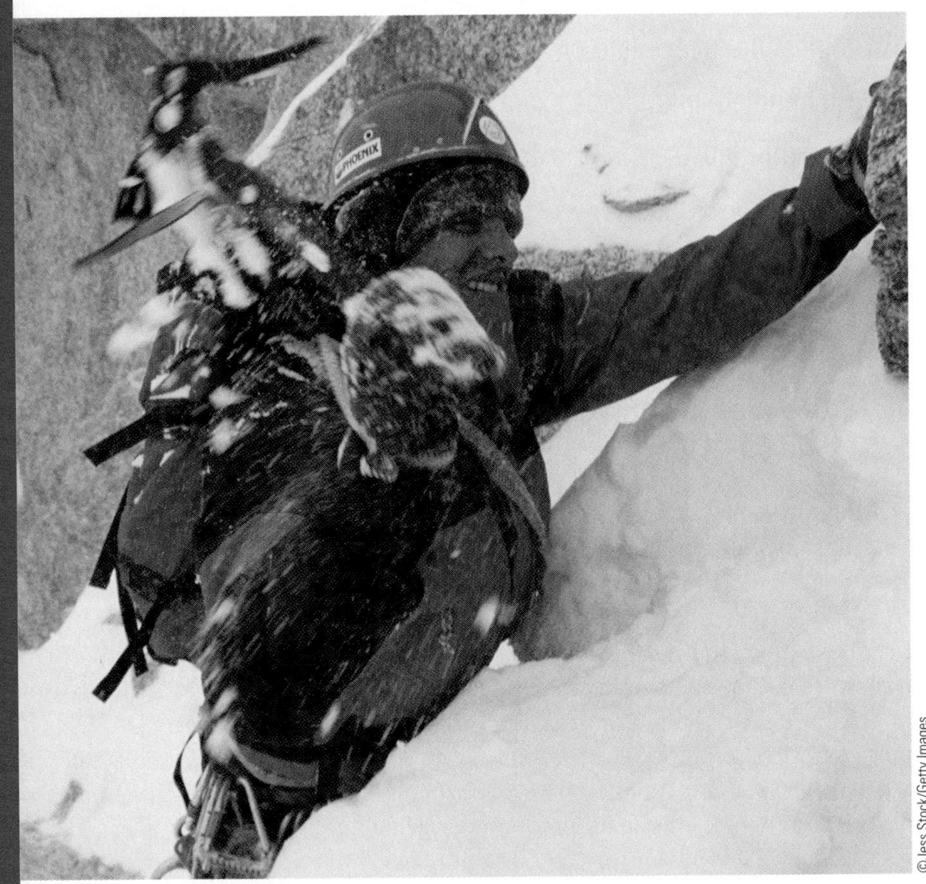

©Jess Stock/Getty Images

Jeanne L. Higbee of the University of Minnesota, Twin Cities, contributed her valuable and considerable expertise to the writing of this chapter.

Going Forward: Student Voices

Three tests in the next two days! I am never going to live through this week. I studied hard and I didn't cheat. Now here I am walking into class and my mind is a total blank. Help!

Looking Back: Author Voices

I had a lot of essay exams, and I wrote so quickly that even I had trouble figuring out what the words said. But the important thing was that I had plenty to say, and that told me that I really had gotten involved in the material through assigned readings and class discussions. Jerry Jewler

In this chapter, YOU WILL LEARN

- How to prepare for an exam
- Study tips that will help improve your grades
- How to do better on essay exams
- Strategies for succeeding on various kinds of objective tests
- How to handle a take-home exam
- How cheating hurts you, your friends, and your college

Now that you've learned how to listen and take notes in class and how to read and review your notes and assigned readings, you're ready to use those skills to score high on tests and exams. You can prepare for exams in many ways, and certain methods are more effective depending on your preferred learning style. In this chapter you'll find advice on preparing physically, academically, and emotionally for exams.

Regardless of the study method you use, your goal always will be to seek the truth. Many students entering college assume that every problem has a single right answer and the instructor or the textbook is always a source of truth. Yet some questions may have more than one correct answer, and your teachers will accept a number of answers as long as they correctly answer the question. See Table 6.1, How Your Approach and Attitude Toward a Test Affects Your Performance.

Since college instructors expect you to use higher-level thinking skills such as analysis, synthesis, and evaluation, they continually use tests and exams to ask for reasons, for arguments, for the assumptions on which a given position is based, and for the evidence that confirms or discounts it. They want you to be able to support your opinions, to see *how* you think. You can cough up a list of details from lecture notes or readings, but unless you can make sense of them, you probably won't get much credit.

Exams: The Long View

You actually began preparing for a test on the first day of the term. All your lecture notes, assigned readings, and homework were part of that preparation. As the test day nears, you should know how much additional time you will need to review, what material the test will cover, and what format the test will take.

Three things will help you study well:

- *Ask your instructor.* Have you learned from your instructor the purpose, conditions, and content of the exam? Have you talked with your instructor to clarify any misunderstandings you may have about the content of the course? Ask your instructor whether it will be essay, multiple-choice, true/false, or another kind of test. Ask if the test covers the entire term's worth of material, or just the material since the last test. Ask how long the test will last and how it will be graded. Some instructors may let you see copies of old exams, so you can see the types

Self-Assessment
Test Taking

Place a check mark in front of the items that best describe you:

1. ________ I always study for essay tests by predicting possible questions and outlining the answers.
2. ________ I always begin studying for an exam at least a week in advance.
3. ________ I usually study for an exam with at least one other person.
4. ________ I usually know what to expect on a test before I go into the exam.
5. ________ I usually finish an exam early or on time.
6. ________ When I finish early, I use the remaining time to recheck my paper.
7. ________ I usually know that I have done well on an exam when I finish.
8. ________ I usually perform better on essay tests than on objective tests.
9. ________ I usually perform better on objective tests than on essay tests.
10. ________ I usually find that my class notes are very helpful when I'm preparing for an exam.

Table 6.1 How Your Approach and Attitude Toward a Test Affects Your Performance

Approach	Attitude	Decision	Outcome
The easy way out	I don't know why I had to take this course. I learned nothing. *(I skipped a few classes and didn't take notes or read the assignments.)*	So I'll get the answers from someone who took the test earlier and memorize them.	Not only did I bomb this one, I realize I haven't learned one thing in this class. Except maybe never to cheat again.
The defeatist approach	This course has been rough. I've been getting so-so grades. I can't seem to understand what's being taught. *(I never joined a study group or asked my teacher for guidance.)*	So I'll cram the night before and hope for the best.	Blew the exam, too. Barely passed the course. Didn't learn much. *(Only have myself to blame. Oh, well. There's always next time.)*
The sensible approach	I'm here to learn all I can. Who knows what I'll need to get a job? Besides, it's expensive to go to college.	My schedule lets me study longer for my toughest classes. And I've been reviewing my notes all term.	Got a B+. More important, studying with a group and writing the exam helped me understand things I might have missed.

of questions they use. Never miss the last class before an exam, because your instructor may summarize valuable information.

- *Manage your time wisely.* Have you laid out a schedule that will give you time to review effectively for the exam, without waiting until the night before? Is your schedule flexible, allowing for the unexpected distraction?
- *Sharpen your study habits.* Have you created a body of material from which you can effectively review what is likely to be on the exam? Is that material organized in a way that will enable you to study efficiently? If you are an interactive learner, have you collaborated with other students in a study group or as study partners to share information? If you are a visual learner, have you created maps (see how to do this later in this chapter), lists, diagrams, flash cards, tables, or other visual aids that will enhance memory?

Planning Your Approach

Physical Preparation

1. **Maintain your regular sleep routine.** Don't cut back on your sleep in order to cram in additional study hours. Remember that most tests will require you to *apply* the concepts that you have studied, and you must have all your brain power available. Especially during final exam weeks, it is important to be well rested in order to remain alert for extended periods of time. This is no time for partying.
2. **Maintain your regular exercise program.** Walking, jogging, swimming, or other aerobic activities are effective stress reducers, may help you think more clearly, and provide positive—and needed—breaks from studying.
3. **Eat right.** You really are what you eat. Avoid drinking more than one or two caffeinated drinks a day or eating foods that are high in sugar or fat. Eat a light breakfast before a morning exam. Greasy or acidic foods might upset your stomach. To maintain a good energy level, choose fruits, vegetables, and other foods (peas, beans, and whole grains) that are high in complex carbohydrates. Consider a banana or a slice of cantaloupe or other foods that are high in potassium to help prevent muscle cramps. You also might bring a bottle of water to the exam.

Emotional Preparation

1. **Know your material.** If you have given yourself adequate time to review, you will enter the classroom confident that you are in control. Study by testing yourself or quizzing one another in a study group so you will be sure you really know the material.
2. **Practice relaxing.** Some students experience upset stomachs, sweaty palms, racing hearts, or other unpleasant physical symptoms before an exam. See your counseling center about relaxation techniques. If you have trouble getting to sleep the night before an exam, try mental imagery. Create your own peaceful scene. It can be real or imaginary—the beach, the woods, the mountains—as long as it is a setting in which you would feel completely relaxed. Use your five senses to take yourself there—what would you see, hear, taste, smell, and feel if you were there?
3. **Use positive self-talk.** Instead of telling yourself, "I never do well on math tests" or "I'll never be able to learn all the information for my history essay exam," make positive statements, such as "I have attended all the lectures, done my homework, and passed the quizzes. Now I'm ready to pass the test!"

Design an Exam Plan

Use the information about the test as you design a plan for preparing. Build that preparation into a schedule of review dates. Develop a to do list of the major steps you need to take in order to be ready.

The week before the exam, set aside a schedule of one-hour blocks for review, along with notes on what you specifically plan to accomplish during each hour.

SEE EXERCISE 6.1: DESIGNING AN EXAM PLAN

Join a Study Group

Study groups can help students develop better study techniques. In addition, group members can benefit from different views of instructors' goals, objectives, and emphasis; have partners to quiz them on facts and concepts; and gain the enthusiasm and friendship of others to help sustain their motivation.

SEE EXERCISE 6.2: FORMING A STUDY GROUP

Ask your instructor, advisor, or campus tutoring or learning center to help you identify interested students and decide on guidelines for the group. Study groups can meet throughout the term, or they can review for midterms or final exams. Group members should complete their assignments before the group meets and prepare study questions or points of discussion ahead of time. If your study group decides to meet just before exams, allow enough time to share notes and ideas.

Together, devise a list of potential questions for review. Then spend time studying separately to develop answers, outlines, and mind maps (discussed below). The group should then reconvene shortly before the test to share answers and review.

Tutoring and Other Support

If you think tutoring is just for failing students, you're wrong! Often, excellent students seek tutorial assistance to ensure their A's. In the typical large lecture classes for first-year students, you have limited opportunity to question instructors. Tutors know the highlights and pitfalls of the course. Most tutoring services are free. Ask your academic advisor or counselor or campus learning center. Most academic support centers or learning centers have computer labs that can provide assistance for course work. Some offer walk-in assistance for help in using word processing, spreadsheet, or statistical computer programs. Frequently computer tutorials are available to help you refresh basic skills. Math and English grammar programs may also be available, as well as access to the Internet.

Now It's Time to Study

Through the consistent use of proven study techniques, you will already have processed and learned most of what you need to know. Now you can focus your

Speaking of Careers

How many of the suggestions in this chapter for studying can be applied to the workplace? Nearly all of them: being honest, knowing the rules, seeking help, getting sleep and exercise, eating properly, knowing how to handle an emergency, reviewing information, finding a system of memorizing that works. Interview someone who works full-time and ask him or her to react to this list. You might even get a paper out of this.

study efforts on the most challenging concepts, practice recalling information, and familiarize yourself with details.

Review Sheets, Mind Maps, and Other Tools

To prepare for an exam covering large amounts of material, you need to condense the volume of notes and text pages into manageable study units. Review your materials with these questions and hints in mind:

- Is this one of the key ideas in the chapter or unit?
- Will I see this on the test? You may prefer to highlight, underline, or annotate the most important ideas, or you may create outlines, lists, or visual maps containing the key ideas.
- Use large pieces of paper to summarize main ideas chapter by chapter or according to the major themes of the course. Look for relationships between ideas. Try to condense your review sheets down to one page of essential information. Key words on this page can bring to mind blocks of information. A *mind map* is essentially a review sheet with a visual element. Its word and visual patterns provide you with highly charged clues to jog your memory. Because they are visual, mind maps help many students recall information more easily.

Figure 6.1 shows us what a mind map might look like for a chapter on listening and learning in the classroom. See if you can reconstruct the ideas in the chapter by following the connections in the map. Then make a visual mind map for this chapter and see how much more you can remember after studying it a number of times.

In addition to review sheets and mind maps, you may want to create flash cards or outlines. Also, do not underestimate the value of using the recall column from your lecture notes to test yourself or others on information presented in class.

Emergency? Your Instructor Needs to Know

Things happen. Even if your instructor has warned you that there is no excuse for missing a quiz or turning in a paper late, he or she may bend the rules in a true emergency. Even if you missed an important quiz or deadline for dubious reasons, it's better to admit you overslept or forgot that a paper was due or left an essay at home. Your instructor may be willing to help. In a real emergency, however, here's what you can do:

1. **Let your instructor know about a recurring medical condition that may occasionally keep you at home.** Find out if the instructor requires documentation from your doctor. Make it clear you are asking not to be excused from required work, but for some allowance for turning in work late if necessary. If you have a medical condition, you may qualify for services from your campus office for disability services. Often, disability services staff members serve as advocates for students who must miss class for medical reasons.
2. **Get phone numbers and/or e-mail addresses for your instructors in advance.** Most faculty have e-mail and voice mail. Leave a number where you can be reached or the number of a friend or relative who will be able to contact you. Some colleges can distribute a memo to your instructors to inform them of your situation, especially if you'll be out for a week or more. Find out whom to contact for this service.
3. **When you know in advance that you can't make class, tell the instructor as soon as possible.** In any event, contact your instructor to explain why you're absent. This thoughtful action may result in your instructor's allowing you to turn in work early or make up work when you return.

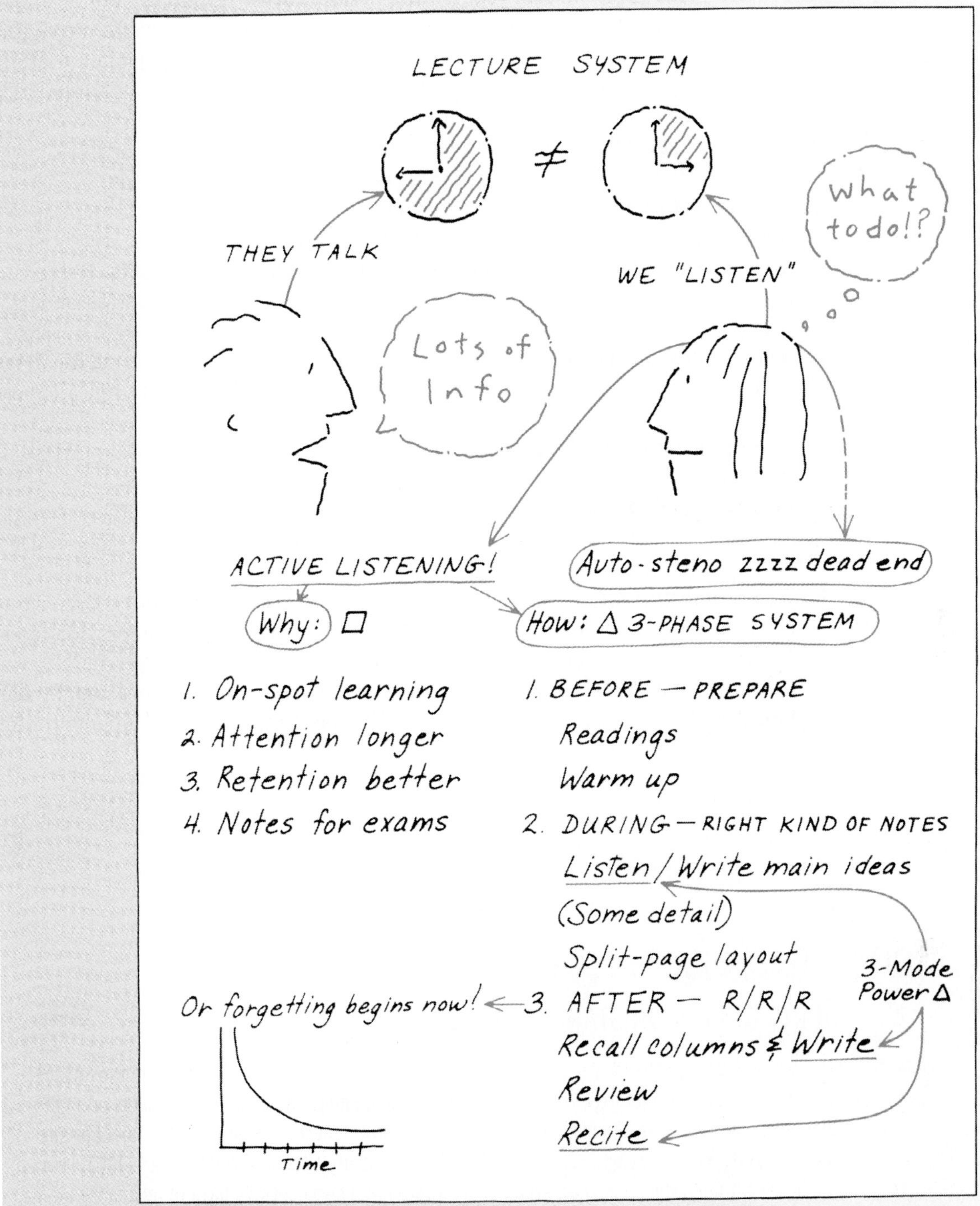

Figure 6.1 **Sample Mind Map on Listening and Learning in the Classroom**

Summaries

A written summary can be helpful in preparing for essay and short-answer exams. By condensing the main ideas into a concise written summary, you store information in your long-term memory so you can retrieve it to answer an essay question. Here's how:

1. **Predict a test question from your lecture notes or other resources.** For example, one of the major headings in this chapter reads, "Join a Study Group." From this you might predict a question such as, "Discuss the merits of joining a study group." Or for "Planning Your Approach," you might predict, "Name three kinds of preparation for a test and give at least one example of each."
2. **Read the chapter, article, notes, or other resources.** Underline or mark main ideas as you go, make notations, or outline them on a separate sheet.
3. **Analyze and abstract.** What is the purpose of the material? Does it compare, define a concept, or prove an idea? What are the main ideas?
4. **Make connections between main points and key supporting details.** Reread to identify each main point and supporting evidence. (Use an outline to assist you.) Analyze the author's argument for bias or insufficient details.
5. **Select, condense, order.** Review underlined material and begin putting the ideas into your own words. Number what you underlined or highlighted in a logical order.
6. **Write your ideas precisely in a draft.** In the first sentence, state the purpose of your summary. Follow with each main point and its supporting ideas.
7. **Review your draft.** Read it over, adding missing transitions or insufficient information. Check the logic of your summary. Annotate with the material you used for later reference.
8. **Test your memory.** Put your draft away and try to recite the contents of the summary to yourself out loud, or explain it to a study partner who can provide feedback on the information you have omitted.
9. **Schedule time to review summaries and double-check your memory shortly before the test.** You may want to do this with a partner, but some students prefer to review alone.

Setting Goals for Success

DOING BETTER ON STANDARDIZED TESTS

Chances are that you took some sort of standardized test to get into college: The ACT and the SAT are the two most common ones. Maybe you took a test for students learning English as a foreign language, or an AP exam to "place out" of a college course. Standardized tests evaluate your general knowledge of a subject or subjects, not what was covered recently in class. Because of their general nature, standardized tests are difficult to study for. If you plan to continue your schooling beyond an undergraduate degree, you'll have to take more exams with acronyms like GRE, GMAT, LSAT, and MCAT. There are ways to be better prepared, less nervous, and more successful on standardized tests. Set some goals for future testing:

My goal for standardized tests is to: ______________________________

I can achieve this goal by: ______________________________

I want to achieve this goal because: ______________________________

It's important because: ______________________________

I may encounter these obstacles: ______________________________

My strategy for accomplishing this goal is to: ______________________________

Taking the Test

1. **Write your name on the test** (unless directed not to) and answer sheet.
2. **Analyze, ask, and stay calm.** Take a long, deep breath and slowly exhale before you begin. Read all the directions so that you understand what to do. Ask for clarification if you don't understand something. Be confident. Don't panic. Answer one question at a time.
3. **Make the best use of your time.** Quickly survey the entire test and decide how much time you will spend on each section. Be aware of the point values of different sections of the test. Are some questions worth more points than others?
4. **Answer the easy questions first.** Expect that you'll be puzzled by some questions. Make a note to come back to them later. If different sections consist of different types of questions (such as multiple-choice, short answer, and essay), complete the type of question you are most comfortable with first. Be sure to leave enough time for any essays.
5. **If you feel yourself starting to panic or go blank, stop whatever you are doing.** Take a long, deep breath and slowly exhale. Remind yourself you will be okay and that you do know the material and can do well on this test. Then take another deep breath. If necessary, go to another section of the test and come back later to the item that triggered your anxiety.
6. **If you finish early, don't leave.** Stay and check your work for errors. Reread the directions one last time. If using a Scantron answer sheet, make sure that all answers are bubbled completely and correctly.

Essay Questions

Although you will take objective (multiple-choice, matching, and true/false) exams in college, many college teachers, including the writers of this book, have a strong preference for the essay exam because it promotes higher-order critical thinking, whereas other types of exams tend to be exercises in memorization. Some instructors use objective tests in large classes. Grading more than 100 essay exams can take days, whereas objective exams can be machine-scored and returned quickly. Generally, the closer you are to graduation, the more essay exams you'll take. To be successful on essay exams, follow these guidelines:

1. **Budget your exam time.** Quickly survey the entire exam and note the questions that are the easiest for you, along with their point values. Take a moment to weigh their values, estimate the approximate time you should allot to each question, and write the time beside each number. Be sure you know whether you must answer all the questions or choose among questions. Start with the questions that are easiest for you, and jot down a few ideas before you begin to write. Remember, it can be a costly error to write profusely on easy questions of low value and take up precious time you may need on more important questions. Wear a watch so you can monitor your time, including time at the end for a quick review.
2. **Develop a very brief outline of your answer before you begin to write.** Then use your first paragraph to introduce the main points, and subsequent paragraphs to describe each point in more depth. If you begin to lose your concentration, you will be glad to have the outline to help you regain your focus. If you find that you are running out of time and cannot complete an essay, at the very least provide an outline of key ideas. Instructors usually assign points based on your coverage of the main topics from the material. Thus, you will usually earn more points by

responding to all parts of the question briefly than by addressing just one aspect of the question in detail.

3. **Write concise, organized answers.** Many well-prepared students write fine answers to questions that may not have been asked because they did not read a question carefully or did not respond to all parts of the question. Others hastily write down everything they know on a topic. Answers that are vague and rambling tend to be downgraded by instructors.
4. **Know the key task words in essay questions.** Being familiar with the key word in an essay question will help you answer it more specifically. The following key task words appear frequently on essay tests. Take time to learn them, so that you can answer essay questions more accurately and precisely.

Analyze. To divide something into its parts in order to understand it better. To show how the parts work together to produce the overall pattern.

Compare. To look at the characteristics or qualities of several things and identify as well as to define how they are alike and how they are different.

Contrast. To identify the differences between things.

Criticize/Critique. To analyze and judge something. Criticism can be positive, negative, or both. A criticism should generally contain your own judgments (supported by evidence) and those of other authorities who can support your point.

Define. To give the meaning of a word or expression. Giving an example sometimes helps to clarify a definition, but an example by itself is not a definition.

Describe. To give a general verbal sketch of something, in narrative or other form.

Discuss. To examine or analyze something in a broad and detailed way. Discussion often includes identifying the important questions related to an issue and attempting to answer these questions. A good discussion explores all relevant evidence and information.

Evaluate. To discuss the strengths and weaknesses of something. Evaluation is similar to criticism, but the word *evaluate* places more stress on the idea of how well something meets a certain standard or fulfills some specific purpose.

Explain. To clarify something. Explanations generally focus on why or how something has come about.

Interpret. To explain the meaning of something. In science, you might explain what an experiment shows and what conclusions can be drawn from it. In a literature course, you might explain—or interpret—what a poem means beyond the literal meaning of the words.

Critical Thinking

Essay questions may require quite different responses, depending on their key task words. Answer and then discuss the following questions in class. In your discussion, include what each task word is asking you to do and how it differs from the other two listed here:

1. How would you *define* the purposes of this chapter?

   ____

2. How would you *evaluate* the purposes of this chapter?

   ____

3. How would you *justify* the purposes of this chapter?

   ____

Justify. To argue in support of some decision or conclusion by showing sufficient evidence or reasons in its favor. Try to support your argument with both logical and concrete examples.

Narrate. To relate a series of events in the order in which they occurred. Generally, you will also be asked to explain something about the events you are narrating.

Outline. To present a series of main points in appropriate order. Some instructors want an outline with Roman numerals for main points followed by letters for supporting details. If in doubt, clarify with the instructor whether he or she wants a formal outline.

Prove. To give a convincing logical argument and evidence in support of some statement.

Review. To summarize and comment on the main parts of a problem or a series of statements. A review question usually also asks you to evaluate or criticize.

Summarize. To give information in brief form, omitting examples and details. A summary is short yet covers all important points.

Trace. To narrate a course of events. Where possible, you should show connections from one event to the next.

Multiple-Choice Questions

Preparing for multiple-choice tests requires you to actively review all the material covered in the course. Reciting from flash cards, summary sheets, mind maps, or the recall column in your lecture notes is a good way to review these large amounts of material.

Take advantage of the many cues that multiple-choice questions contain. Careful reading of each item may uncover the correct answer. Always question choices that use absolute words such as *always, never,* and *only*. These choices are often incorrect. Also, read carefully for terms such as *not, except,* and *but* that are introduced before the choices. Often, the answer that is the most inclusive is correct. Generally, options that do not agree grammatically with the first part of the item are incorrect.

Some students are easily confused by multiple-choice answers that sound alike. The best way to respond to a multiple-choice question is to read the first part of the item and then predict your own answer before reading the options. Choose the letter that corresponds to the option that best matches your prediction.

If you are totally confused by a question, leave it and come back later, but always double-check that you are bubbling in the answer for the right question. Sometimes, another question will provide a clue for a question you are unsure about. If you have absolutely no idea, and there is no penalty for guessing (ask your instructor), look for an answer that at least contains some shred of information.

True/False Questions

Remember, for the question to be true, every detail of the question must be true. Questions containing words such as *always, never,* and *only* are usually false, whereas less definite terms such as *often* and *frequently* suggest the statement may be true. Read through the entire exam to see if information in one question will help you answer another. Do not begin to second-guess what you know or doubt your answers because a sequence of questions appears to be all true or all false.

Matching Questions

The matching question is the hardest type of test to answer by guessing. In one column you will find the term, in the other the description of it. Before answering any question, review all the terms or descriptions. Match those terms you are sure of first. As you do so, cross out both the term and its description, and then use the process of elimination to assist you in answering the remaining items. Flash cards and lists (remember to "chunk" them in groups of five, seven, or nine) are excellent ways to prepare for matching questions.

Fill-in-the-Blank Questions

Fill-in-the-blank tests seem a lot easier than they really are. First, decide what kind of answer is required. Be certain that your answer completes the sentence grammatically as well as logically (e.g., don't use a verb when a noun is required). Look for key words in the statement that could jog your memory.

Machine-Scored Tests

Don't make extra marks or doodles on the answer sheet. The machine can't tell the difference. Make certain you're bubbling in the right dot in the right row. If you decide to change an answer, erase the original mark completely. Otherwise, it may cancel out both choices.

Take-Home Tests

A take-home test, by its nature, is virtually an open-book test. This means your instructor will expect precise and comprehensive answers, since you are (1) not under the pressure of time and (2) able to look up facts without penalty. Our suggestions are: Don't procrastinate, don't underestimate the difficulty of the test, and take as much time as you need to be certain your paper is the best it can be. Take-home tests usually require a lot more of your time than the one or two hours of an in-class exam.

Academic Honesty

Colleges and universities have academic integrity policies or honor codes that clearly define cheating, lying, plagiarism, and other forms of dishonest conduct, but it is often difficult to know how those rules apply to specific situations. Is it really lying to tell an instructor you missed class because you were "not feeling well" (whatever "well" means) or because you were experiencing vague "car trouble"? (Some people think car trouble includes anything from a flat tire to difficulty finding a parking spot.)

Types of Misconduct

Institutions vary widely in how they define broad terms such as lying or cheating. One university defines cheating as "intentionally using or attempting to use unauthorized materials, information, notes, study aids, or other devices . . . [including] unauthorized communication of information during an academic exercise." This would apply to looking over a classmate's shoulder for an answer, using a calculator when it is not authorized, procuring or discussing an exam (or individual questions from an exam) without permission, copying lab notes, purchasing term papers over the Internet, watching the video instead of reading the book, and duplicating computer files.

Plagiarism, or taking another person's ideas or work and presenting them as your own, is especially intolerable in academic culture. Just as taking someone else's property constitutes physical theft, taking credit for someone else's ideas constitutes intellectual theft.

Examining Values

Which of the following mottos describes your attitude toward your education: "The end justifies the means." "Cheaters never prosper."

Think about what each of those expressions means and discuss this with others in your group. Is cheating ever justified?

On most tests, you do not have to credit specific individuals. (But some instructors do require this; when in doubt, ask!) In written reports and papers, however, you must give credit any time you use (1) another person's actual words, (2) another person's ideas or theories—even if you don't quote them directly, and (3) any other information not considered common knowledge.

Many schools prohibit other activities besides lying, cheating, unauthorized assistance, and plagiarism. For instance, the University of Delaware prohibits intentionally inventing information or results; the University of North Carolina outlaws earning credit more than once for the same piece of academic work without permission; Eastern Illinois University rules out giving your work or exam answer to another student to copy during the actual exam or to a student in another section before the exam is given in that section; and the University of South Carolina prohibits bribing in exchange for any kind of academic advantage. Most schools also outlaw helping or attempting to help another student commit a dishonest act.

Reducing the Likelihood of Problems

To avoid becoming intentionally or unintentionally involved in academic misconduct, consider the reasons it could happen:

- *Ignorance.* In a survey at the University of South Carolina, 20 percent of students incorrectly thought that buying a term paper wasn't cheating. Forty percent thought using a test file (a collection of actual tests from previous terms) was fair behavior. Sixty percent thought it was all right to get answers from someone who had taken a similar or identical exam earlier in the same, or a prior, term.
- *Cultural and campus differences.* In other countries and on some U.S. campuses, students are encouraged to review past exams as practice exercises. Some campuses permit sharing answers and information for homework and other assignments with friends.
- *Different policies among instructors.* Because there is no universal code that dictates such behaviors, ask your instructors for clarification. When a student is caught violating the academic code of a particular school or teacher, pleading ignorance of the rules is a weak defense.
- *A belief that grades—not learning—are everything,* when actually the reverse is true. This may reflect our society's competitive atmosphere. It also may be the result of pressure from parents, peers, or teachers. In truth, grades are nothing if one has cheated to earn them.
- *Lack of preparation or inability to manage time and activities.* Before you consider cheating, ask an instructor for an extension of your deadline.

Here are some steps you can take to reduce the likelihood of problems:

1. **Know the rules.** Learn the academic code for your school. Study course syllabi. If a teacher does not clarify his or her standards and expectations, ask.

2. **Set clear boundaries.** Refuse to "help" others who ask you to help them cheat. You don't owe anyone an explanation for why you won't participate in academic dishonesty. In test settings, cover your answers, keep your eyes down, and put all extraneous materials away.
3. **Improve time management.** Be well prepared for all quizzes, exams, projects, and papers. This may mean unlearning habits such as procrastination.
4. **Seek help.** Get help with study skills, time management, and test taking. If your methods are in good shape but the content of the course is too difficult, see your instructor, join a study group, or visit your campus learning center or tutorial service.
5. **Withdraw from the course.** Your school has a policy about dropping courses and a last day to drop without penalty. You may decide only to drop the course that's giving you trouble. Some students may choose to withdraw from all classes and take time off before returning to school if they find themselves in over their heads or if a long illness, a family crisis, or some other unexpected occurrence has caused them to fall behind. Before you withdraw, you should ask about campus policies as well as ramifications in terms of federal financial aid and other scholarship programs. See your advisor or counselor.
6. **Reexamine goals.** Stick to your own realistic goals instead of giving in to pressure from family or friends to achieve impossibly high standards. You may also feel pressure to enter a particular career or profession of little or no interest to you. If so, sit down with counseling or career services professionals or your academic advisor and explore alternatives.

Reassess Yourself

Now that you've learned some strategies for taking tests more successfully, go back to the self-assessment that appears at the beginning of this chapter. This is an opportunity for you to measure your progress, to check in with yourself and see how reading this chapter may have changed your approach to studying and taking exams. Which of the items on page 97 did you check? Would you change any of your answers as a result of reading this chapter? If so, which ones, and why?

How Cheating Hurts Everyone

It Hurts Individuals

- *Cheating sabotages academic growth.* Because the grade and the instructor's comments apply to someone else's work, cheating makes accurate feedback impossible.
- *Cheating sabotages personal growth.* Educational accomplishments inspire pride and confidence. What confidence will students have when their work is not their own?
- *Cheating can have long-term effects.* Taking the easy way out in college may spill over into graduate school, jobs, and relationships. Would you want a doctor, lawyer, or accountant who had cheated on exams to handle your affairs?

It Hurts the Community

- *Widespread cheating causes honest students to become cynical and resentful,* especially if grades are curved and the cheating directly affects other students.
- *Widespread cheating devalues a college degree.* Alumni, potential students, graduate students, and employers learn to distrust degrees from schools where cheating is widespread.
- *Widespread cheating creates an environment of mistrust.* Would you want to live in a community when you doubt the integrity of its citizens?

Where to Go for Help

ON CAMPUS

Learning assistance support center. Every campus has one of these and helping students study for tests is one of their specialties. The best students and good students who want to be the best students as well as students with academic difficulties, use learning centers. These services are offered by both full-time professionals and highly skilled student tutors.

Fellow college students. Often, the best help we can get is the closest to us. Keep an eye out in your classes, residence hall, co-curricular groups, and so forth for the best students, those who appear to be the most serious, purposeful, and directed. Hire a tutor. Join a study group. Students who do these things are much more likely to be successful.

ONLINE

<http://www.uic.edu/depts/counselctr/ace/examprep.htm>. Visit this site for some sound advice from the Academic Center for Excellence, University of Illinois at Chicago.

<http://www.lc.unsw.edu.au/onlib/exam.html>. Learn how they do it down under. This site is maintained by the Learning Centre of the University of New South Wales in Sydney, Australia. Includes the popular SQ3R method.

<http://owl.english.purdue.edu/handouts/research/r_plagiar.html>. This Web site from the Purdue University Online Writing Lab describes how plagiarism occurs, gives tips for avoiding it, and even includes an interactive quiz on the subject.

ON INFOTRAC® COLLEGE EDITION

"Take an Active Approach When Studying for Final Exams." Kathy Mathers, *Knight Ridder/Tribune News Service*, May 11, 1994 p. 0511K7966. This InfoTrac® College Edition article offers yet another way to study. You can ignore the "kid tip" at the bottom, by the way.

"Study Secrets for College Success: Three Profs Offer Fool-Proof Tips for Making the Grade and More." (Life at College). Josh Johnson, *Campus Life*, February 2002, 60, no. i7: 66(5). Learn how to read your professors, plan ahead, and use better study habits to get through "monster" exams.

Exercises

Each of these exercises will let you further explore the topic of this chapter. You'll find all of these exercises, plus Internet and InfoTrac® College Edition exercises, on the CD-ROM that accompanies this book.

EXERCISE 6.1 Designing an Exam Plan

Use the following guidelines to design a plan for the next test in one of your courses:

1. What type of exam will be used?
2. What material will be covered?
3. What type of questions will it contain?
4. How many questions do you think there will be?
5. What approach will you use to study for the exam?
6. How many study sessions—and how much time—will you need?

Now list all material to be covered and create a study schedule for the week prior to the exam, allowing as many one-hour blocks as you will need.

EXERCISE 6.2 Forming a Study Group

Use the goal-setting process from Chapter 1 to form a study group for at least one of your courses. Think about your strengths and weaknesses in a learning or studying situation. For instance, do you excel at memorizing facts but find it difficult to comprehend theories? Do you learn best by repeatedly reading the information or by applying the knowledge to a real situation? Do you prefer to learn by processing information in your head or by participating in a hands-on demonstration? Make some notes about your learning and studying strengths and weaknesses here.

Strengths: ______________________________

Weaknesses: ______________________________

In a study group, how will your strengths help others? What strengths will you look for in others that will help you?

How you can help others: ______________________________

How others can help you: ______________________________

In your first study group session, suggest that each person share his or her strengths and weaknesses and talk about how abilities might be shared for everyone's benefit.

EXERCISE 6.3 The Temptation to Cheat

a. Mary tells you she got a copy of tomorrow's exam from her boyfriend, who took the same exam today. She asks if you want a copy.

What should your answer be? ______________________________

What would you do if you were certain nobody would find out? ______________________________

Defend your answers ______________________________

If caught cheating in this manner, what should your punishment be? ______________________________

b. Ted has a micro tape recorder with a small earplug. He has recorded notes from the book and from the lectures, and plans to sneak this device into the classroom for the test.

What should your reaction be? ______________________________

What reasons would you give him for what you have said? ______________________________

Defend your stance. ______________________________

If Ted is caught, what should the punishment be? ______________________________

If he confesses that you knew about his behavior the night before but did not report him, should you be penalized? How severely? ______________________________

WORKING TOGETHER EXERCISE
Defining Plagiarism on Your Campus

Working in teams of five to eight, use your campus Web site, interview appropriate faculty and staff, and so forth to determine what constitutes plagiarism on your campus and what the penalties are. Each group should report to every other group, just in case some groups have different information.

See the CD-ROM for these additional exercises as well as all other exercises appearing in this chapter

Exercise 6.4	Writing a Summary
Internet Exercise 6.1	Examining Institutional Values
InfoTrac® College Edition Exercise 6.1	Researching Good Study Habits
InfoTrac® College Edition Exercise 6.2	Testing Key Words and Subjects

Part 3

GO

(The Extra Mile)

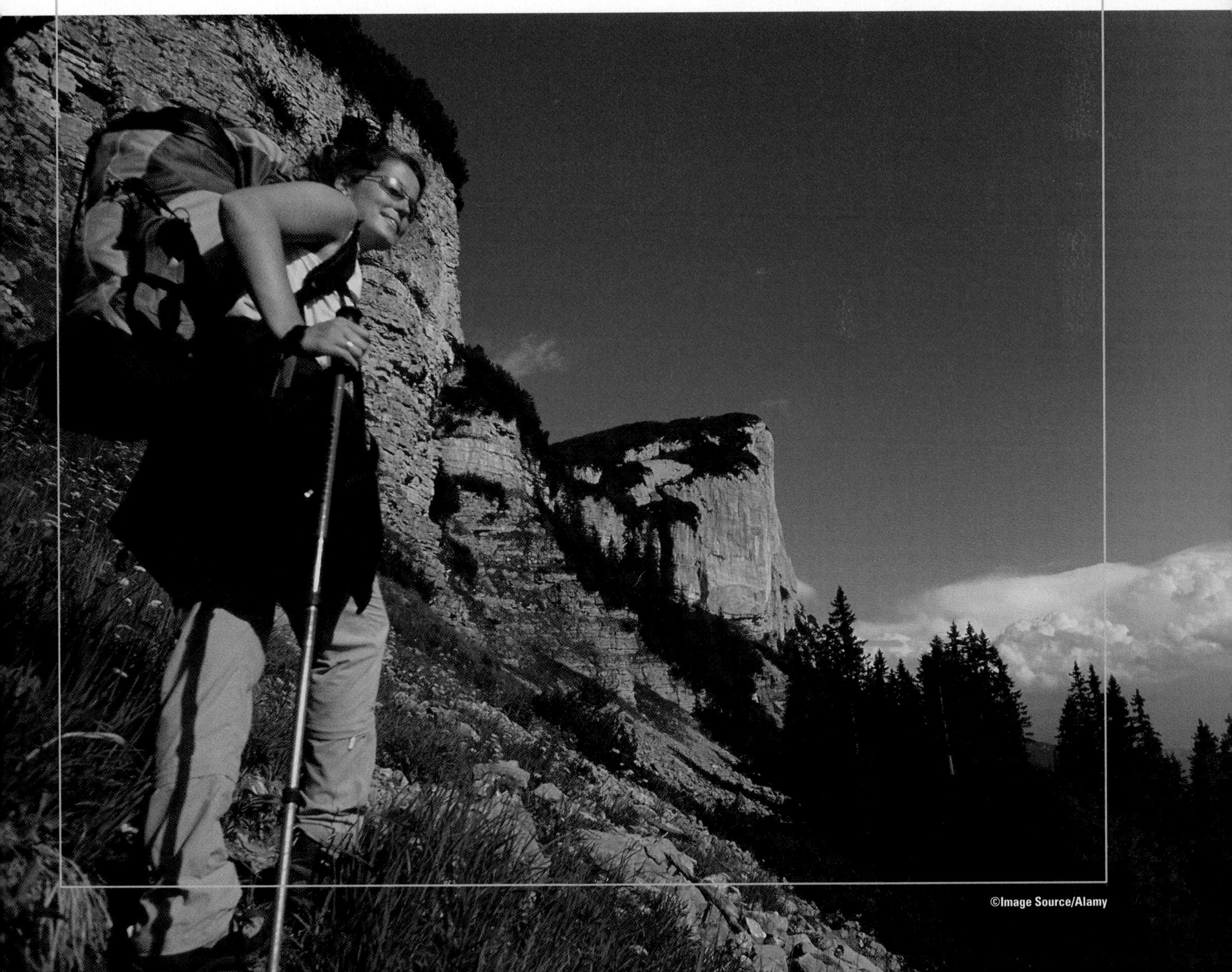

7 Developing Values

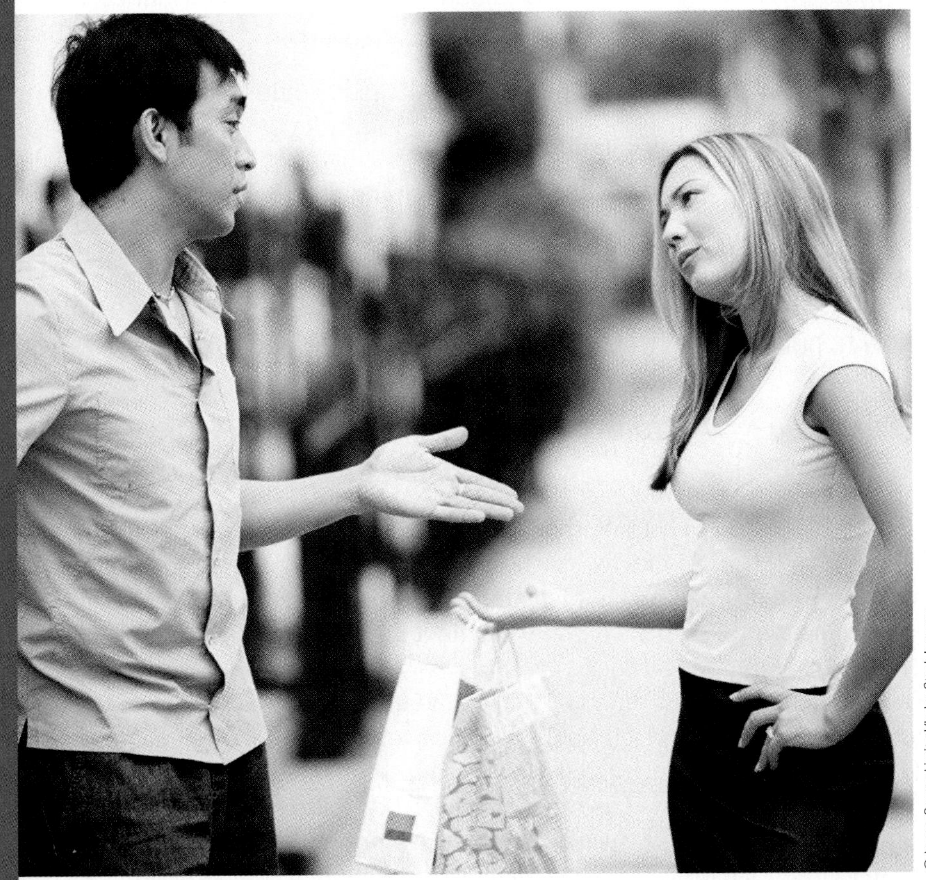

© Image Source Limited/Index Stock Imagery

John M. Whiteley and James B. Craig of the University of California, Irvine, and Edward Zlotkowski of Bentley College contributed their valuable and considerable expertise to the writing of this chapter.

Going Forward: Student Voices

One of my friends thinks nothing of bragging about all the people he's slept with. Another friend admits to cheating on exams, while another feels guilty if he misses church, and another admits he plagiarized material for his term paper. Me? I'm just a normal person. I don't cheat, and I keep my private life to myself. Who's right, anyway?

Looking Back: Author Voices

When I look back at the impact of my college experience, the biggest and longest-lasting effect was its influence on my values, especially my political and spiritual values. Wow. Did I change? You bet, and my parents weren't always happy about it either. But these changes were a better fit for who I was and was becoming. **John Gardner**

In this chapter, YOU WILL LEARN

- How to define values
- Different usages of the term *values*
- Distinctions between moral values and aesthetic and performance values
- Distinctions between instrumental and intrinsic values
- How societal values are in conflict
- How changes in American society have forced changes in societal values
- The difficulties of basing our behaviors on certain societal values
- How to put values to the test through service learning

Unlike most of the chapters in this text, this chapter deals with an abstract concept—the concept of values. If you don't already know, you'll find out why values are an integral part of who you are. We hope that by understanding how your values and the values of others may conflict with each other, you will gain a greater understanding of yourself, your friends, your family, and society.

The word *values* means different things to different people. For some, the word refers to specific views a person holds on controversial moral issues such as capital punishment. For others, it refers to whatever is most important to a person, such as a good job, a fancy car, or the welfare of one's family. For still others, it refers to abstractions such as truth, justice, or success. In this chapter, we offer definitions of values, provide a framework for thinking about values, and explore ways to discover your values and apply them not only to the college experience but also to life after college.

Defining Values

Perhaps we can best define a value as an important attitude or belief that commits us to take action, to do something. We may not necessarily act in response to others' feelings, but when we truly hold a value, we act on it.

For instance, we might watch a television program showing starving people and feel sympathy or regret but take no action whatsoever. If our feelings of sympathy cause us to take action to help those who are suffering, those feelings qualify as values. Actions do not have to be overtly physical. They may involve thinking and talking continually about a problem, trying to interest others in it, reading about it, or sending letters to officials regarding it. The basic point is that when we truly hold a value, it leads us to do something.

We can also define values as beliefs that we accept by choice, with a sense of responsibility and ownership. Much of what we think is simply what others have taught us. Many things we have learned from our parents and others close to us will count as our values, but only after we fully embrace or accept them ourselves.

Self-Assessment
Values

Read the following statements and check those that apply to you:

1. ________ I am under pressure from family and friends to make the "right" choices.
2. ________ So far, college life is not challenging my existing beliefs.
3. ________ I am concerned about the continuing changes in society that are affecting the family.
4. ________ Based on what I've seen of other relationships (those of my family and friends), I am pretty sure what I will seek in a "significant other."
5. ________ I believe our country could do more for the poor and disabled who cannot take care of themselves.
6. ________ There is no excuse for poverty. Anyone can find a job if he or she really makes an effort. We should not support poverty by giving free handouts.
7. ________ If two people choose to have a sexual relationship, it's nobody's business but their own.
8. ________ I know some people cheat in school. That's why I don't feel so bad about cheating—that is, if I have to do it for a good grade.
9. ________ In order to be beneficial, any work I do must be for pay.

Finally, the idea of affirmation or prizing is an essential part of values. We are proud of our values and the choices to which they lead, and want others to know it. We also find ourselves ready to sacrifice for them and to establish our priorities around them. Our values govern our loyalties and commitments.

In summary, then, our values are those important attitudes or beliefs that we (1) accept by choice, (2) affirm with pride, and (3) express in action.

When Australian actor Russell Crowe was interviewed backstage at the 2001 Oscar ceremony after winning the Best Actor award for his role in *Gladiator*, he recalled some advice he had received from his father: "You know, I'd really like you to do something at a technical college or do some kind of apprenticeship—to fall back on." Such advice from a father is not atypical. Crowe's father was reflecting the hope that his son would always have the skills to support himself and his family, and would not have to worry about where the proverbial "next meal" was coming from. This valuing of security and of developing skills to help a young person fit productively into society is an example of the values that one generation, with the best of intentions and beliefs, attempts to pass on to the next. But for the next generation, these are what we call "smuggled values."

SEE EXERCISE 7.1: EVIDENCE OF VALUES

As you know, Russell Crowe chose to reject his father's advice. He chose his own direction for life in terms of his own hierarchy of values, which were different from those of his father. He recalled that he told his father: "Mate, I'm really certain in my life that I'm gonna fall on my face, but it's highly unlikely that I'm ever gonna fall back." At a pinnacle of success in his career as an actor, he was expressing quite a different set of values for himself in defining his own uniqueness.

We will attempt to help you discern your own unique values in the context of a society whose basic institutions "smuggle" or put pressure on you to choose what they believe are the "correct" values when in fact those values are often in conflict with your own.

Crowe chose to make public this brief episode from his life. But every one of us has had some version of that conversation with significant others in our lives. Pressures from family and friends to make the "right" value choices often come with the best of intentions. But within a democratic free society, a basic human right is to choose your own values. This chapter will empower you to understand more about the origins and forms of pressures on you to make particular value choices and to help you define your uniqueness.

The nature of the human condition is that we are like all other people in some respects, we are like some other people in many respects, and we are like no one else in our special uniqueness. How we choose to establish values different from those of our friends, our family, our society, and its institutions is what helps us become unique.

Another Way of Looking at Values

The word *values* is used so differently in scientific and popular literature that we need to begin by explaining how we are using the concept. Values define what is deemed desirable and describe the standards someone employs to determine future directions and evaluate past actions. Authors J. P. Shaver and W. Strong state: "Values are our standards and principles for judging worth. They are the criteria by which we judge 'things' (people, objects, ideas, actions, and situations) to be good, worthwhile, desirable; or, on the other hand, bad, worthless, despicable; or of course, somewhere in between these extremes."[1] Milton Rokeach, an important researcher whose field is the nature of values, believes that the ultimate function of human values is to provide "a set of standards to guide us in all our efforts to satisfy our needs and at the same time maintain and, insofar as possible, enhance self-esteem."[2]

Conceived in this way, values are central to determining human behavior and to influencing public and private action. Values also are basic to understanding the many differences in how both people and institutions choose to act. On the institutional level, values guide decisions about where resources ought to be allocated, what policies should be formulated, and what directions institutions ought to pursue.

Challenges to Personal Values in College

Most students find that college life challenges their existing personal and moral values. New students are often startled at the diversity of personal moralities found on campus. For instance, you may have been taught that it is wrong to drink alcohol, yet you find that friends whom you respect and care about see nothing wrong with drinking. At the same time, students from more liberal backgrounds may be astonished to discover themselves forming friendships with classmates whose personal values are very conservative.

When you don't approve of some aspects of a friend's way of life, do you try to change his or her behavior, pass judgment on the person, or withdraw from the relationship? Often, part of the problem is that the friend demonstrates countless good qualities and values that make the troublesome conduct seem less significant. In the process, your own values may begin to change under the influence of a new kind of

[1]J. P. Shaver and W. Strong, *Facing Value Decisions: Rationale-Building for Teachers*, New York: Teachers College Press, 1982, pp. 17–34.
[2]M. Rokeach, *Understanding Human Values: Individual and Societal,* New York: The Free Press, 1979.

relativism: "I don't choose to do that, but I'm not going to make any judgments against those who do." In cases where a friendship is affected by differing values, tolerance is generally a good goal.

Tolerance for others is a central value in our society and one that often grows during college. Even so, it is easy to think of cases in which tolerance gradually becomes an indulgence of another's destructive tendencies. It is one thing to accept a friend's responsible use of alcohol at a party and quite another to fail to challenge a drunk who plans to drive you home. Sexual intimacy in an enduring relationship may be one thing; a never-ending series of one-night stands is quite another. Remember, the failure to challenge destructive conduct is no sign of friendship.

Your challenge is to balance your personal welfare, your tolerance for diversity, and your freedom of choice. It can be very enriching and rewarding to talk about values with those whose values seem to be in conflict with your own. What are the other person's true values (consciously identified, freely chosen, and actively expressed)? Do his or her current behaviors correspond to those values? Each of you can learn a great deal from talking about why you value what you do. Many people flee from diversity and fail to confront conflicting value systems when, realistically, the values of our society change over time and many deeply held societal values are in serious conflict. Adopting a set of values that truly make sense to you can help you move ahead with your life and enable you to consciously analyze and reflect on what is taking place in society.

Types of Values

There are a number of useful ways of thinking about values in practice. One approach is to distinguish among moral values, aesthetic values, and performance values. Another is to consider ends versus means.

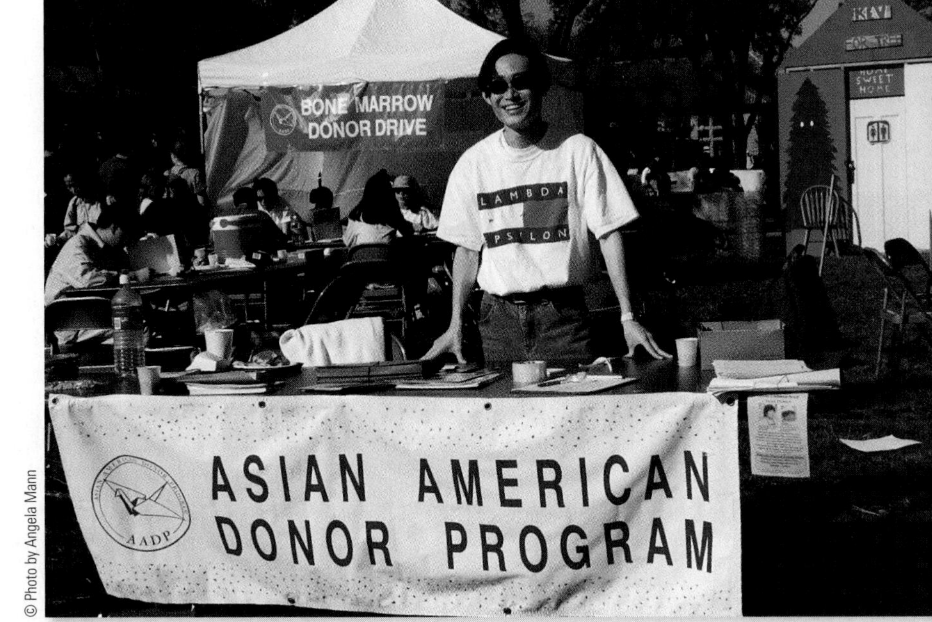

As you clarify your values in college, you can choose activities that affirm several of them at the same time. What different values can you guess are important to this student volunteer? (Two seem obvious; what others do you see?)

© Photo by Angela Mann

Moral Values

Moral values are those personal values that we generally do not attempt to force on others, but which are of immense importance to ourselves as individuals, such as, "I believe it is wrong to lie because lying shows disrespect for other people." These moral values are used to justify our own behavior toward others (as well as to privately judge others). The college years represent a significant opportunity to focus on the choice of moral values to live by, often for the first time away from the influences of parents, siblings, and previous peer groups.

Aesthetic Values

Aesthetic values are the standards by which we judge beauty. Beauty, as used here, refers to a broad set of judgments about nature, art, music, literature, personal appearance, and so on. For example, people make different value judgments about music, about what is of value artistically, and about what types of books are worth reading. Within society, vast differences of opinion exist about the definition of proper aesthetic values and how to judge beauty—or even what beauty is.

Performance Values

There is less difference of opinion about nonmoral performance values, or how well a person performs to some standard, at least within most campus and other institutional cultures. The definition of performance may vary from person to person or context to context, but representative performance values are accuracy, speed, accomplishment, reward, and discipline.

These performance values can have a moral component when judgments are made about specific individuals or groups of people with similar characteristics and how they measure up to some performance standard.

Performance values influence college students through the expectations of important people in their lives. No example is closer to home for college students than the expectations of parents and teachers for a high level of academic performance. Some significant others—parents, teachers, and so forth—tend to make negative moral evaluations when someone does not measure up to their own performance standards.

Means Values Versus Ends Values

Values may also be classified as means values versus ends values. Ends, or intrinsic values, refer to the ultimate goals toward which it is worth striving. Rokeach identified a list of 18 ends values that included a world at peace, a comfortable life, freedom, wisdom, and true friendship. Means, or instrumental values, are values that are used to help one attain other values. Rokeach also identified 18 means values ranging from responsible, obedient, loving, and imaginative to ambitious, independent, and honest.[3] When you think about your values, you should realize that values do not always separate clearly into means and ends categories. The fundamental American value of equality of opportunity, for example, is frequently offered as an intrinsic value that distinguishes the United States from totalitarian countries. But equality of opportunity can also be instrumental in the achievement of other intrinsic values, such as the enhancement of human dignity, the realization of human potential, and the liberation of the human spirit, putting it in the category of a means value.

Societal Values in Conflict: Value Dualisms

> *"Poverty is deplorable and should be abolished."*
> *But: "There never has been enough to go around," and the Bible tells us that "the poor you have always with you."*[4]

A basic reality of analyzing values is that the values held by a society are not necessarily consistent. And it is the nature of the human condition that individuals do not easily recognize value conflicts in themselves. Therefore, it is useful to understand that the process of choosing your values does not exist apart from the culture in which you live, and that the values in your culture and in the broader society are frequently in conflict.

Your conflicting beliefs, or value dualisms, may derive from many different experiences, from childhood through adolescence and into adulthood. This prolonged

[3]Rokeach.
[4]Robert S. Lynd, *Knowledge for What?*, Princeton, NJ: Princeton University Press, 1939, p. 62.

period of time during which you may have acquired parts of your value dualisms, coupled with the very different sources from which they derive, may help explain why such conflicts remain largely unexamined. Formal education apparently has little effect on helping you reconcile your value dualisms.

Two of the conflicting value assumptions identified by Robert Lynd relate to poverty and welfare. You just read the first one. Here is another:

> *"No man deserves to have what he hasn't worked for."*
> *"It demoralizes him to do so."*
> *But: "You can't let people starve."*[5]

Now apply this dualism to a contemporary problem in American society. Children under 16 years of age living in poverty reached 16.7 percent in 2001. By 2002, more than 12 percent of adults over age 65 were living below the poverty level. Given the immense wealth of the United States, to leave substantial percentages of its most vulnerable populations, children and the aged, to subsist in poverty is simply not a rational value choice. Yet the citizens of our country have not reached a consensus on how to solve the problems of poverty and welfare, or demonstrated the political will to insist that the problems be solved.

Another pair of assumptions cited by Lynd refers to America's view of its place in the world and the role of individualism:

> *"The United States is the best and greatest nation on earth and will always remain so."*
>
> *"Individualism, 'the survival of the fittest,' is the law of nature and the secret of America's greatness; and restrictions on individual freedom are un-American and kill initiative."*
>
> *But: "No man should live for himself alone; for people ought to be loyal and stand together and work for common purposes."*[6]

The reality of the United States in the world of the twenty-first century is that it is far from approaching its potential. With respect to being the "best and greatest nation on earth," based on the values associated with the Bill of Rights and the aspirations for the United States reflected in President Abraham Lincoln's Gettysburg Address, most of us would agree that the United States still has a long way to go.

The value of individual freedom is essentially synonymous with the values of the United States. When seen from the perspective of people in nations where the rights of the state take precedence over the rights of the individual, the contrast is striking and clear. It is less clear when one examines what is happening in American society.

The values embedded in people working for common purposes is documented in the Index of Social Health, a composite measure of these 16 indices:

1. Infant mortality
2. Health insurance coverage
3. Child abuse
4. The elderly in poverty
5. Children in poverty
6. Health insurance for the elderly
7. Teen suicide
8. Highway deaths due to alcoholism
9. Drug abuse
10. Homicides
11. High school dropouts
12. Food stamp coverage

[5]Lynd, p. 62.
[6]Lynd, pp. 60, 284.

Critical Thinking

Most Americans agree on their country's most serious problems, and yet differing values systems have prevented us from working together to overcome them. Do value dualisms within American society contribute to the failure to formulate needed reforms? What are those dualisms? Brainstorm how people might get beyond their conflicts to solve problems.

13. Average weekly earnings
14. Housing
15. Unemployment
16. The gap between rich and poor

Since 1970, social health in the United States has declined more than 45 percent, with 11 of the 16 indices worsening over this time period, including child abuse, unemployment, health insurance coverage, average weekly earnings, poverty for those aged 65 or older, out-of-pocket health costs for the population over 65, and the gap between rich and poor.[7]

Changing Society, Changing Values

Changes in society dramatically affect both individual values and the values of society itself. Societal change was the hallmark of the twentieth century. With the information technology revolution and globalization already bringing fundamental changes to the worlds of business and education throughout the world, there is every reason to believe that change will be even more rapid in the twenty-first century.

Consider the changes identified in the book *America at Century's End.*[8] Using the 1950s and 1960s as a baseline, Alan Wolfe and his colleagues document a series of changes in some of the fundamental institutions of American society, including family, religion, education, and the United States' place in the global marketplace. He reminds us that these changes will have the most profound implications for values and value change in both individuals and society.

Examining Values

Robert S. Lynd's original insights into value dualisms in American culture were formulated more than half a century ago. Are his basic insights relevant to the college campus and college student culture of today? We believe the answer is yes, and offer this example:

> "Earning excellent grades in college is critical to success in life."
>
> But: "The most important decision you make in college is about the kind of person you want to be."[9]

Reflect on this dualism. Do you find yourself holding both values? Do your friends? Can you prove that no dualism exists here. If it does exist, what should you and your friends do about it? What other value dualisms exist in your campus culture?

[7]*Index of Social Health: Monitoring the Social Well-Being of the Nation,* New York: Fordham Institute for Innovation in Social Policy, 1994.
[8]Alan Wolfe, ed., *America at Century's End*, Berkeley: University of California Press, 1991.
[9]Ibid.

For example, one of the major changes in American society over the past half-century has been a new demographic profile due to immigration from Latin America and Asia as well as a population shift to the South and West. Another major area of change has been the extensive political realignments and major transformations in the American and world economies. Social and technological changes have reinforced each other in governing how people work, how they use their leisure time, and how they travel. Both upward and downward mobility have increased to create a larger middle class. For the first time we can remember, children may not achieve the economic level of their parents, and dual-career families have become a reality.

Moreover, agreement at the local level may contrast sharply with values held at state and national levels. New ethical challenges affecting moral values are coming from such diverse sources as computer hacking, AIDS, white-collar crime, abortion, and the bioethical implications of genetic engineering.

If values did not (or could not) change with the changing societal structure, we would never have progress. At the same time, it is all the more difficult to define enduring values. For example, in the institutions of business and the economy, conditions at work have been almost completely transformed. One implication is that the wife, rather than staying at home as she did in the majority of cases in the 1950s, now works full-time. Wolfe notes that "for more and more Americans, everything about work is negotiated constantly—between husbands and wives and between employees and employers."[10] From these new situational changes spring profound value dilemmas.

© Andersen Ross/Photodisc/Getty Images

When a parent values education, he or she must make some difficult values choices.

The traditional family of an earlier generation does not serve as a model for society today. In 1950, 60 percent of American households contained male breadwinners and female homemakers, with or without children. By 2000, more than 69 percent of married women with children under 18 were in the labor force, whereas nearly 13 percent of women were single parents and 26 percent of householders lived alone.[11] Such statistics have changed family demographics dramatically since the 1950s.

In attempting to characterize the nature of the family in the United States, J. Stacey calls it "diverse, fluid, and unresolved."[12] By inference, one might conclude that family values possess similar characteristics.

In the same study, Kathleen Gerson reports that women still retain responsibility for the lion's share of household labor but also experience discrimination in the workplace, with the result that "the structural conflicts between family and work

[10]Wolfe, p. 4.

[11]U.S. Census Bureau American Community Survey Office, 2003.

[12] J. Stacey, "Backward Toward the Postmodern Family: Reflections on Gender, Kinship, and Class in the Silicon Valley," In Alan Wolfe, ed., *America at Century's End*, Berkeley: University of California Press, 1991.

continue to make it difficult for either women or men to combine child rearing with sustained employment commitment."[13] Although some women have gained access to highly rewarding careers, most women are constrained within ill-rewarded, female-dominated occupations, and most men continue to enjoy significant economic advantages. Yet many women have joined the workforce as a result of a higher divorce rate as well as stagnant wages for their husbands. Ironically, gender inequality at work makes domesticity an inviting alternative for those women who have trouble earning a decent wage. Despite all the talk about "women's rights," the data indicate that women have a long way to go.

If continuing changes in society are affecting values within families, what are the implications for today's college students? What do we mean by a "generation gap" between this generation of college students and the generation represented by their parents and their friends' parents? If men's and women's experiences with family continue to change, how does someone in college decide what enduring values will "work" for him or her? What enduring values should you be seeking in a "significant other"?

Implementing Societal Values

In his book *The State of the Nation*, Derek Bok, President Emeritus of Harvard University, offers a historical and comparative assessment of how well the United States is doing in meeting the goals of its citizens.[14] He contends that "Americans remain surprisingly united on what the basic goals of the society ought to be." One of the values that Americans say they cherish most is individual freedom in the exercise of political and personal liberties. Accepting such a value carries with it a responsibility to respect the legitimate rights and interests of others. When polled, most Americans say they want to help the poor, indicate concern that the sense of individual responsibility is eroding, and point to the controversy over the value of particular social welfare programs.

Bok observes that a distinguishing feature of Americans' treatment of freedom is the contrast between the "elaborate protection given to political, intellectual and artistic freedoms on the one hand, and the absence of any affirmative constitutional rights" to such basic necessities as food, jobs, shelter, and health care on the other.

He notes that the constitutions of Japan and Germany, for example, make explicit mention of such rights. The Swedish constitution states that "the personal, economic and cultural welfare of the individual shall be the fundamental aims of the community. In particular, it shall be incumbent on the community to secure the right to work, to housing and to education, and to promote social care and security as well as favorable living experience." Bok observes that the percentage of American adults who say they trust other people dropped by one-third from the 1960s to the 1990s. Three-fourths of Americans are unhappy with the "honesty and ethical standards of other citizens." The statement that "most Americans try to avoid taking responsibility for their actions" is endorsed by 75 percent of respondents under 20 years of age and 70 percent of respondents between 30 and 44.

SEE EXERCISE 7.2: FRIENDS AND VALUES

Values and the Family

The family is an important institution for considering social values in the United States, notes Bok, because of the inherent basic obligations it entails toward others and the bridge the family provides between social and personal values. Do fathers

[13] K. Gerson, "Coping with Commitment: Dilemmas and Conflicts of Family Life," In Alan Wolfe, ed., *America at Century's End*, Berkeley: University of California Press, 1991.
[14] Reprinted by permission of the publisher from Derek Bok, *The State of the Nation*, Cambridge, MA: Harvard University Press. Copyright © 1996 by Derek Bok.

have a basic obligation to their children? If so, how is that obligation reflected in behavior? A study of 1,000 teenage children of divorced parents found that more than 40 percent had not seen their fathers in more than a year. Only half of all divorced mothers received any child support, an issue of both personal and social values. Of that half, just over half received the full amount due.

Values and the Community

Bok also explores how the United States has been doing on such fundamental indices of responsibility to the community as voting in elections and contributing time to community organizations. In 1960, 63 percent of potential voters cast ballots.

In the sharply contested presidential election of 2000, the percentage was around 50 percent of potential voters. In contrast, Bok reports that the average turnout among 18 European nations from 1945 to 1989 ranged between 80 and 85 percent. A long and valued tradition in the United States is volunteer participation, contributing time and energy to improving communities. This was noted historically in 1835 by Alexis de Tocqueville in *Democracy in America*, and its continued presence is documented by Bok, who cites evidence that nearly half of all adult Americans have engaged in some form of volunteer activity. Robert Putman provides countervailing evidence in a controversial article called "Bowling Alone: America's Declining Social Capital,"[15] in which he reports that membership in the League of Women Voters has declined by 42 percent since 1969 and Boy Scout volunteers have declined by 26 percent. Thus, conflicting evidence exists on this dimension of the intersection of personal and societal values.

Values and Personal Responsibility

In assessing changes in various aspects of American life from the early 1960s through the early 1990s, Bok found that indices of personal responsibility had declined. He described these six dimensions of personal responsibility as having worsened:

- Obeying the law
- Children born out of wedlock
- Cheating on exams
- Income given to charity
- Community service (remember this when you read about service learning later in this chapter)
- Voting rates

Bok notes that some of the value problems that concern society today—such as the environment, poverty, and gender discrimination—went largely unrecognized from World War II until the 1960s. He compared progress in the United States on selected values dimensions with that of six other industrialized democracies: Canada, France, West Germany, Japan, Sweden, and the United Kingdom. Among these seven democracies, the United States scored only average. On the dimension of providing for the poor and disadvantaged—measured by percentage of the population with incomes below the poverty line, severity of poverty, and effectiveness of government transfer programs—the United States was at or near bottom. On the percentage of children born out of wedlock, the U.S. score was average (in absolute terms, 28 percent of U.S. children are born out of wedlock). The United States was also at or near the bottom on the following critical dimensions:

[15] Robert Putman, "Bowling Alone: America's Declining Social Capital," *Journal of Democracy*, January 1995, 65(1).

Speaking of Careers

The three basic elements in career choice (in contrast to a specific job choice, which can be based on opportunity or economic necessity) are aptitude, personality, and values.

Aptitude does not mean whether you are intelligent compared to people in general (college students are an elite group, after all), but what your special pattern of intellectual competencies is compared to other bright people. Salespeople are usually quite different from production engineers or financial managers in how they relate to people and problems. That's personality. As for values, your career center can help you take a test that compares your pattern of values with those associated with different careers. Looking at the results may help you narrow your present list of career possibilities.

- Violations of criminal laws (57.6 crimes per 1,000 people)
- Incidence of teenage pregnancy (64 pregnancies per 1,000 girls ages 15–19)
- Voting rates

Bok's summary of the evidence was not encouraging:

> *Whether one looks at stealing, cheating on exams, paying taxes, charitable giving, paying child support, voting, births out of wedlock, or community service, it is hard to find a single case in which our record today is as strong as it was in 1960.*

Service Learning and Values

At the beginning of this chapter, we noted that its focus would be on the relatively abstract "concept of values." Yet one of the most effective ways to explore values is through a concept that is anything but abstract, called *service learning*.

Service Learning Defined

Service learning is a teaching method that combines meaningful service to the community with curriculum-based learning.

Serving

The service itself should address a genuine community need, as determined by existing or student-led community assessments. The service should be thoughtfully organized to solve, or make a positive contribution toward solving, a problem.

Linking

In quality service learning, the service project is designed to meet not only a real community need, but also classroom goals. By ensuring strong linkages between the service and the learning, students are able to improve their academic skills and apply what they learn in school to the broader community and vice versa. Through service learning, students demonstrate to teachers what they are learning and how they are meeting specific academic standards.

Learning

Reflection is a key element of service learning. The teacher structures time and methods for students to reflect on and analyze their service experience. Through

Setting Goals for Success

SERVICE LEARNING

Becoming more engaged with your community and country is a worthy goal. But how do you turn such a general concept into a specific plan of action? Should you work on a short-term goal, such as enrolling in a service learning course next term, or a long-term goal, such as building community service into your long-range career plans? To begin the process, select a goal for applying your values to some sort of outreach and devise a plan to implement your goal.

My service learning or community service goal is: ____________________

I can achieve this goal by: ____________________

I want to achieve this goal because: ____________________

It's important because: ____________________

I may encounter these obstacles: ____________________

My strategy for accomplishing this goal is to: ____________________

this process, students learn and understand the complexity of community issues. In addition, students understand how to view such issues in their broader social, political, and economic contexts. Reflection and analysis help reinforce the connection between the students' service and the curriculum content.

In other words, service learning is both related to and yet different from two kinds of off-campus activity with which you are probably familiar: community service and internships. Like community service, service learning seeks to help others, to contribute to the common good. Indeed, students involved in service learning and community service often work at the same community site. At the same time, service learning shares with internships a strong emphasis on student development—including some of the very career-related skills students develop through internships.

But there are also important differences, such as service learning's emphasis on reflection (careful thought, especially the process of reconsidering previous actions, events, or decisions) and reciprocity (something done mutually or in return) as "key concepts." Although a student may learn a lot through traditional community service, service learning does not leave such learning to chance. Instead, it surrounds the service experience with carefully designed reflection activities to help students prepare for, process, and synthesize different aspects of their experience. Without such reflective activities, service learning loses much of its educational effectiveness.

In the same way, reciprocity helps ensure that service learning doesn't lose its social effectiveness. Unlike internships designed primarily with student development in mind, service learning seeks to achieve a balance between student and community benefits. Hence, service learning educators sometimes distinguish between "placements" and "partnerships," using the partnership concept to underline the fact that collaboration, communication, and mutual respect are central to the service learning experience.

Because reflection and reciprocity require some kind of formal structure to make them effective, service learning often takes place in and through specially designed academic courses.

Here are some reasons more and more students are making service learning an important part of their education:

Values Clarification

There is probably no better way for people to clarify what they really value than to put themselves in situations where their assumptions and beliefs are "tested." Suppose you've always assumed that you wanted to be an accountant. You take a course with a service learning requirement that asks you to "reconcile the books" at a local nonprofit. You set about introducing some "method" into their "madness"—and you LOVE it! Or, you HATE it!! In either case, you've now got some important additional information with which to make your career choice. Why wait until your senior year to learn whether you really do like working with kids or patients, or numbers or machines? Service learning helps you experience such options before you've reached the proverbial "point of no return." Consider how you can integrate service learning into a comprehensive career exploration plan.

Assistance with Value Dualisms

Earlier in this chapter we discussed *value dualisms*, explicit—or more often implicit—conflicts between different things someone professes to believe. Service learning is one of the most powerful tools we have to bring such conflicts to consciousness. In other words, it helps an individual better understand his or her personal value system and the strength of his or her stated beliefs. For example,

1. Student A professes to have no racial or ethnic prejudices but finds the idea of working with a certain group different from her own very anxiety-producing. What's in conflict here?
2. Student B has been brought up to believe there's a right and a wrong answer to everything, but now he finds himself somehow very sympathetic to people he'd always dismissed as simply "misguided." What needs reassessment here?
3. Student C has always considered herself pretty responsible when it comes to the environment, but after an entire term working with the city parks service, she finds herself questioning a lot of habits she took for granted. Does she need to review her old assumptions from a new perspective?

Although most students find the very experience of being on a campus a good opportunity to reexamine their personal values, it's also true that most of us quickly seek out others more or less similar to us. Service learning helps to ensure that your college years really do teach you to stretch and move outside your comfort zone.

Skills Development

Still another set of benefits associated with service learning has to do with skills and competencies. You know you'll need to be able to think on your feet once you graduate—but how do you learn to do that in a course where the teacher does most of the talking? You'd like to improve your public speaking skills, but will in-class presentations provide you with the practice you need? And what about writing, time management, and intercultural communication for the "real world"? For many students, service learning means knowing not just about things but how to do them. It juxtaposes theories and ideas with concrete personal experience, and in doing so, helps students learn how to act on their knowledge and put theory to the test. Hence, it is an especially effective way to develop critical thinking skills.

Indeed, service learning will not only help you develop important new skills, it will also give you a good measure of the reliability of what you think you know. Is your understanding of concepts in math, biology, or nutrition good enough to allow you to teach them to others? Can you design a playground that is both fun and safe? When you step outside the traditional role of knowledge "consumer" and become a knowledge "producer" in your own right, you will be taking a huge step toward becoming a "lifelong" learner—one who knows how to learn outside the bounds of a formal classroom.

Civic Engagement

In February 2003, a group of Oklahoma students issued what they called a "Civic Engagement Resolution." Visit the Oklahoma Higher Education Service Learning Web site and click on VOICE to view the complete resolution: *http://www.okhighered.org/service-learning.* In it they complained that " . . . higher education institutions do not provide adequate education and knowledge about our civic responsibilities. Higher education's primary focus is to produce professionals, when instead they should be producing citizens."

Although it has become common to criticize the younger generation as politically apathetic, surveys indicate that more young people today are engaged in community service than at any time in the past. Yet they are given little guidance on how to develop their service activity into genuine civic engagement. As the Oklahoma students point out, higher education certainly is not doing its part. Indeed, facilitating civic engagement is one of service learning's most important benefits. Getting a chance not only to do things in the community but also to reflect on your experiences from a civic as well as a technical and a personal perspective can help build the very kind of knowledge you need to become an effective citizen as well as a competent professional. As you prepare to become one of our country's future leaders, you should insist that this critical dimension of being a citizen is not missing from your education.

Where to Go for Help

ON CAMPUS

Counselors, chaplains, academic advisors, your own college teachers–all are great resources for helping you sort out and think through the challenges you face in dealing with values in college: your own and those of others around you. In fact, anyone who has gotten to know you might be a person with whom you could converse on this critical topic of growth and change during college. The most important thing is to reflect on this topic and then talk about it with others. Find out if any of your teachers use service learning projects as part of class.

ONLINE

Read about the development of service learning programs at **<http://www.compact.org/faculty/special report.html>**. See the Big Dummy's Guide to Service Learning at **<http://www.fiu.edu/~time4chg/Library/bigdummy.html>**. Although this site is maintained for faculty, it contains valuable information on service learning for students as well.

ON INFOTRAC® COLLEGE EDITION

On InfoTrac® College Edition, read "College Teaches Values with Free Money. (Experiment: Giving 100 College Students $50 Each)," *Capper's*, October 29, 2002, 124, i 22: 14(1). Also on InfoTrac® College Edition, read "The Real Values of Mentoring: Reaching Out to Help." (Career Development from the Compass Group North America offers mentoring program), Susie Stephenson, Food Service Director, September 15, 2002, 15, no. 9: 72(1).

Service Learning and Learning Styles

Awareness of the many ways in which learning styles affect individual success in college and beyond has been one of the most important educational developments of the recent past. Service learning is one of the very few teaching-learning strategies that gives all kinds of learners an equal opportunity to succeed—not only students who learn well from books and who are perceptive listeners, but also students who learn best through active experimentation and hands-on projects. That is why so many students seek out such courses. Even students who excel at more traditional learning strategies find themselves excited by the prospect of an assignment that offers a change from the traditional term paper and test. Service learning directly addresses a question often on the tip of a student's tongue: Why do I have to learn this? Through service learning, students can see the utility of their knowledge even as they develop it.

SEE EXERCISE 7.3: YOUR VALUES AND YOUR FAMILY'S VALUES

SEE WORKING TOGETHER EXERCISE: SHARED VALUES?

Practical Suggestions and Useful Resources

If you find willing instructors and appropriate courses, you should make sure what you are being offered is really service learning: an opportunity to reflect and discuss as well as to act, a chance to develop citizenship as well as professional skills. Never confuse service learning with ordinary community service tacked on to a class or with internships or practica that have simply been relabeled. If your school has a service learning office, it can help you find faculty who really know what they're doing. Even if your school doesn't have such an office, you can easily do a little research on your own.[16]

Reassess Yourself

Now that you've read about values and service learning, go back to the self-assessment that appears at the beginning of this chapter. This is an opportunity for you to measure your progress, to check in with yourself and see how reading this chapter may have changed your approach to your college, community, and country. Which of the items on page 117 did you check? Would you change any of your answers as a result of reading this chapter? If so, which ones, and why?

Exercises

The exercises at the end of this chapter will help you sharpen what we believe are the critical skills for college success. You can further explore the topic of each chapter by completing the Internet and InfoTrac® College Edition exercises on the CD-ROM that accompanies this book.

[16] *Note:* For more information on service learning, go to the Web site of the W. K. Kellogg Foundation at *<http://learningindeed.org/about/index.html>*. Courtesy of the W. K. Kellogg Foundation. Reprinted with permission.

EXERCISE 7.1 Evidence of Values

Another way to start discovering your values is by defining them in relation to some immediate evidence or circumstances. List 15 items in your room (or apartment or house) that are important or symbolize something important to you.

Now cross out the ten items that are least important—the ones you could most easily live without. Of the remaining five, cross out two more. Rank-order the final three items from most to least important. What has this exercise told you about what you value?

EXERCISE 7.2 Friends and Values

A. Consider several friends and think about their values. Pick one who really differs from you in some important value. Write about the differences.

B. In a small group, discuss this difference in values. Explore how it's possible to be friends with someone so different.

EXERCISE 7.3 Your Values and Your Family's Values

The process by which we assimilate values into our own value systems involves three steps:

1. Choosing (selecting freely from alternatives after thoughtful consideration of the consequences)
2. Prizing (cherishing the value and affirming it publicly)
3. Acting (consistently displaying this value in behavior and decisions)

A. List three values your family has taught you are important. For each, document how you have completed the three-step process to make their value yours.

B. If you haven't completed the three steps, does it mean you have not chosen this value as your own? Explain your thoughts on this.

Working Together Exercise: Shared Values?

List all the reasons you chose to attend college. Share your reasons in a small group.

Attempt to get a consensus about the five most important reasons people choose to attend college. Rank the top five, from most important to least important.

My Group's Top Five Reasons	Different Reasons Other Groups Listed
1. ____________	**6.** ____________
2. ____________	**7.** ____________
3. ____________	**8.** ____________
4. ____________	**9.** ____________
5. ____________	**10.** ____________

Share your final rankings with other groups in the class. How similar were the results of those other groups? How different? How easy or hard was it to reach a consensus in your group? In other groups? What does this exercise tell you about the consistency of values among members of the class?

See the CD-ROM for these additional exercises as well as all other exercises appearing in this chapter

Internet Exercise 7.1	**Obligations to Society**
Internet Exercise 7.2	**Do Students Want Values Programs?**
InfoTrac® College Edition Exercise 7.1	**Is Service Learning Worth It?**
InfoTrac® College Edition Exercise 7.2	**Fifty Dollars of Values**
Exercise 7.4	**Values in Conflict**
Exercise 7.5	**Discovering the Value of Service Learning**

Exploring Courses and Careers

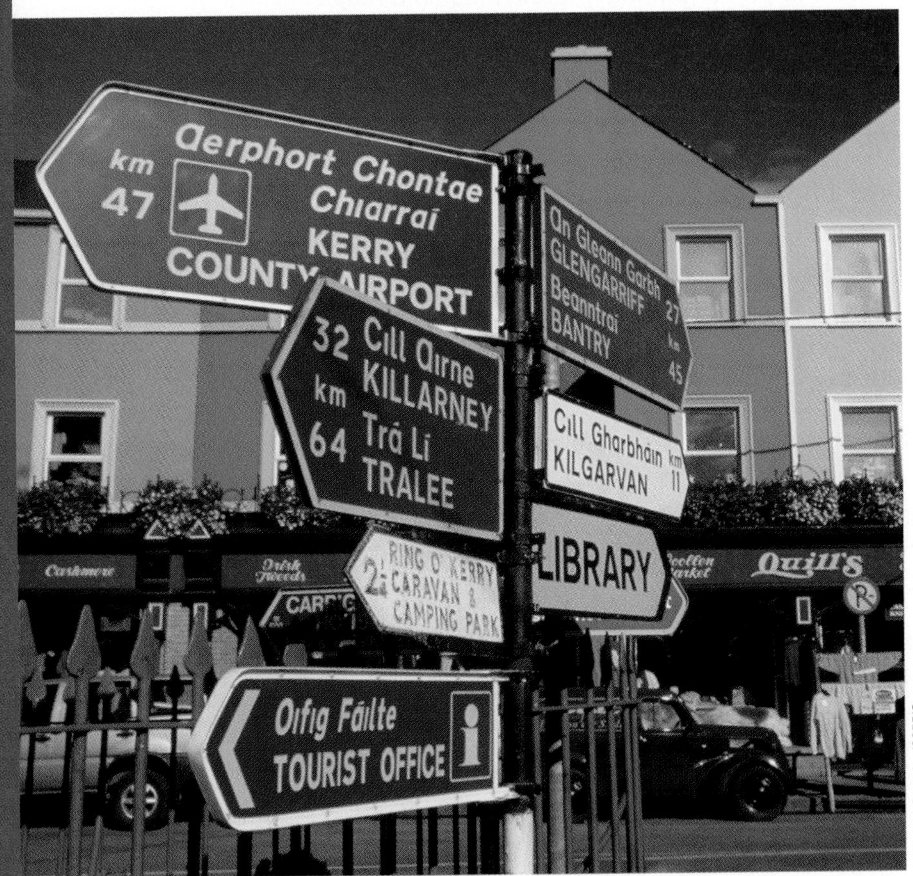

© Richard Cummins/CORBIS

Philip Gardner of Michigan State University, Linda Salane of Columbia College, and Stuart Hunter of the University of South Carolina at Columbia contributed their valuable expertise to this chapter.

Going Forward: Student Voices

Don't know why I chose English as a major. Probably because I've always liked my English classes. Off the top of my head, I can't think of any job that requires an English degree. Maybe Lila was right. She chose management, not because she's thrilled about it, but it sure will make her more marketable than me.

Looking Back: Author Voices

I never had any "career counseling" in college in the 1960s because there wasn't any! Instead, I got a really lucky break while I was in the Air Force during the Vietnam era, when I was ordered to do part-time evening college teaching. This led me to discover my calling: how to earn a living doing the four things I most love to do: read, write, talk, and help people. **John Gardner**

In this chapter, YOU WILL LEARN

- How majors and careers are linked–but not always
- Surprising things about careers and liberal arts majors
- Factors in career planning and choosing a major
- How to prepare a résumé and cover letter
- How your academic advisor and college catalog can be helpful references
- How internships and co-op programs can pave the way to employment

Sara entered college with thoughts of majoring in the sciences because she enjoyed working in a laboratory. Her concern for helping others led her to choose nursing as a major, a good career path that combined her two primary interests. Sara sailed through the first two years, excelling in her science classes. During her junior year, she began her nursing courses and spent more time observing nursing practice. After a summer working in various departments of her hometown hospital, Sara confessed that she did not like being around sick people every day and wanted to change her major but had no idea what she wanted to do.

John explored several majors during his first two years in college by choosing his elective courses with careers in mind and talking to his friends. He settled on business as a major, focusing on finance. John had high aspirations of working for a Fortune 500 company and earning a six-figure salary within five years of graduation. He performed above average in his academic work, although he was occasionally slack with assignments and frequently missed class. He interned with two prominent companies and eventually accepted a position at a Fortune 500 company. To his surprise, he was laid off nine months later because he was frequently late for work and on two occasions missed important deadlines.

Like Sara and John, students planning for careers frequently encounter bumps along the way. Choosing a career is a process of discovery, involving a willingness to remain open to new ideas and experiences. Many of the decisions you make early in college will have an impact on where you end up in the workplace.

Careers and the New Economy

Since the 1990s, companies have restructured and assumed new shapes to remain competitive. As a result, major changes have taken place in how we work, where we work, and the ways we prepare for work while in college. The following characteristics more or less define the economy of the early twenty-first century:

- *Global.* Increasingly, national economies have gone multinational, not only moving into overseas markets but also seeking cheaper labor, capital, and resources abroad. Factories around the world can be built to similar standards and turn out essentially the same products. Your career is bound to be affected by the global economy, even if you never leave the United States.

Self-Assessment

Majors and Careers

Place a check next to the statements that best describe your present situation. Circle the items you need help with:

1. ______ I have made contact with my academic advisor.
2. ______ I have found useful information in my college catalog.
3. ______ I have declared a major, but don't know how it will lead to a career.
4. ______ I have declared a major, but now I'm not sure I made the right choice.
5. ______ I'm not sure I have the necessary skills to pursue the major of my choice.
6. ______ I have visited the career center to learn how to research various careers.
7. ______ I have gone on a few informational interviews.
8. ______ I chose my major primarily because of the potential to earn lots of money.
9. ______ I chose my major primarily because I enjoy this subject.
10. ______ I know how to read a job posting and to research the company and career.

- *Boundaryless.* Teams of workers within an organization need to understand the missions of other teams because they most likely will have to work together. U.S. companies also have partners throughout the world. DaimlerChrysler, the result of a merger of the U.S. Chrysler organization with the German Mercedes-Benz group, is a recent example. Also, you may be an accountant and find yourself working with the public relations division of your company, or you may be a human resources manager who does training for a number of different divisions and in a number of different countries. You might even find yourself moved to a unit with a different function—as opposed to climbing up the proverbial and narrow career ladder.
- *Customized.* More and more, consumers are demanding products and services tailored to their specific needs. One example is the "health food supermarket" that has sprung up in many cities, offering complete grocery shopping for the segment of the market that demands natural or healthful foods. Another is the seemingly endless varieties of a single brand of shampoo or soup crowding your grocer's shelves. Such market segmentation requires constant adaptation of ideas to identify new products and services as new customer demands emerge.
- *Fast.* When computers became popular, people rejoiced because they believed the computer would reduce their workloads. Actually, the reverse happened. Where secretaries and other support workers performed many tasks for executives, now executives are designing their own PowerPoint presentations because, as one article put it, "it's more fun to work with a slide show than to write reports." For better or worse, "we want it now" is the cry in the workplace, with product and service delivery time cut to a minimum. Being fast requires constant thinking outside the box to identify new approaches.
- *Unstable.* Terrorist attacks, the war in Iraq, and the scandals within the highest echelons of major companies placed the stock market into a spin and caused

massive layoffs. The travel industry experienced a slump after 9/11 that is still felt today. Drops in state and federal funding have negatively affected shopping. Although, as history has taught us, the situation will get better, it's important to know about the economy, especially in times like these.

Surviving in a Changing Economy

According to *Fast Company* magazine, the new economy has changed many of the rules about work. Leaders are now expected to teach and encourage others as well as head up their divisions. People who can second-guess the marketplace are in demand. Change has become the norm. Workers are being urged to continue their learning, and companies are volunteering to play a critical role in the welfare of all people through the sponsorship of worthy causes. With the lines between work and life blurring, workers need to find healthy balances in their lives. Bringing home work may be inevitable at times, but it shouldn't be the rule.

As you work, you'll be continually enhancing and expanding your skills and competencies. You can accomplish this on your own, by taking evening courses, or by attending conferences and workshops. As you prepare over the next few years to begin your career, remember that:

- *You are, more or less, solely responsible for your career.* At one time, organizations provided structured "ladders" that an employee could climb in his or her moves to a higher professional level. In most cases, such ladders have disappeared. Companies may assist you with assessments and information on available positions in the industry, but the ultimate task of engineering a career path is yours.
- *To advance your career, you must accept the risks that accompany employment and plan for the future.* Organizations will continually restructure, merge, and either grow or downsize in response to economic conditions. As a result, positions may be cut. Because you can be unexpectedly unemployed, it will be wise to keep other options in mind and to invest and save what you can on a regular basis.
- *A college degree does not guarantee employment.* Of course, you'll be able to hunt through opportunities that are more rewarding, financially and otherwise, than if you did not have a degree. But just because you want to work at a certain organization doesn't mean there's a job for you there. And as the economy rises and falls and rises, and so forth, you may find yourself laid off from a job that fits you to a "T."

Critical Thinking

From talking with your parents, teachers, and other people, you've no doubt learned that the work world doesn't provide the kind of safe, permanent employment it once did. Workers must take more responsibility for managing not only their careers, but also their security, including company-related health benefits and long-term savings.

The employment outlook varies depending on the profession you've chosen and the current state of the economy. Brainstorm some issues you might face in the career you're considering. Are jobs plentiful or will you have to compete seriously to get one of the several slots available? What sorts of concerns do you have about salary, benefits, workload, and security? What might you do to improve any or all of these areas?

- *A commitment to lifelong learning will help keep you employable.* In college you have been learning a vital skill: how to learn. *Gradus,* the Latin root of *graduation,* means moving to a higher level of responsibility. Your learning has just begun when you receive your diploma.

Now the good news. Thousands of graduates find jobs every year. Some may have to work longer to get where they want to be, but persistence pays off. If you start now, you'll have time to build a portfolio of academic and co-curricular experiences that will begin to add substance to your career profile. This Rudyard Kipling couplet from *The Just So Stories* (1902) is an easy way to remember how to navigate for career success:

> *I keep six honest serving men*
> *(They taught me all I knew)*
> *Their names are what and why and when*
> *And how and where and who.*

The knowledge to manage your career comes from you (why, who, how) and from an understanding of the career you wish to enter (what, where, when):

- *Why?* Why do you want to be a . . . ? Knowing your goals and values will help you pursue your career with passion and an understanding of what motivates you. Never say "because I'm a people person" or "because I like to work with people." Sooner or later, most people have to work with people. And your interviewer has heard this much too often.
- *Who?* Network with people who can help you find out what you want to be. Right now, that might be a teacher in your major or an academic advisor or someone at your campus career center. Later, network with others who can help you attain your goal. Someone will always know someone else for you to talk to.
- *How?* Have the technical and communications skills required to work effectively. Become a computer whiz. Learn how to do PowerPoint presentations or improve your PowerPoint skills. Take a speech course. Work on improving your writing. More than likely, your future job will require many or all of these skills.
- *What?* Be aware of the opportunities an employer presents, as well as such unforeseen occurrences as relocation overseas. Clearly understand the employment requirements for the career field you have chosen. Know what training you will need to remain in your chosen profession.
- *Where?* Know the points of entry into the field. For example, you can obtain on-the-job experiences through internships, co-ops, or part-time jobs.
- *When?* Know how early you need to start looking. Find out if certain professions hire at certain times of the year.

Making Major Decisions: Your Academic Advisor or Counselor

SEE EXERCISE 8.1: YOUR ACADEMIC ADVISOR/COUNSELOR

A key individual in your search for majors and careers is your academic advisor or counselor. A mounting body of evidence suggests that poor academic advising is a major reason students become dissatisfied with college during the first year.

An effective academic advisor will go beyond recommending classes for you to take next term. He or she will take time to learn about your interests and concerns, and, without making decisions for you, will help steer you towards the majors and careers that seem to fit you best. Should you ever feel frustrated about a class or classes, should you ever begin to think you're in the wrong major, should a medical emergency force you to miss classes beyond the drop date, or should you find your-

Examining Values

WHAT ARE YOU LOOKING FOR IN YOUR ACADEMIC ADVISOR/COUNSELOR?

This graph from a study of students at Harvard shows that men and women tend to seek different qualities in advisors. When asked about advising, men want an advisor who "knows the facts." Or "if he doesn't know the data, he knows where to get it or to send me to get it." Or one who "makes concrete and directive suggestions, which I am free to accept or reject." Women more often want an advisor who "will take the time to get to know me personally." Or who "is a good listener and can read between the lines if I am hesitant to express a concern." Or who "shares my interests so that we will have something in common."

What values do you look for in an advisor? Are you looking for a friend, an expert, or a problem solver? What can you do to ensure that you get the advisor who is best for you? Write down three attributes that you would seek in a counselor or advisor.

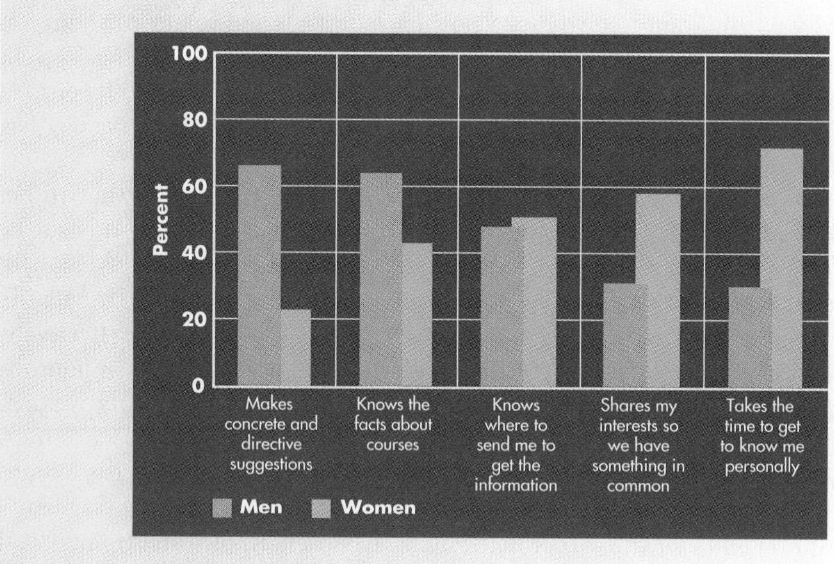

Figure 8.1 What Students Want from Academic Advisors

Source: Richard J. Light, *The Harvard Assessment Seminars, First Report*, Cambridge, MA: Harvard University Graduate School of Education and Kennedy School of Government, 1990.

self in a situation where it's impossible for you to focus on your studies, contact this person asap. One way or another, he or she can probably help.

For example, your advisor may put your mind at ease by telling you that it is perfectly fine to enter college as an undecided major. Most college students change their majors at least once, and some change more often. It may even be better to shop around before you make the important decision.

So make it a point to meet this important person and be sure the match is comfortable. If not, find someone else. Ask one of your favorite instructors or check with your department head or dean's office. Never stay in an advising/counseling relationship that isn't working for you.

Connecting Careers and Majors

Once you have explored your interests, you can begin to connect them to academic majors. If you're still not sure, take the advice of Patrick Combs, author of *Major in Success,* who recommends that you major in a subject that you are really passionate about. Most advisors would agree.

Hold on. Choose something like history because I love history? Where will that put me in the job market? The reality is that most occupational fields do not require a specific major and graduates have found a number of ways to use their majors.

Today, English majors are designing Web pages, philosophy majors are developing logic codes for operating systems, and history majors are sales representatives and business managers. You do not have to major in science to gain admittance to medical school. Of course, you do have to take the required science and math courses, but medical schools seek applicants with diverse backgrounds.

Some fields do require specific degrees, such as nursing, accounting, engineering, and pharmacy, because certification in these fields is directly tied to a degree.

Hold On to Your College Catalog

The catalog in use at the time of your matriculation (the day you enrolled for the first time) will generally stand as your individual contract with the institution. Since colleges and universities are constantly changing admissions standards, degree requirements, academic calendars, and so on, it's important to keep "your" catalog in a safe place until you finish college.

Most college catalogs include a current academic calendar, which shows the beginning and ending dates of academic terms, holidays, and important deadlines. If you are not doing well in a particular class, you may want to drop the course rather than receive a failing grade, but you must do so before the deadline for withdrawal.

Don't rely on secondhand grapevine information. Become familiar with general academic regulations directly from the catalog. If you don't understand something in the catalog, seek clarification from an official source, such as your academic advisor.

By far the lengthiest part of most catalogs is the section on academic programs. It summarizes the various degrees offered, the majors within each department, and the requirements for each discipline. The academic program section also describes all courses offered at your institution, along with the course number, the course title, units of credit, prerequisites for taking the course, and a brief statement of the course content. For more detailed academic information, check with individual departments.

Exploring Your Interests

SEE EXERCISE 8.2: USING YOUR CATALOG AND STARTING A FILE

Dr. John Holland, a psychologist at Johns Hopkins University, has developed a number of tools and concepts including this Self-Directed Search, that can help you identify your various dimensions so that you can determine potential career choices.

Holland separates people into six general categories based on differences in their interests, skills, values, and personality characteristics—in short, their preferred approaches to life[1]:

SEE EXERCISE 8.3: WHAT ARE YOUR LIFE GOALS?

Realistic (R) These people describe themselves as concrete, down-to-earth, and practical doers. They exhibit competitive/assertive behavior and show interest in activities that require motor coordination, skill, and physical strength. They prefer situations involving action solutions rather than tasks involving verbal or interpersonal skills, and they like to take a concrete approach to problem solving rather than rely on abstract theory. They tend to be interested in scientific or mechanical areas rather than cultural and aesthetic fields.

[1]Adapted from John L. Holland, *Self-Directed Search Manual,* Lutz, FL: Psychological Assessment Resources, 1985. Copyright 1985 by PAR, Inc. Reprinted with permission.

Investigative (I). These people describe themselves as analytical, rational, and logical problem solvers. They value intellectual stimulation and intellectual achievement and prefer to think rather than to act, to organize and understand rather than to persuade. They usually have a strong interest in physical, biological, or social sciences. They are less apt to be people-oriented.

Artistic (A). These people describe themselves as creative, innovative, and independent. They value self-expression and relations with others through artistic expression and are also emotionally expressive. They dislike structure, preferring tasks involving personal or physical skills. They resemble investigative people but are more interested in the cultural or aesthetic than the scientific.

Social (S). These people describe themselves as kind, caring, helpful, and understanding of others. They value helping and making a contribution. They satisfy their needs in one-to-one or small group interaction using strong speaking skills to teach, counsel, or advise. They are drawn to close interpersonal relationships and are less apt to engage in intellectual or extensive physical activity.

Enterprising (E). These people describe themselves as assertive, risk-taking, and persuasive. They value prestige, power, and status and are more inclined than other types to pursue it. They use verbal skills to supervise, lead, direct, and persuade rather than to support or guide. They are interested in people and in achieving organizational goals.

Conventional (C). These people describe themselves as neat, orderly, detail-oriented, and persistent. They value order, structure, prestige, and status and possess a high degree of self-control. They are not opposed to rules and regulations. They are skilled in organizing, planning, and scheduling and are interested in data and people.

Holland's system organizes career fields into the same six categories. Career fields are grouped according to what a particular career field requires of a person (skills and personality characteristics most commonly associated with success in those fields) and what rewards those fields provide (interests and values most commonly associated with satisfaction). Here are a few examples:

Realistic (R). Agricultural engineer, electrical contractor, industrial arts teacher, naval officer, fitness director, package engineer, electronics technician, computer graphics technician

Investigative (I). Urban planner, chemical engineer, bacteriologist, flight engineer, genealogist, laboratory technician, marine scientist, nuclear medical technologist, obstetrician, quality control technician, computer programmer, environmentalist, physician, college professor

Artistic (A). Architect, film editor/director, actor, cartoonist, interior decorator, fashion model, graphic communications specialist, journalist, editor, orchestra leader, public relations specialist, sculptor, media specialist, librarian, reporter

Social (S). Nurse, teacher, social worker, genetic counselor, marriage counselor, rehabilitation counselor, school superintendent, geriatric specialist, insurance claims specialist, minister, travel agent, guidance counselor, convention planner

Enterprising (E). Banker, city manager, FBI agent, health administrator, judge, labor arbitrator, salary and wage administrator, insurance salesperson, sales engineer, lawyer, sales representative, marketing specialist

Conventional (C). Accountant, statistician, census enumerator, data processor, hospital administrator, insurance administrator, office manager, underwriter, auditor, personnel specialist, database manager, abstractor/indexer

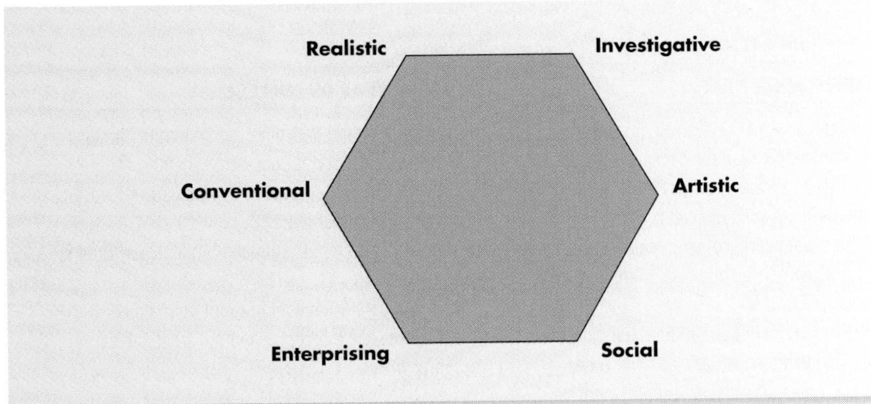

FIGURE 8.2 Holland's Hexagonal Model of Career Fields

Your career choices ultimately will involve a complex assessment of the factors that are most important to you. To display the relationship between career fields and the potential conflicts people face as they consider them, Holland's model is commonly presented in a hexagonal shape (Figure 8.1). The closer the types, the closer the relationships among the career fields; the farther apart the types, the more conflict between the career fields.

Holland's model can help you address the problem of career choice in two ways. First, you can begin to identify many career fields that are consistent with what you know about yourself. Once you've identified potential fields, you can use the career library at your college to get more information about those fields, such as daily activities for specific jobs, interests and abilities required, preparation required for entry, working conditions, salary and benefits, and employment outlook.

Second, you can begin to identify the harmony or conflicts in your career choices. This will help you analyze the reasons for your career decisions and be more confident as you make choices.

Never feel you have to make a decision simply on the results of one assessment. Take time to talk your interests over with a career counselor. Another helpful approach is to shadow an individual in the occupation that interests you.

Starting Your Career-Planning Program

The process of making a career choice begins with:

- Understanding your values and motivations
- Identifying your interests
- Linking your personality and learning styles to those interests
- Using this information to decide on an appropriate academic major
- Researching possible occupations that match your skills, your interests, and your academic major
- Building on your strengths and developing your weaker skills
- Preparing a marketing strategy that sells you as a valued member of a professional team
- Writing a convincing résumé and cover letter

Table 8.1 provides a guide to what you should be doing during each year of college (if you are in a two-year program, you will have to do more during your second year than this table suggests).

You may proceed through these steps at a different pace than your friends, and that's okay. What you want is to develop your qualifications, make good choices, and

Table 8.1 Your Career Itinerary

A. NO MATTER WHAT YEAR

- Get a job. Even a part-time job will develop your skills and may help you make decisions about what you like—and what you don't—in a work environment. In any job, you can learn vital skills such as teamwork, communication, and interpersonal, computer, and time management skills.
- Register with your college's online job listing system to find listings for part- and full-time, internship, co-op, and seasonal employment.
- Find on-campus interviewing opportunities for internships in your early years and for full-time employment as a senior.
- Network with family, friends, instructors, friends of family, and acquaintances to find contacts in your field(s) of interest so that you can learn more about those areas.
- Volunteer! This can help you explore careers, and get some experience in an area that interests you as you help others.
- Conduct occupational and industrial research for your field or area of geographic interest. Look for other options within and beyond those fields.
- Explore career options through informational interviews (interviewing to find out about a career) and job shadowing (getting permission to observe someone as he or she works).
- Prepare a draft of your résumé and have it critiqued by your career counselor and perhaps by a professional in your chosen field.
- Get involved in clubs and organizations; work toward leadership positions.
- Explore overseas study possibilities to gain a global perspective and learn a foreign language.
- Attend career fairs to connect with employers for internships and other career-related opportunities as well as to develop a professional network.

B. FIRST YEAR OF COLLEGE

- Take the Holland Self-Directed Search or similar interest inventory at your career center.
- Take a variety of classes to get exposure to various skill and knowledge areas.
- Attend your campus' annual job fair to see what is being offered.
- Talk to a career counselor about your skills, aptitudes, and interests. Find out what the career center offers.

C. SECOND YEAR OF COLLEGE

- Attend career fairs to learn more about employers who hire graduates in your major.
- Spend some time talking with your college advisor or career counselor to discuss your career plans.

D. THIRD YEAR OF COLLEGE

- Take an advanced computerized assessment (SIGI Plus or FOCUS II) to discover further career options and to refine your career plans. Visit your career center.
- Take on a leadership role in a club or organization.
- Participate in mock interview activities to improve your interviewing skills.
- Attend workshops to learn more about résumé writing, looking for an internship, interviewing, and other job search skills.
- Explore the option of graduate school.
- Develop a top ten list of employers of interest.

E. LAST YEAR OF COLLEGE

- Check on-campus interviewing opportunities on a daily basis, beginning in the fall term. Interview with organizations recruiting for your major.
- Research organizations of interest to you, interview with those coming to campus, and contact human resources professionals who represent organizations that won't be on campus. Find out if you can interview with those groups.
- Attend career fairs to network with employers and set up interviewing opportunities.
- Find a local professional who will allow you to shadow him or her during working hours.
- If you're thinking about graduate school, request applications early in the fall and send them out throughout the fall term.
- Target your geographic areas of interest by contacting local chambers of commerce and using local newspapers, phone books, and Internet resources.

Source: Used by permission of Career Passport, Michigan State University.

take advantage of any opportunities on campus to learn more about the career search. Keep your goals in mind as you select courses and seek employment, but also remember that the route you think you want to take ultimately may not be the best one for you.

Some Career Do's and Don'ts

Some first-year students come to college with a strong sense of self-knowledge and a focus on a specific interest. Others have no idea what their interests might be and are sorting through their values, interests, and skills in an attempt to define themselves. Such self-definition is an ongoing experience that, for many of us, continues well beyond college. It helps to keep a journal of such thoughts because reviewing these early interests later in life may lead to long-forgotten career paths just when you need them.

As you start examining your aspirations and interests, keep in mind these simple do's and don'ts:

DO'S

1. Do explore a number of career possibilities and academic majors.
2. Do get involved through volunteer work, study abroad, and student organizations—especially those linked to your major.
3. Do follow your passion. Learn what you love to do, and go for it.

DON'TS

1. Don't just focus on a major and blindly hope to get a career out of it. That's backward.
2. Don't be motivated primarily by external stimuli, such as salary, prestige, and perks. All the money in the world won't make you happy if you hate what you're doing every day.
3. Don't select a major just because it seems "cool."
4. Don't choose courses simply because your roommate said they were easy. That's wasting your valuable time, not to mention tuition.

Factors Affecting Career Choices

Some people have a definite self-image when they enter college, but most of us are still in the process of defining (or redefining) ourselves throughout life. We can look at ourselves in several useful ways with respect to possible careers:

- *Interests.* Interests develop from your experiences and beliefs and can continue to develop and change throughout life. You may be interested in writing for the college newspaper because you wrote for your high school paper. On the other hand, it's not unusual to enter Psych 101 with a great interest in psychology and realize halfway through the course that the field of psychology is not what you imagined.
- *Skills.* Skills, or the ability to do some things better than most people, can usually be improved with practice.
- *Aptitudes.* Aptitudes, the foundation for skills, are inherent strengths, often part of your biological heritage or the result of early training. We each have aptitudes we can build on. Build on your strengths.

Where to Go for Help

ON CAMPUS

Career center. Every college campus has a career center where you can obtain free counseling and information on careers. A career professional will work with you to help you define your interests, to interpret the results of any assessment you complete, and to coach you on interview techniques and critique your résumé. Make an appointment to discuss such things.

By the end of your first year you should be familiar with the career center–where it is located and the counselor responsible for your academic major or interests. You might also find opportunities for internships, practicums, and work shadowing here.

Academic advising. Many advisors can help you see beyond individual classes to help you plan a career search. Talking to your advisor is often the best place to start. If you have not declared a major–which is true of many first-year students–your advisor may be able to help you with that decision as well.

Faculty. On many campuses, faculty take an active role in helping students connect academic interests to careers. A faculty member can recommend specific courses in this regard. Faculty in professional curricula, such as business and other applied fields, often have direct contact with companies and serve as contacts for internships. If you have an interest in attending graduate school, faculty sponsorship is critical to admission. Developing a mentor relationship with a faculty member can open doors in a number of ways.

The library. Some campuses have a separate library in the career center staffed by librarians whose job it is to help you locate career-related information resources. Of course, all campuses have a main library containing a wealth of information on careers. This is perhaps the best place to start, and the person who will be glad to help you is the reference librarian at the main desk.

Upper-class students. Resident assistants and senior mentors can help you navigate courses and find important resources. They may also have practical experience from internships and volunteering. Their insights can extend the theoretical aspects of academic work into the practical realm.

Student organizations. Professional student organizations that focus on specific career interests meet regularly throughout the year. Join them now. Not only will they put you in contact with upper-class students, but their programs often include employer representatives, helpful discussions on searching for internships or jobs, and exposure to current conditions in the workplace.

ONLINE

<http://www.employmentguide.com/site/index. html>. Go to this Web site for a list of jobs in a number of categories. As you browse, be certain to find out whether or not a fee is charged for its services.

<http://www.collegerecruiter.com/>. A site similar to the one listed above, but focuses on entry-level jobs for college graduates. Again, check carefully for fees.

<http://www.csp.msu.edu/pages/main/students.cfm>. A Michigan State University Web site, created by Philip Gardner, one of the contributors to this chapter, that contains valuable and up-to-date information on career trends.

ON INFOTRAC® COLLEGE EDITION

Do a search using "choosing careers" as your subject and you will find articles such as the following: Alan Bernstein, "Choosing a Career: What 'Color' Is Your Ideal Career Path?" *Careers and Colleges*, Jan.-Feb. 2004 v24, i3, p.6(4).

- *Personality.* The personality you've developed over the years makes you *you* and can't be ignored when you make career decisions. The quiet, orderly, calm, detail-oriented person probably will make a different work choice than the aggressive, outgoing, argumentative person.
- *Life goals and work values.* Two factors influence our conclusions about success and happiness: (1) knowing that we are achieving the life goals we've set for ourselves and (2) finding that we gain satisfaction from what we're receiving

Setting Goals for Success

Where do you want to be in five years? Ten years? Twenty years? In the space below, describe the occupation you want to have at those milestones (In graduate school? Managing a restaurant? Caring for your children?) and two or three things you will have to accomplish before then in order to meet those goals.

YEARS	OCCUPATION	ACTIONS TO TAKE
5 years		
10 years		
20 years		

from our work. If your values are in conflict with the organizational values where you work, you may be in for trouble.

Getting Experience

Now that you have a handle on your interests, it's time to test the waters and do some exploring. Your campus has a variety of activities and programs in which you can participate to confirm those interests, check your values, and gain valuable skills. Here are some examples:

- *Volunteer/service learning.* Some instructors build service learning into their courses. Service learning allows you to apply academic theories and ideas to actual practice. Volunteering outside of class is a valuable way to encounter different life situations and to gain work knowledge in areas such as teaching, health services, counseling, and tax preparation. A little time spent each week can provide immense personal and professional rewards.
- *Study abroad.* Take courses in another country and learn about a different culture at the same time. Learn to adapt to new traditions and a different pace of life. Some study abroad programs also include options for both work and service learning experiences.
- *Internships and co-ops.* Many employers now expect these work experiences. They want to see that you have experience in the professional workplace and have gained an understanding of the skills and competencies necessary to succeed. Check with your academic department and your career center on the internships that are available in your major. Many majors offer academic credit for internships. And remember: With an internship on your résumé, you'll be a step ahead of students who ignore the possibility of this valuable experience.
- *On-campus employment.* On-campus jobs may not provide much income, yet this type of employment gives you a chance to practice good work habits. Some campus jobs have direct connections to employment. More important, on-campus employment brings you into contact with faculty and other academic professionals whom you can later consult as mentors or ask for references.
- *Student projects/competitions.* In many fields, students engage in competitions based on what they have learned in the classroom. Civil engineers build concrete canoes and marketing majors develop campaign strategies, for example. They might compete against teams from other schools. In the process, they learn teamwork, communication, and applied problem-solving skills.

SEE EXERCISE 8.4: FINDING YOUR INTERESTS

- *Research.* An excellent way to extend your academic learning is to work with a faculty member on a research project. Research extends your critical thinking skills and provides insight on a subject above and beyond your books and class notes.
- *Informational interviewing.* One way to learn more about a career is to talk directly with the people in it. By arranging to meet with people who would be your peers, as well as those who are doing the hiring, you'll learn more about job requirements and the workplace environment.

Time for Action

In addition to being well educated, you'll also need the following qualities and skills:

1. Communication skills that demonstrate solid oral, written, and listening abilities.
2. Presentation skills, including the ability to respond to questions and serious critiques of your presentation material.
3. Computer/technical aptitudes at the level required for the position being filled. Computer ability is now perceived as a given core skill, right up there with reading, writing, and mathematics. Expectations for computer knowledge and application continue to rise.
4. Leadership skills, or the ability to take charge or relinquish control according to the needs of the organization.
5. Team skills, the ability to work with different people while maintaining autonomous control over some assignments.
6. Interpersonal abilities that allow you to relate to others, inspire others to participate, or mitigate conflict between coworkers.
7. Personal traits, including showing initiative and motivation, being adaptable to change, having a work ethic, being reliable and honest, possessing integrity, knowing how to plan and organize multiple tasks, and being able to respond positively to customer concerns.
8. Critical thinking and problem solving—the ability to identify problems and their solutions by integrating information from a variety of sources and effectively weighing alternatives.
9. Intelligence and common sense.
10. A willingness to learn quickly and continuously.
11. Work-related experiences in college that provide an understanding of the workplace and allow you to apply classroom learning.

Speaking of Careers

Since this entire chapter is about careers, we want to shift the emphasis to your next summer job. Certainly, many of you will be working then to help offset the costs of college. But what if you could gain experience–even without pay–by working in your intended field? Can't afford it? Think again. Without the pressures of school, you might be able to work a limited number of hours "interning" in your field and use the remaining time to earn cash. Find the person in your major who runs internship or practicum programs and ask if he or she has any ideas. Even though you may not qualify for credit, the experience may help you decide whether or not you belong in this field. If you do like it, you can come back to that same person for a real internship or a job in the future.

Researching Careers

Even if you have followed the many suggestions in this chapter to learn more about careers in general and those that interest you most, there is still another way to become "career-educated," and that is by reading books and checking Internet sources on the career process.

To begin, check out these and other Web sites that provide information on careers:

<http://www.jobweb.com/joboutlook/2004outlook/>
<http://dir.yahoo.com/Business_and_Economy/Business_to_Business/Labor/Statistics/Salary_Information/>
<http://www.bls.gov/bls/blswage.htm>
<http://www.collegegrad.com/offer/index.shtml> (Avoid the salary report that costs money, but use other parts of this site for solid information on benefit packages, general salary ranges by career, etc.)

Also check your library to see if they have the following books and similar ones:

Barbara Moses. *The Good News About Careers*, Hoboken, NJ: Wiley, 2000
Linda Gale. *Discover What You're Best At,* New York: Simon and Schuster, 1998
James Barrett, Geoff Williams and Jim Barrett. *Test Your Own Job Aptitude: Exploring Your Career Potential,* New York: Penguin USA, 1995
Donald Asher. *College to Career: Entry-Level Résumés for Any Major From Accounting to Zoology*, Berkeley: Ten Speed Press, 1999

If you want more to read, use a Web site such as *<http://www.bn.com>* or *<http://www.amazon.com>*. Use such search terms as "college and career," "career outlook," "careers in . . . ," and so forth.

Finally, use InfoTrac® to find career articles. One approach is to enter "careers + psychology" or "careers + marketing" or whatever fields you may find of interest. Be sure to use the key word search, not the subject guide search for this approach.

Reassess Yourself

Now that you've read more about courses and careers, go back to the self-assessment that appears at the beginning of this chapter. This is an opportunity for you to measure your progress, to check in with yourself and see how reading this chapter may have changed your approach to choosing your major and plotting your career. Which of the items on page 135 did you check? Would you change any of your answers as a result of reading this chapter? If so, which ones, and why?

Exercises

Each of these exercises will let you further explore the topic of this chapter. You'll find all of these exercises, plus Internet and InfoTrac® College Edition exercises, on the CD-ROM that accompanies this book.

EXERCISE 8.1 Your Academic Advisor/Counselor

Fill in the following information about your academic advisor/counselor:

Name: ____________________

Phone: ____________________

E-mail: ____________________

Office: ____________________

Office hours: ____________________

Then prepare to meet this person by answering the following questions:

1. What is my major? What is my potential career? If I don't have a major, what would I like to major in?
2. What classes do I think I need to take next term?
3. Which classes must I complete before I can take other classes?
4. What problems, if any, am I having this term? What should I do about them?
5. Which of my current teachers do I learn best from? Which do I learn least from? Why?
6. What do I need to know about services on campus, scholarships, internships, co-operative education, and so forth?

EXERCISE 8.2 Using Your Catalog and Starting a File

A. Get a college catalog. Make sure it's the one dated the year you matriculated, not the year you applied for admission or were accepted. Ask your advisor/counselor where to find one or find one online through your campus portal.

B. Start a file (hard copy or soft copy) for your catalog and other documents, including your grade reports, advisement forms, fee payment receipts, schedule change forms, and other proof of financial and academic transactions with your campus. Hang onto these until your diploma is in your hands.

EXERCISE 8.3 What Are Your Life Goals?

The following list includes some life goals that people set for themselves. This list can help you begin to think about the kinds of goals you may want to set. Check the goals you would like to achieve in your life. Next, review the goals you have checked and circle the five you want most. Finally, review your list of five goals and rank them by priority—1 for most important, 5 for least important. Be prepared to discuss your choices in class if your instructor asks.

____The love and admiration of friends
____Good health
____Lifetime financial security
____A lovely home
____International fame
____Freedom within my work setting
____A good love relationship
____A satisfying religious faith
____Recognition as the most attractive person in the world
____An understanding of the meaning of life
____Success in my profession
____A personal contribution to the elimination of poverty and sickness
____A chance to direct the destiny of a nation
____Freedom to do what I want
____A satisfying and fulfilling marriage
____A happy family relationship

____Complete self-confidence

____Other: ______________________________

Source: Adapted from James D. McHolland, *Human Potential Seminar,* Evanston, IL: 1975. Used by permission of the author.

EXERCISE 8.4 Finding Your Interests

A. Complete an interest inventory, such as the Holland Self-Directed Search, at your career center or online at *<http://www.self-directed-search.com/taketest.html>* (there is a fee of around $8.95 to get your results); or visit the *Princeton Review* and take their Career Quiz (*<http://www.review.com>*). List your top five occupational interests based on this test:

1. ______________________________
2. ______________________________
3. ______________________________
4. ______________________________
5. ______________________________

B. Interview a professional in one of these fields. In the interview, find out as much as you can about the education required, skills needed to be successful, typical career opportunities, and outlook for the future. Identify five key points you learned from the interview.

Working Together Exercise

Holland or Not?

1. Each student writes the name of the career field in the Holland model that they most closely affiliate with.
2. Participants group themselves, when possible, into teams containing each of the six fields.
3. Each person reads a description of his or her career field. The others comment on the description. Does this sound like this person or not? What doesn't "match"?
4. After each person has had the chance to read a description and hear comments from other students, the group begins again. This time, each person reads the list of careers matching the career field and comments on whether any of these careers makes sense for him or her. Other participants may offer assistance by citing whether there is an appropriate career field in that group for this person, or whether the person may actually belong in a related career field.

If some members have taken the Holland Career Inventory, they might share what they perceive to be the accuracy of that test with others in the group.

See the CD-ROM for these additional exercises as well as all other exercises appearing in this chapter

Internet Exercise 8.1	**Mission and Vision**
Internet Exercise 8.2	**Internet Career Resources**
InfoTrac® College Edition Exercise 8.1	**Careers**
Exercise 8.5	**Personality Mosaic**
Exercise 8.6	**Holland Hexagon**

9

Creating Diverse Relationships

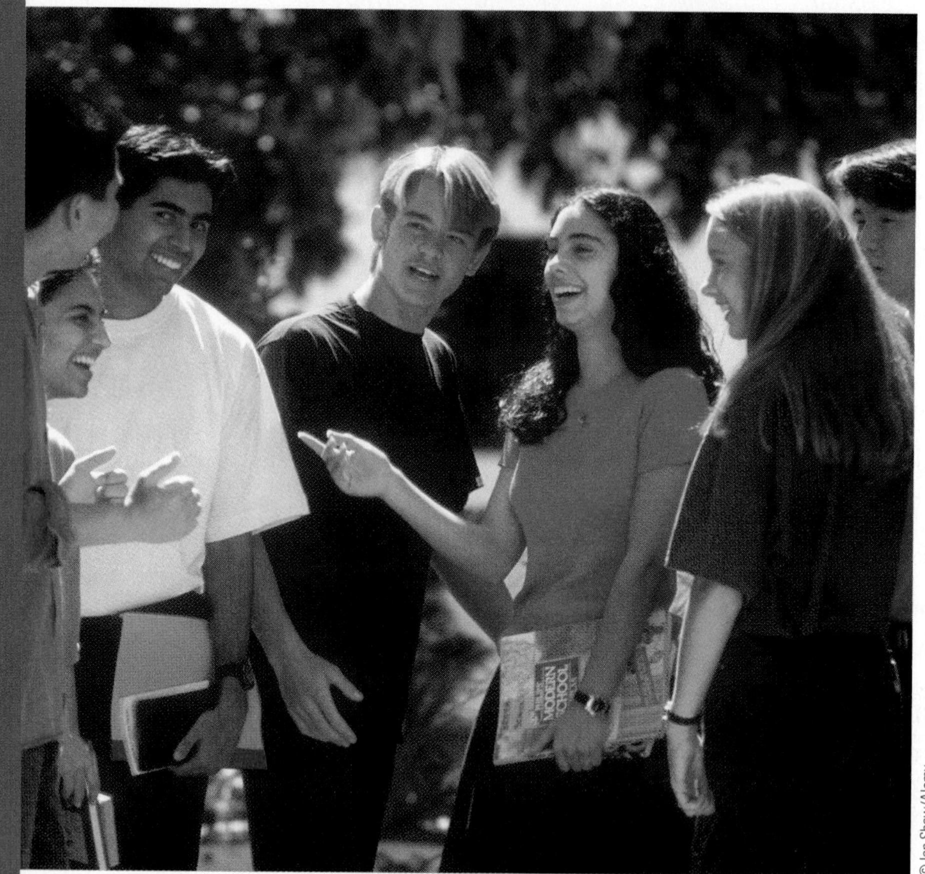
© Ian Shaw/Alamy

Those educators contributed their valuable expertise to this chapter: J. Herman Blake, Iowa State University; Joan Rasool, Westfield State College; Tom Carskadon, Mississippi State University; Tricia Phaup and Sara J. Corwin, University of South Carolina at Columbia

Going Forward: Student Voices

So many different kinds of people here. It's not like my high school class. Should I stick with people who are more like me, or should I try to make friends with a bunch of different kinds of people? Might learn something from them. Then again, what I learn might not be so great, either.

Looking Back: Author Voices

I find it hard to believe, but I never went to school with an African American. Never had an African American professor, and never thought much about it. Today my life has been enriched by friends of every kind. Though we may look different and act differently, the thing we have in common is that we think alike and like each other very much. **Jerry Jewler**

In this chapter, YOU WILL LEARN

- How America is becoming more diverse
- That college is a place where diversity can flourish among all groups
- How to fight discrimination and prejudice on campus
- The stages of relationships
- Factors in sexual decision making
- What to do if your relationship is abusive
- How to avoid sexual assault
- How to integrate parents, marriage, and roommates into your college experience
- The value of co-op programs, service learning, and campus activities

Now that you're in college, classes and studying are supposed to be the first things on your mind. In reality, though, the focus is just as often on relationships—with dates, lovers, spouses, children, friends, roommates, parents, classmates, and coworkers.

Relationships have outcomes far beyond your social life. They strongly influence your survival and success in college. Distracted by bad relationships, you will find it difficult to concentrate on your studies. Supported by good relationships, you will be better able to get through the rough times, reach your full potential, remain in college, and enjoy life. The relationships you form in college are likely to remain part of you long after you've graduated.

The Many Dimensions of Diversity

In present-day U.S. society, race, ethnicity, and national origin are inextricably intertwined. Take the case of Hispanics or Latinos. Often considered an ethnic minority group, they represent not only a variety of racial backgrounds but also a great many different countries of origin. The same is true for those categorized as black or African American. Although most black residents of the United States have been American for many generations, recent immigration patterns add further complexity and variety.

According to one college dean, when a faculty member tells him a student is black, he always asks "American, African, or Caribbean born?" Furthermore, a Caribbean-born black student may also be Hispanic! So even though we may think race and ethnicity are clearly distinct concepts, such is not the case. In fact, race and ethnicity are just convenient social concepts we use to categorize and define people according to their physical appearance or the way they act or sound. *Although we use the term "race" in this book to discuss one aspect of diversity, you should know that there is no biological or scientific foundation for the idea of race.*

Self-Assessment

Creating Diverse Relationships

Place a check next to the statements that best describe what you believe:

1. _______ Culture, ethnicity, and race all mean the same to me.
2. _______ I am not part of any cultural, ethnic, or racial group.
3. _______ I believe in equal rights, but I'm not always comfortable getting to know people who are very different from me.
4. _______ Now that I am in college, asking my parents' advice is a good idea.
5. _______ Roommates are like the weather: You hope for the best, but you take what you get with a smile.
6. _______ I am not sure how to take responsibility for my own sexual decisions or how having sex will change how I feel about myself and others.
7. _______ I am reluctant to tell the person I am dating that I don't want sex.
8. _______ I am uncomfortable asking for help or seeking information about sexually transmitted diseases and contraception.

Even though no scientific foundation exists for the notion of race, the *concept* of race is still powerful in the United States. The consequence is that physical appearance—including skin complexion, hair texture, and eye shape—is an important part of our categorization of others and ourselves. Indeed, race is one of the most pervasive ideas in American society.

The Changing U.S. Population

When the Census Bureau completed its count of the American population in April 2000, we learned that the United States had 281 million people within its 50 states and territories. During the twentieth century, the number of Americans had increased by more than 200 million people, reflecting a phenomenal and unprecedented rate of change.

When the latest figures were revealed, then director of the Census Bureau, Kenneth Prewitt, stated that not only was the United States a dynamic nation in terms of population growth, it was also the only nation in the world where virtually every group represented had its origins in another country. Seldom before have we thought about the diverse origins of the American population as we did in the last portion of the twentieth century. The extraordinary range of countries and continents that have spawned the American population shows the dynamic nature of social change and diversity in creating twenty-first century America.

You undoubtedly will encounter this diversity during college, and most definitely in your postcollegiate life. Social change over the past 100 years has changed the face of America, and the results of these changes will become increasingly apparent in the early part of the new century.

Evidence indicates that social interaction in a diverse setting can significantly improve your education. In a 10-year study of college student success, Harvard University Professor Richard J. Light found that an overwhelming majority of his students reported the impact of diversity on learning was both strong and positive.[1] Such experiences are occurring among college students from all types of institutions. In a letter to his teacher at a university in Iowa, where minorities are a very small percentage of the population, a recent white graduate who is now a corporate executive wrote, "A day doesn't go by that I don't use something I learned from African American Studies."

A Century of Change

Race, country of origin, and ethnicity comprise three specific dimensions of American diversity. An ethnic group is defined by cultural characteristics that are voluntary, such as language, lifestyle, cuisine, or other patterns of social organization. Race and ethnicity intersect in various ways and are much more complex ideas than commonly assumed. In counting the American population in 2000, for example, the Census Bureau used five categories of race, plus two additional categories for people of "some other race" or "two or more races" (see Table 9.1). In responding, nearly half (48%) of all Latinos indicated their race as white. Others described themselves as black or American Indian, and many indicated that they represented two or more races.

People from Hispanic or Latino backgrounds are in fact not considered a race, but an ethnic group. The Census Bureau reports that more than 35 million Americans (12.5% of the total) identify themselves as Hispanic. If we add these numbers to those of other minorities, we see that racial and ethnic minorities together represent more than one-third of the U.S. population at the beginning of the twenty-first century.

These present-day patterns of diversity are significantly different from those of earlier generations. We can get a sense of the dynamic nature of diversity in America by looking at race, ethnicity, and national origin at three points in time: 1900, 1950, and 2000.

Note that although little changed in the first half of the twentieth century, the second half was a different matter. Not only racial distribution changed but the definitions of race also changed. The American Anthropological Association reports that since 1900, more than 30 different racial terms have been used to identify populations in the U.S. Census. Regardless of definitions, however, it is clear that the United States is more diverse than ever before, and this diversity is apparent at most colleges and universities.

SEE EXERCISE 9.1: SHARING YOUR BACKGROUND

Another aspect of present-day American diversity is the dramatic change in the places from which new Americans have come. In 1900, among 10 million foreign-born Americans, 86 percent were from Europe and about 1 percent each from Asia and Latin America. In 1990, of 20 million foreign-born Americans, 22 percent were from Europe, 25 percent from Asia, and 42 percent from Latin America.[2]

By the end of the century, more than 26 million persons of foreign birth were living in the United States, many of them as naturalized citizens. In 1999, 50.7 percent

Table 9.1 Trends in U.S. Population by Race

YEAR	POPULATION	WHITE	BLACK	OTHER
1900	76 million	87.9%	11.6%	0.5%
1950	151 million	89.5%	10.0%	0.5%
2000	291 million	75.1%	12.3%	[a]See below

[a]American Indian/Alaska Native, 0.9; Asian, 3.6; Hawaiian/Pacific Islander, 0.1, some other race, 5.5; two or more races, 2.4.

Source: U.S. Census Bureau.

[1]Richard J. Light, *Making the Most of College: Students Speak Their Minds,* Cambridge, MA: Harvard University Press, 2001, pp. 9–10, and Chap. 7 and 8.
[2]*Statistical Abstract of the United States,* U.S. Government, Washington, DC 1999, Table 1417.

Most colleges make an effort to help students feel welcome, respected, and supported in every way that the students themselves feel is important.

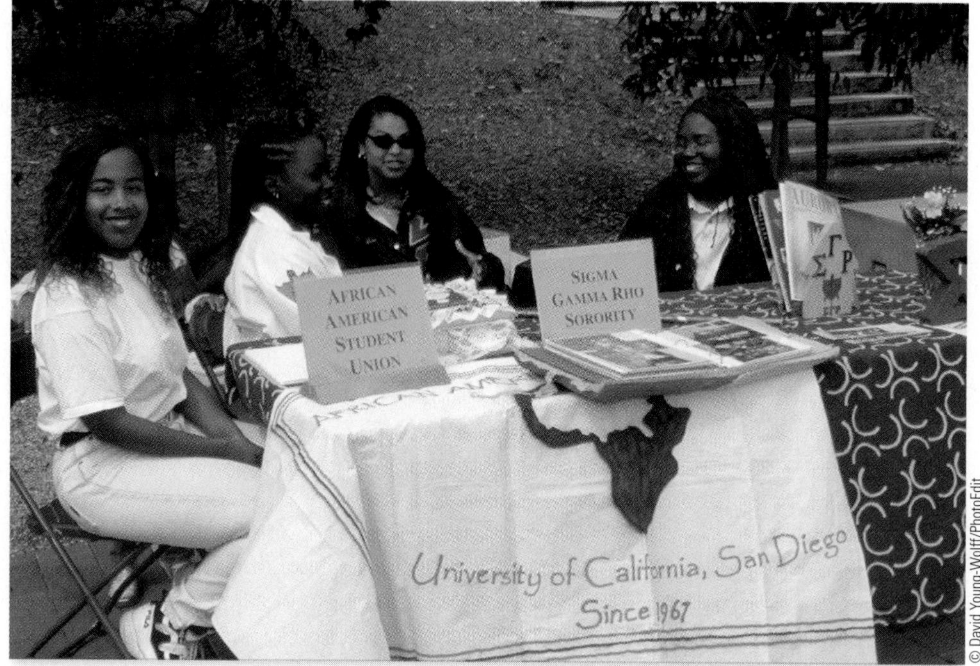

© David Young-Wolff/PhotoEdit

of all foreign-born residents were from Latin America, most of them from Mexico or Central America. Another 27.1 percent were born in Asia, and 15.1 percent were born in Europe. The remaining 6.2 percent were born in other areas of the world.[3]

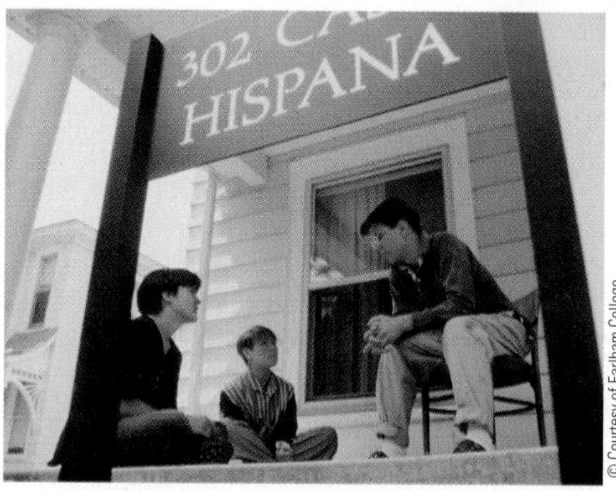

© Courtesy of Earlham College

In the 2000 census, more than 6 million people described themselves as multi-racial. Although most indicated they were of two races, some indicated as many as five races. This multiracial dimension shows the changing nature of American society and the dynamic nature of diversity. It's harder now than ever before to easily categorize any individual.

SEE WORKING TOGETHER EXERCISE: CREATING COMMON GROUND

SEE EXERCISE 9.2: THE IDEA OF "RACE"

SEE EXERCISE 9.3: DIVERSITY ON YOUR CAMPUS

If the present rates of change continue, we can expect minorities to make up 50 percent of the U.S. population by the year 2030. This will mean that when you reach the height of your personal and professional future, half of all Americans will belong to a racial or ethnic group. What will diversity mean then? Will the term "minority" still be appropriate?

The future will be dynamic and different, just as our recent past has been. As Amitai Etzioni points out, "We came in many ships, but now we ride in the same boat."[4] You can prepare for that diverse future by using every opportunity to extend yourself beyond the social patterns that often divide people. With a knowledge and understanding of the past and present, you will find it easier to build bridges to the future.

[3]U.S. Bureau of the Census, "PPL-123, Profile of the Foreign-Born Population in the United States: March 1999," issued August 2000.
[4]Amitai Etzioni, *The Monochrome Society,* Princeton, NJ: Princeton University Press, 2001.

Other Types of Diversity on Campus

Gays and Lesbians

Let's dispel some stereotypes. No matter how keen your vision may be, you can't tell someone's sexual orientation just by appearance. Just because a person is gay or lesbian doesn't mean he or she is attracted to all people of the same sex (are straight people attracted to all people of the opposite sex?). Also, being gay or lesbian is rarely a choice. Each year, scientists find further evidence indicating that sexual orientation may be influenced by genetic as well as environmental factors. Last, most child molesters are white male heterosexuals—not homosexuals.

Returning Students

Adult students (those 25 and older) are enrolling in college courses in record numbers. Women return to school after raising children or while raising children in order to learn skills for a new career. Other adults, men and women, may decide it's time to broaden their horizons or prepare themselves for a better job with a higher starting salary. Many returning students work full-time and attend school either full- or part-time. Their persistence is remarkable, given the potential stressors of family and work. One study actually found that older women in college were less stressed than younger students, partly because they had grown accustomed to wearing two or more hats while raising children, working, and living their own lives. Colleges have accommodated the needs of adults with distance education courses, night courses, and other innovations.

Students with Disabilities

The number of students with physical and/or learning disabilities continues to grow. Improvements in campus services and accommodations have made it possible for more students with disabilities to enter and stay in college. Also, more students are being identified as learning disabled than ever before. Perhaps you are a student with a disability, facing particular challenges, or perhaps you know such a student through your classes or where you live. Maybe you've struggled with your reading assignments or test taking and suspect you may have an undiagnosed learning disability. Maybe, because of an injury or accident, you or a friend is suddenly

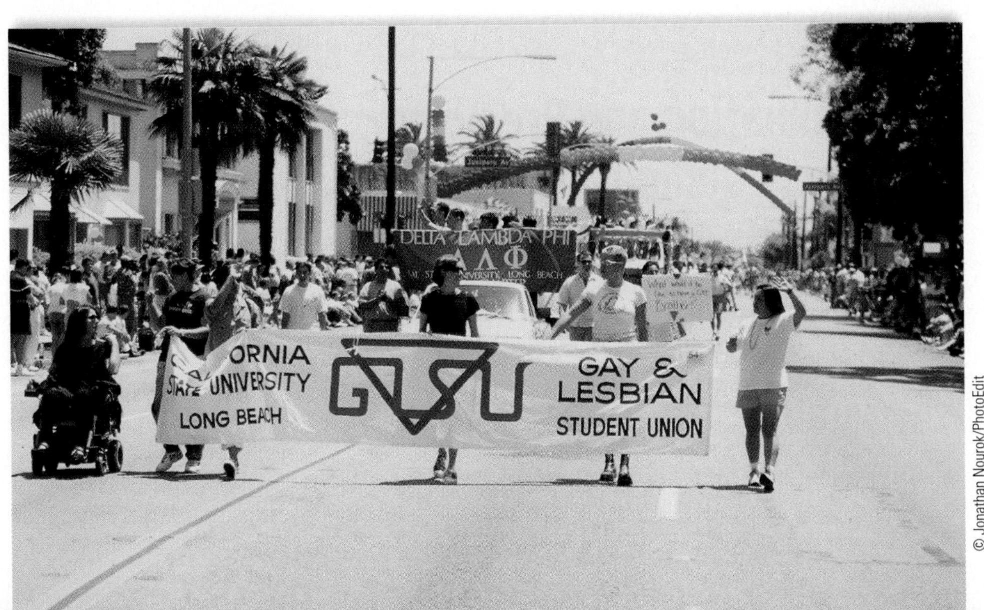

© Jonathan Nourok/PhotoEdit

Diversity is about more than racial or ethnic and religious backgrounds. It also encompasses gay, lesbian, bisexual, and transgender individuals who live in a world that is not always tolerant or accepting, much less affirming. All students grow when they learn to find pride in their own communities and to also accept the diverse groups around them.

Examining Values

Make a list of negative stereotypical judgments you've heard about people of other races, cultures, and sexual orientations as well as older people and people with disabilities. Some of these—all incorrect—are: "All African Americans are angry at white students." "White students look down their noses at anyone who isn't white." "Gays and lesbians are always on the make for anyone they can catch." "Older students are too serious about college." "Handicapped students just want your sympathy all the time." When you've written your own list, reflect on what values instilled in you by family, friends, and experiences have caused you to either accept or reject such thoughts. Write what you have discovered about yourself.

temporarily disabled. Whatever your situation, you should know about the campus services that are available to help. Most campuses have an academic skills center staffed with people who can support all kinds of student needs as well as a center for students with disabilities. Find out where these campus support services are located.

Diversity Resources

Many campuses have separate offices whose sole purpose is to help students sort out diversity-related concerns and to provide learning experiences for students who want to improve their understanding and skills for living, working, and studying in a highly diverse society and world. Check your campus for one or more of the following (this list is not comprehensive):

- Office of Student Affairs
- Office of Diversity
- Office for Disability Services
- Hillel (for Jewish students)
- Affirmative Action Office
- Bisexual, Gay, and Lesbian Student Organization
- Office of Multicultural Student Affairs
- Office of Veterans' Programs
- Muslim Student Organization
- Mecha (for Chicano students)
- Society of Women Engineers
- Campus Chapter of NAACP

Discrimination and Prejudice on College Campuses

Unfortunately, acts of discrimination and incidents of prejudice are rising on college campuses. Although some schools may not be experiencing overt racial conflict, tension still exists; many students report having little contact with students from different racial or ethnic groups.

A national survey, "Taking America's Pulse II," (TAP) conducted for the National Conference for Community and Justice in 2000, indicated the following:

- Only 29 percent of respondents were satisfied with "how well different groups in society get along with each other," and the majority felt that "racial, religious or ethnic tension" was a very serious or somewhat serious problem.

- Self-reports by respondents indicate that discrimination is a common part of the everyday lives of many Americans.

Across six important life domains (education, housing, promotions, access to equal justice, treatment by the police, and fair media attention), opportunity is not seen as equal.

Yet the news is not all bad:

- Interracial/interethnic contact is higher now than during the first TAP survey in 1993.
- Among racial and ethnic groups, most say that their group generally gets along with others.
- The public feels closer to all groups now than in 1996.[5]

You should know that in addition to being morally and personally repugnant, discrimination is illegal. Most colleges and universities have established policies against all forms of racism, anti-Semitism, and ethnic and cultural intolerance. These policies prohibit racist actions or omissions, including verbal harassment or abuse, which might deny someone his or her rights to equity, dignity, culture, or religion. Anyone found in violation of such policies faces corrective action, including appropriate disciplinary action.

If college is a place where you seek an education and develop values for life, appreciating people who are different from you is one of its major lessons. Regardless of the "group" you belong to, all college graduates share one thing in common: a degree that is the mark of an educated person. If you avoid the chance to know people from other groups, you'll be missing out on many of the benefits of your education.

Speaking of Careers

Being aware of diversity doesn't stop when you graduate from college. In the world of work, employers and employees must continue striving for equity and balance. When problems arise, know that the law is on the side of equal rights. The federal Equal Employment Opportunity Commission enforces laws prohibiting employment discrimination. Among those laws are:

- Title VII of the Civil Rights Act of 1964 prohibits employment discrimination based on race, color, religion, sex, or national origin.
- The Equal Pay Act (EPA) of 1963 protects men and women who perform substantially equal work in the same establishment from sex-based wage discrimination.
- The Age Discrimination in Employment Act (ADEA) of 1967 protects individuals who are 40 years of age or older.
- Title I and Title V of the Americans with Disabilities Act (ADA) of 1990 prohibit employment discrimination against qualified individuals with disabilities in the private sector, and in state and local governments.
- Sections 501 and 505 of the Rehabilitation Act of 1973 prohibit discrimination against qualified individuals with disabilities who work in the federal government.
- The Civil Rights Act of 1991, among other things, provides monetary damages in cases of intentional employment discrimination.

For more information, visit the following Web site: <*http://www.eeoc.gov/facts/qanda.html*>.

[5] "Taking America's Pulse II (Summary)." National Conference for Community and Justice (formerly National Conference of Christians and Jews), <*http://www.nccj.org/nccj/nccj.nsf/article/4537?opendocument&1#874*>.

Dating and Mating

Perhaps in high school your parents had strict rules about dating. Or maybe you didn't feel ready to date. Maybe, like a large number of people, you are happily single—a "quirkyalone"[6] who is more comfortable without a partner.

For many young people, their first romantic relationship occurs in college when they're legally adults, when their parents loosen the reins, and when they meet new and exciting people. The opportunities for relationships on campus are like a banquet table: Some people choose to sample a little of everything and others find one thing they love and choose only that. Either way, it's a growing experience for you and those you become involved with.

Stages of a Relationship

Usually, relationships go through the following stages, according to social psychologist Elaine Walster:

- *The passionate stage.* This stage is marked by dramatic highs and lows. Early in a relationship, you may be wildly "in love." You may find yourself preoccupied—if not obsessed—with the other person, with feelings of intense longing when you are apart. When you are together, you may feel thrilled and blissful, yet also insecure and demanding. You are likely to idealize the other person, yet you may overreact to faults or disappointments. If the relationship goes awry, your misery is likely to be intense, and the only apparent relief from your pain lies in the hands of the very person who rejected you.
- *Companionate love.* A successful relationship will move on to a calmer, more stable stage. At this next stage, your picture of your partner is much more realistic. You feel comfortable and secure with each other. Your mutual love and respect stem from predictably satisfying companionship.
- *Intimacy.* If sexual activity would violate your morals or values, don't do it. And don't expect others to violate theirs. If you are sexually active, it's important that you get professional advice about avoiding sexually transmitted infections (STIs) and pregnancy prevention. A pregnancy will drastically curtail your freedom and social life, and finding time for your studies will be much harder.

  Here are some warning signs that should concern you:

- Having sex when you don't really want to
- Feeling guilty or anxious afterward
- Having sex because your partner expects or demands it
- Having sex with people to attract or keep them near
- Becoming physically intimate when what you really want is emotional intimacy

Believe it or not, a thorough review of the literature on happiness finds no evidence that becoming sexually active increases your general happiness. Sex relieves horniness, but it doesn't ensure happiness. Loving relationships, on the other hand, are powerfully related to happiness.

- *Getting serious.* You may have a relationship you feel is really working. Should you make it exclusive? Ask yourself why you want this relationship to be exclusive. For security? To prevent jealousy? To reduce your risk of contracting a sexually transmitted disease? To build depth and trust? As a prelude to a permanent commitment? Before you make the decision to see only each other, make sure it is the best thing for each of you. You may find that you treat each other better and appreciate each other more when you are able to explore other relationships.

[6]See <*http://www.quirkyalone.net*>.

If you are seriously considering marriage, consider this: Studies show that the younger you are, the lower your odds of a successful marriage. It may also surprise you to learn that trial marriage or living together does not decrease your risk of later divorce.

Above all, beware of what might be called "the fundamental marriage error." Many 18- to 20-year-olds change their outlook and life goals drastically. If you want to marry, the person to marry is someone you could call your best friend—the one who knows you inside and out, the one you don't have to play games with, the one who prizes your company without physical rewards, the one who over a period of years has come to know, love, and respect who you are and what you want to be.

- *Breaking up.* In a national study of 5,000 college students, 29 percent reported they had ended a romantic relationship during their first year in college.

Breaking up is hard, but if it is time to end things, do it cleanly and calmly. Don't be impulsive or angry. Explain your feelings and talk them out. If you don't get a mature reaction, don't join someone else in the mud. If you decide to reunite after a trial separation, and if things fail a second time, then you really need to forget it.

You may want to remain friends with your partner, especially if you have shared a lot and invested time and effort in the relationship. You can't really be friends, however, until both of you have healed from the hurt and neither of you wants the old relationship back. That usually takes a year or two.

If you are having trouble getting out of a relationship or dealing with its end, get help. Your college counselors have assisted many students through similar difficulties. In fact, relationship problems are the most common student concern that college counselors hear about. It is also a good time to get moral support from friends and family. Read a good book on the subject, such as *How to Survive the Loss of a Love* by Melba Cosgrove, Harold H. Bloomfield, and Peter McWilliams.

Sexual Decision Making

Although the sexual revolutions of the 1960s and 1970s may have made premarital sex more socially acceptable, people have not necessarily become better equipped to deal with sexual freedom. The rate of STIs among college students has increased, and unwanted pregnancies are too common.

Students are given a lot of powerful messages about sex, some that encourage and others that discourage.

Encouragers	**Discouragers**
Hormones	Family values/expectations
Peer pressure	Religious values
Alcohol/other drugs	Sexually transmitted infections
Curiosity	Fear of pregnancy
The media	Concern for reputation
An intimate relationship	Feeling of unreadiness
Sexual pleasure	Fear of being hurt or used

SEE EXERCISE 9.4: PERSONAL REFLECTIONS ON SEXUALITY

With such powerful pressures on each side, some people become confused and overwhelmed and fail to make any decisions. Often, sex "just happens" and is not planned.

For your protection, try to clarify your own values and then act in accordance with them. Those who do this usually wind up happier with their decisions.

Where to Go for Help

IF YOUR RELATIONSHIP IS ABUSIVE

- Tell your abuser the violence must stop.
- If you don't want sex, say no firmly.
- Have a safety plan handy: Call the police at 911, consult campus resources (women's student services, the sexual assault office, and so forth), call a community domestic violence center or rape crisis center, or call someone else on campus you can trust.
- Find a counselor or support group on campus or in the community.
- Obtain a restraining order through your local magistrate or county court. If the abuser is a student at the same institution, schedule an appointment with your campus judicial officer to explore campus disciplinary action.
- Get prepared. Evidence indicates that violence tends to escalate once the abused person decides to make a break. Should you reach that point, it's wise to remove yourself from the other person's physical presence. This may include changing your daily patterns.

For further advice, contact your counselor to find out about restraining orders, listing the abuser's name at the front desk, changing your locks, securing windows, and taking other precautions.

To support a friend whose relationship is abusive, be there. Listen. Help your friend recognize the abuse. Be nonjudgmental. Help your friend contact campus and community resources for help. If you become frustrated or frightened, seek help for yourself as well.

Unhealthy Relationships

Off Limits!

Some "fishing grounds" are strictly off limits. Never become romantically involved with your teacher or someone who works over or under you. Many of these relationships end in a breakup. And imagine if your ex still had power or control over you! If you date a subordinate, when the relationship ends, you may find yourself accused of sexual harassment, fired, or sued. Even dating coworkers carries major risks; it will be much harder to heal from a breakup if you must continue to work together. Be wise, think ahead—and fish elsewhere.

Intimate Partner Violence

Some individuals express their love in strange and improper ways—ways that should be reported to the authorities. It's called relationship, or intimate partner, violence: emotional, abusive, and violent acts occurring between two people who presumably care very much for each other. First-year students are at particular risk because they are in a new and unfamiliar environment, may not realize the risks, are anxious to fit in, and may appear to be easy targets.

Approximately one-third of all college-age students will experience a violent intimate relationship. Almost every 15 seconds, a woman in the United States is battered by her boyfriend, husband, or live-in partner. And nearly half a million women report being stalked by a partner in the previous year.

Women ages 16 to 24, according to the July 2000 National Institute of Justice *Findings from the National Violence Against Women Survey,* experience the highest per capita rates of intimate relationship violence. Although statistics indicate that the majority of abusers involved in intimate partner violence are male, females can also be physically, emotionally, and verbally abusive to their partners.

It's important to recognize the warning signs and know what to do if you find yourself (or know a friend) in an abusive relationship.

- An abuser typically has low self-esteem, blames the victim and others for what is actually his or her own behavior, can be pathologically jealous of others who approach the partner, may use alcohol or drugs to manage stress, and views the partner as a possession.
- A battered person typically has low self-esteem, accepts responsibility for the abuser's actions, is passive but has tremendous strength, believes no one can help, and thinks no one else is experiencing such violence.

How to Tell If Your Relationship Is Abusive

- You're frightened by your partner's temper and afraid to disagree.
- You apologize to others for your partner's abusive behavior.
- You avoid family and friends because of your partner's jealousy.
- You're afraid to say no to sex, even if you don't want it.
- You're forced to justify everything you do, every place you go, and every person you see.
- You're the object of ongoing verbal insults.
- You've been hit, kicked, shoved, or had things thrown at you.

Sexual Assault

Tricia Phaup of the University of South Carolina offers this advice on avoiding sexual assault:

- Know what you want and do not want sexually.
- Go to parties or social gatherings with friends, and leave with them.
- Avoid being alone with people you don't know very well.
- Trust your gut.
- Be alert to unconscious messages you may be sending.
- Be conscious of how much alcohol you drink, if any.
- If you are ever tempted to force another person to have sex, realize that it is *never* okay to force yourself sexually on someone.
- Don't assume you know what your date wants.
- If you're getting mixed messages, ask.
- Be aware of the effects of alcohol.
- Remember that rape is legally and morally wrong.

Regardless of whether a victim chooses to report a rape to the police or get a medical exam, it is very helpful to seek some type of counseling to begin working through this traumatic event.

The following people or offices may be available on or near your campus to deal with a sexual assault: campus sexual assault coordinator, local rape crisis center, campus police department, counseling center, student health services, student affairs professionals, women's student services office, residence life staff, local hospital emergency rooms, and campus chaplains.

The Keys to Healthy Relationships

- *Communicate effectively.* Think before you speak. Avoid language that may appear hostile or critical by other people. Tell the truth. You don't have to reveal everything about yourself, but be truthful about the things you choose to say. If

Critical Thinking

Review the section on "You and Your Parents." Now think about all the things you do that may not seem like serious risks to you, but would make your parents shudder. Can you guess some of the reasons they would feel this way? Can you honestly say they have no reason to worry?

Put yourself in their shoes, and write down what they might be thinking or telling each other when they're worried about you. Seek resources on teenage behavior during the years your parents were in their teens. Next, as if you were writing to your parents, draft a letter that calmly justifies your behaviors in a logical and reassuring way. Now read what you've written. Does it sound defensive? Would it be convincing? Have you accepted at least a share of blame yourself? Keep revising the letter until you could honestly speak these words to your parents without sounding defensive.

it's true, let the person know you enjoyed chatting with him/her. If it isn't, excuse yourself and say you hope to run into one another soon.

- *Develop self-esteem.* Use your journal to sing your praises. No one will see this, so it's not bragging. Write about what you're good at, about your relationship with your family, about your accomplishments, and so forth. Make the picture complete. Than read it aloud to yourself and say, "I am a worthy human being and deserve to be treated as such." Repeat the process regularly.
- *Keep your emotions in check.* Even if your mind tells you to cry or scream, you don't have to listen. Instead, look at the problem logically. If you anticipate an encounter, make a list of what you might say to calm down both yourself and the other person. Pick the best ideas from that list and come up with logical (not emotional) defenses for each one ("I can't go away with you this weekend. It would make me very uncomfortable and it would be awkward to tell my parents where I was. I don't lie to my parents."). Even if your friend yells, try to ignore it and just continue talking calmly.
- *Learn to assert yourself.* Assertiveness means being nonaggressive and nonpassive. Aggressive statements put the listener down and open the door to emotional arguments. Passive statements ("I don't know why I can't handle this") invite others to talk you into doing what you don't want to do. An assertive statement indicates respect for yourself, and others, and is specific ("Joe, we need to talk. I'm having trouble going out with you on a regular schedule. Sometimes I have to tend to other things. And sometimes I just need to be by myself. Could we sit down and talk this over and come up with a compromise? I sure would like that.")
- *Use common sense.* You know what's best for you. Never "give in" because others might think less of you if you didn't.

Other Kinds of Relationships

You and Your Parents

If you are on your own for the first time, your relationship with your parents is going to change. Home will never be as you left it, and you will not remain who you were before. So how can you have a good relationship with your parents during this period of major change? The most common perceptions parents have about their children are:

- Parents fear you'll harm yourself. You may take risks that make older people shudder. You may shudder, too, when you look back on some of your stunts. Sometimes, your parents have reason to worry.

- Parents think their daughter is still a young innocent. Yes, the old double standard (differing expectations for men than women, particularly those regarding sex) is alive and well.
- Parents know you're older but picture you as much younger. Somehow, the parental clock always lags behind reality. Maybe it's because they loved you so much as a child, they can't erase that image.

SEE WORKING TOGETHER EXERCISE: STUDENT-PARENT GRIPES

Parents mean well. Most love their children, even if it doesn't always come out right; very few are really indifferent or hateful. The old have been young, but the young haven't been old. Parental memories of youth may be hazy, but at least they've been there. A younger student has yet to experience their adult perspective.

Not every family functions well. If love, respect, enthusiasm, and encouragement are just not in the cards, look around you. Other people will give you these things, and you can create the family you need. With your emotional needs satisfied, your reactions to your real family will be much less painful.

Married Life in College

Both marriage and college are challenges. With so many demands, it is critically important that you and your partner share the burdens equally; you cannot expect a harried partner to spoil or pamper you. Academic and financial pressures are likely to put extra strain on any relationship, so you are going to have to work extra hard at attending to each other's needs.

If you are in college but your spouse is not, it's important to bring your partner into your college life. Share what you're learning in your courses. See if your partner can take a course, too—maybe just to audit for the fun of it. Take your partner to cultural events—lectures, plays, concerts—on your campus. If your campus has social organizations for students' spouses, try them out.

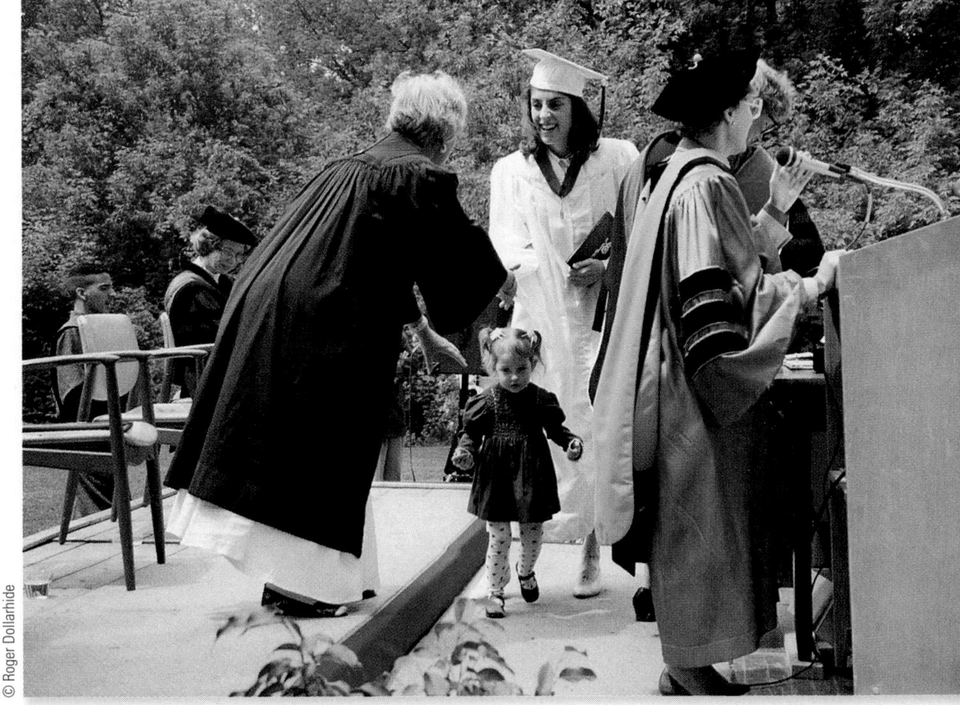

© Roger Dollarhide

If you are married or have children, take steps to involve your loved ones in your college life.

You obviously will not profit if you gain your degree but lose your family. It's very important to schedule time for your partner and family just as carefully as you schedule your work and your classes.

Electronic Relationships

Nowadays, through electronic mail, message boards, interest groups, dating sites, and chat groups, it is possible to form relationships with people you have never met. This can be fun as well as educational. At times, it can also be dangerous. You can interact with a variety of people you might never meet otherwise.

For instance, imagine having regular e-mail correspondence with the following group, as one student does, who all met online: an aspiring screenwriter in New Jersey, an undercover narcotics agent in Michigan, a professional animator in Georgia, a college teacher in Connecticut, a high school student in Arizona, a librarian in California,

Setting Goals for Success

Having read about the various types of relationships college students can have in their lives, spend some time thinking about your relationship goals. Brainstorm some goals for better relationships. Use the goal-setting steps you read about in the Introduction to determine what your goals will be and how you should pursue them.

My goal is to improve my relationship with ______________________

I can do this by: ______________________

I want to achieve this goal because: ______________________

It's important because: ______________________

I may encounter these obstacles: ______________________

My strategy for accomplishing this goal is to: ______________________

a strip-club bartender in Tennessee, a mother in Pennsylvania, a police officer in Australia, a flight attendant in Illinois, an entrepreneur in Louisiana, a psychologist in Colorado, a physician in training in Texas, a schoolteacher in Canada, and college students in five states and three countries.

The downside? People may not be what they seem. Meeting them in real life may be delightful—or disastrous. Some people assume false "electronic" identities. You could literally be corresponding with a state prisoner! Be very cautious about letting strangers know your name, address, telephone number, or other personal information, and about considering face-to-face meetings.

If you find yourself spending hours every day with people on the computer, you are probably overdoing it. Don't let electronic relationships substitute for "real" ones in your life. Your college counselors have experience dealing with students suffering from "computer addiction."

Roommates

Adjusting to a roommate on or off campus often presents difficulties. A roommate doesn't have to be a best friend—just someone with whom you can share your living space comfortably. Your best friend may not make the best roommate. In fact, many students have lost friends by rooming together.

With any roommate, establish your mutual rights and responsibilities in writing. Many colleges provide contract forms that you and your roommate can use. If things go wrong later, you will have something to point to.

If you have problems, talk them out promptly. Talk directly—politely but plainly. If problems persist, or if you don't know how to talk them out, ask your residence hall counselor for help; he or she is trained to do this.

Normally, you can tolerate (and learn from) a less than ideal situation, but if things get really bad and do not improve, insist on a change. If you are on campus, your residence counselor will have ways of helping you.

On-Campus Involvement

New students who become involved with at least one campus organization are more likely to survive their first year and remain in college.

Fraternities and sororities can be a rich source of friends and support. But some students may find them demanding of time and finances, and/or too constricting. If Greek life is not for you, a residence hall, a coeducational service fraternity, or another club or organization may be a good option.

Co-op Programs

Many schools have co-op programs in which you spend some terms in regular classes and other terms in temporary job settings in your field. Although they usually prolong your education somewhat, these programs offer an excellent preview of what work in your chosen field is actually like, thus helping you know if you have made the right choice. They give you valuable experience and contacts that help you get a job when you finish school; in fact, many firms offer successful co-op students permanent jobs when they graduate.

Service Learning Opportunities

Service learning integrates community service with academic study. Students work as volunteers, then reflect on their experiences.

Service learning might include tutoring children or adults, helping in medical establishments and psychological services, building or repairing housing for disadvantaged citizens, or helping out in soup kitchens and homeless shelters. Such service is mandatory, requires that you write or speak about what you have learned, and counts in the compilation of your course grade. If you prefer to volunteer on your own, you could spend a year or two in VISTA (Volunteers in Service to America) or the Peace Corps.

If your college has a service learning office, head for it to learn about opportunities. Or check with your school's career/placement center or student activities center, your local United Way, and various religious organizations. Or search the Web for thousands of more choices.

Reassess Yourself

Let's go back to the self-assessment that appears at the beginning of this chapter. This is an opportunity for you to measure your progress, to check in with yourself and see how your approach to college, relationships, and diversity may have changed upon learning more about these topics. Which of the items on page 152 did you check? Would you change any of your answers as a result of reading this chapter? If so, which ones, and why?

Exercises

Each of the exercises below will help you further explore the topics of this chapter. You'll find all these exercises, plus Internet and InfoTrac® College Edition exercises, on the CD-ROM that accompanies this book.

EXERCISE 9.1 Sharing Your Background

Write a two-part essay. In the first part, describe the racial or ethnic groups to which you belong. Can you belong to more than one? Absolutely. Be sure to include some of the beliefs, values, and norms in your cultural background. How do you celebrate your background? What if you don't feel a strong attachment to any group? Write what you know about your family history and speculate on why your ethnic identity isn't very strong.

In the second part of your essay, discuss a time when you realized that your racial or ethnic background was not the same as someone else's. For example, young children imagine that their experiences are mirrored in the lives of others. If they are Jewish, everyone else must be too. If their family eats okra for breakfast, then all families do the same. Yet at some point they begin to realize differences. Share your essays with other members of the class. In what ways are your stories similar? In what ways are they different?

EXERCISE 9.2 Racism and Other Forms of Hate

This chapter takes a strong stand against the idea that there is any biological or scientific foundation for the idea of race. If so, why is there so much racism in the world? Why do different ethnic or religious groups find it difficult to tolerate each other? Look at the Middle East. Look at South Africa. Look within the United States. In practically every corner of the world, you find animosity against people who belong to other ethnic groups, religions, or "races." You also find the idea that some of these groups are superior or inferior to other groups. Although an educated person would argue these points, why do you suppose so many people still hang on to them?

EXERCISE 9.3 Diversity on Your Campus

How diverse is your campus? In what specific ways does your school encourage all students to feel welcome? Ask your instructor where to locate materials or appropriate people to interview on these two questions: (1) How easy is it for students to express their culture and to learn about their backgrounds or the backgrounds of others on this campus? (2) In what ways does our school try to make all students feel welcome? Groups should report their findings to the class.

EXERCISE 9.4 Personal Reflections on Sexuality

A. Have you taken time to sort out your own values about sexual activity? If you aren't willing to commit to a particular plan of action at this time, what keeps you from doing so? If you are sexually active, do your values take into account your own and your partner's health? If that's not a priority for you, what would it take to get you to a point where safer sex took priority over unsafe sex?

B. Write down some of your thoughts about and intentions on sexuality. This should be for you alone to read. The act of writing may help you organize your thoughts. Committing your values to paper may also help you live by them when faced with tough decisions.

Working Together Exercises
Creating Common Ground

Examine the items in the following chart. For each item, decide whether you would describe your preferences, habits, and customs as reflecting the mainstream (macroculture) or a specific ethnic microculture. Enter specific examples of your own preferences in the appropriate column (two examples are given). For a given item, you may enter examples under both macroculture and microculture, or you may leave one or the other blank. In filling out the chart, you may want to look back at the essay you wrote in Exercise 9.1.

CATEGORY	MACROCULTURE	MICROCULTURE
Language		
Food	*hamburgers*	*sushi*
Music (for your peer group)		
Style of dress (for your peer group)		
Religion		
Holidays celebrated		
Heroes/role models		
Key values		
Lifestyle		
Personal goals		

Compare answers in a small group. Do most people in the group agree on what should be considered an example of the macroculture and what is an example of a microculture? Does anyone identify completely with the macroculture? Does anyone feel completely disconnected from the macroculture? What do you and others in your class regard as significant differences among you? In what areas do you share common ground?

Working Together Exercise
Student-Parent Gripes

A. Student Gripes In surveys, these are the most frequent student gripes about parents. Check the ones that hit closest to home for you:

____Why are parents so overbearing and controlling, telling you everything from what to major in to whom to date?

____Why do parents treat me like a child?

____Why are they so overprotective?

____Why do parents worry so much?

____Why do parents complain so much about money?

____Parents say they want to know what's going on in my life, but if I told them everything, they'd go ballistic and you'd never hear the end of it!

Reflect on the gripes you checked. Why do you think your parents are like that? How do your thoughts affect your relations with them?

B. Parent Gripes Looking at things from the other side, students report the following as the most common gripes their parents have about them. Check off those that ring true for your parents:

____Why don't you call and visit more?

____Why don't you tell us more about what is going on?

____When you are home, why do you ignore us and spend all your time with your friends?

____Why do you spend so much time with your boyfriend (or girlfriend)?

____Why do you need so much money?

____Why aren't your grades better, and why don't you appreciate the importance of school?

____Why don't you listen to us about getting into the right major and courses? You'll never get a good job if you don't.

____What have you done to yourself? Where did you get that (haircut, tattoo, style of clothes, etc.)?

____Why don't you listen to us and do what we tell you? You need a better attitude!

How do such statements affect you? What do you think your parents are really trying to tell you? In small groups, compare your answers.

See the CD-ROM for these additional exercises as well as all other exercises appearing in this chapter

Internet Exercise 9.2	**Questions about Homosexuality**
Internet Exercise 9.3	**Breaking Down Stereotypes**
InfoTrac® College Edition Exercise 9.1	**Dissecting Hate**
InfoTrac® College Edition Exercise 9.2	**Ending Discrimination Against Women**
Exercise 9.5	**Combating Discrimination and Prejudice on Campus**
Exercise 9.6	**Five over 30**

10 Staying Healthy

© Ryan McVay/Photodisc/Getty

Sara J. Corwin, Bradley H. Smith, Rick L. Gant, Georgeann Stamper, JoAnne Herman, Tricia Phaup, and Danny Baker, all of the University of South Carolina at Columbia, contributed their valuable expertise to this chapter

Going Forward: Student Voices

Now that I'm on my own, I'm always eating in a rush between classes which means junk food most of the time. I don't have time to exercise, unless lifting a pint of beer at night to try to relieve the stress counts as exercise. I think I've gained ten pounds in three months.

Looking Back: Author Voices

When I went to college, some things were very different. For instance, I did not drink at all because I was a varsity athlete whose crew coach kicked off the team anybody who drank even a drop. It just went without saying that alcohol was forbidden. Performance-enhancing drugs like steroids weren't even in the picture. Students today are confronted with more temptations, and that means having to be sensible about their choices because the wrong choice might keep them from graduating. John Gardner

In this chapter, YOU WILL LEARN

- How to achieve and maintain good physical and mental health
- The importance of maintaining balance in your life
- The many choices you have for contraception
- Ways to prevent sexually transmitted infections
- Two reasons college students drink
- The realities of abusing tobacco and prescription drugs
- The agony of Ecstasy and other illegal drugs
- The most common health problems college students face
- How to deal with depression and anxiety
- How to stay safe on campus

College is a great time to explore. It's an opportunity to exercise your mind and expand your horizons. Unfortunately, for too many students it becomes an opportunity to stop exercising the body and begin expanding the waistline! Because of the newness of the college environment, you may find yourself forgetting to take care of yourself.

Most students can handle the transition to college just fine using various coping mechanisms. Others drink too much or smoke too much. Some overeat or develop an eating disorder like bulimia or anorexia. Some become so stressed that their anxiety overwhelms them. Some ignore their sexual health, and then have to face a sexually transmitted disease or pregnancy.

This chapter explores the topic of *wellness*, which is a catchall term for taking care of your mind and body. Wellness means making healthy choices and achieving balance. Wellness includes maintaining sexual health, taking a sensible approach to alcohol and other drugs, reducing stress, keeping fit, keeping safe, eating sensibly, getting enough slep, and avoiding unnecessary risks.

Sexual Health

We know from numerous studies that about 75 percent of traditional-age college students have engaged in sexual intercourse at least once.

Regardless of whether you are part of this percentage, it can be helpful to explore your sexual values and to consider whether sex is right for you at this time. If it is, we hope you will choose a birth control method and adopt some strategies for avoiding sexually transmitted infections (STIs). That's the bottom line.

Sexually Transmitted Infections

The problem of STIs on college campuses has received growing attention in recent years as epidemic numbers of students have become infected. In general, STIs continue to increase faster than other illnesses on campuses today, and approximately

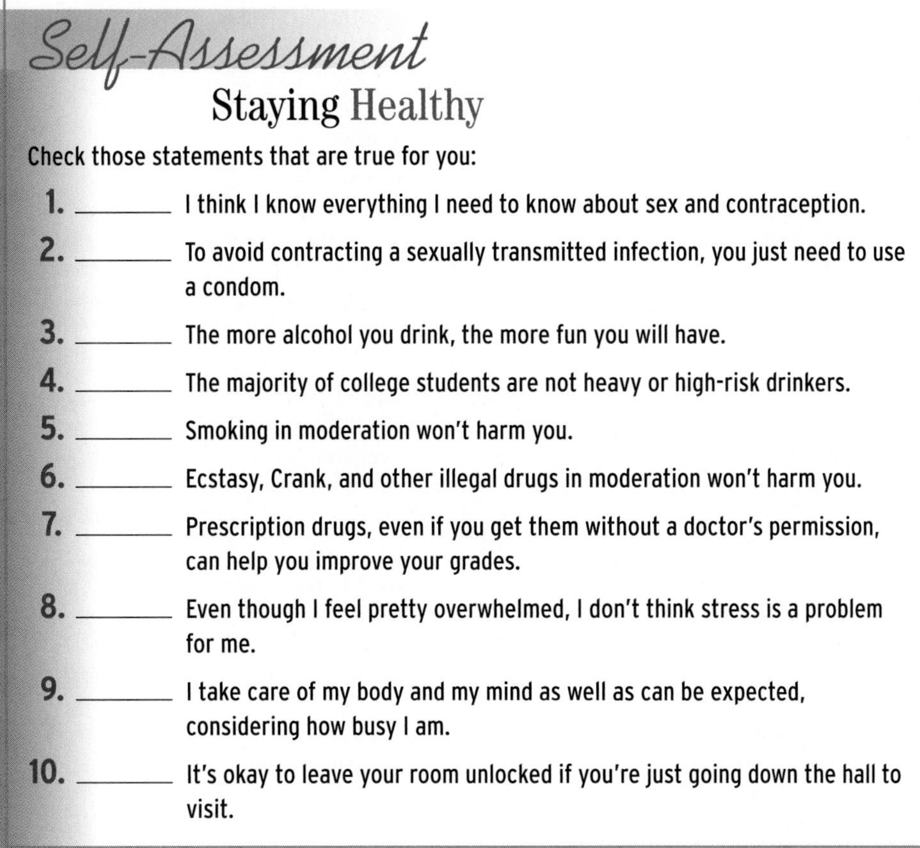

Self-Assessment

Staying Healthy

Check those statements that are true for you:

1. _______ I think I know everything I need to know about sex and contraception.
2. _______ To avoid contracting a sexually transmitted infection, you just need to use a condom.
3. _______ The more alcohol you drink, the more fun you will have.
4. _______ The majority of college students are not heavy or high-risk drinkers.
5. _______ Smoking in moderation won't harm you.
6. _______ Ecstasy, Crank, and other illegal drugs in moderation won't harm you.
7. _______ Prescription drugs, even if you get them without a doctor's permission, can help you improve your grades.
8. _______ Even though I feel pretty overwhelmed, I don't think stress is a problem for me.
9. _______ I take care of my body and my mind as well as can be expected, considering how busy I am.
10. _______ It's okay to leave your room unlocked if you're just going down the hall to visit.

5 to 10 percent of visits by U.S. college students to college health services are for the diagnosis and treatment of STIs. The belief that nice young men and women don't catch these sorts of infections is inaccurate and potentially more dangerous than ever before. If you choose to be sexually active, particularly with more than one partner, exposure to an STI is a real possibility.

STIs are usually spread through the following types of sexual contact: vaginal-penile, oral-genital, hand-genital, and anal-genital. Sometimes, however, STIs can be transmitted through mouth-to-mouth contact. There are more than 20 known types of STIs; Table 10.1 outlines the most common ones on campuses.

Options for Safer Sex

There are several ways to avoid STIs. The most obvious is to not have sex. Even if 75 percent of college students are having sex, that still leaves 25 percent who are not. Celibacy or abstinence are options for you to consider. For some people, masturbation is a reasonable alternative to sex with a partner.

If you are sexually active, you'll be safer (in terms of STIs) if you have only one partner. Yet, you may feel that you're at a point in your life where you should date several people. Whether you're monogamous or not, you should use condoms.

Condoms

In addition to being a contraceptive, the condom can help prevent the spread of STIs, including HIV. The condom's effectiveness against disease holds true for anal, vaginal, and oral intercourse. The most current research indicates that the rate of protection provided by condoms against STIs is similar to its rate of protection against pregnancy (90–99%) when used correctly and consistently for each and

Table 10.1 Sexually Transmitted Infections

Sexually Transmitted Infection	What It Is	Symptoms	Treatment	Dangers	How to Avoid It
Chlamydia	Bacterial infection	Include mild abdominal pain, discharge, and pain and burning with urination. In some people, no symptoms appear.	Antibiotics	In women, can progress to pelvic inflammatory disease (PID) and lead to infertility.	Abstinence or monogamy with an uninfected partner. Condoms reduce but do not eliminate the risk of infection.
Human Papilloma Virus	Virus	None. Warts can be detected by a physician during physical exam.	No cure. Treatment includes burning, freezing, chemical destruction, or laser surgery.	Causes venereal warts. HPV has been associated with cervical cancer in women.	HPV can spread even when condoms are used. Routine screening for HPV by a physician is advised.
Gonorrhea	Bacterial infection	In men, burning sensation during urination, discharge from penis, swollen testicles. In women, discharge from vagina, vaginal bleeding between periods. Can also infect anus and throat, in cases of transmission via oral/anal intercourse.	Antibiotics	If untreated, gonorrhea can cause pelvic inflammatory disease, male infertility, difficult urination, and life-threatening spread to blood or joints.	Abstinence or monogamy with an uninfected partner. Condoms reduce but do not eliminate the risk of infection.
Herpes	Virus	Blisters or lesions on the genital area. In some cases, no symptoms appear.	No cure. Medications can reduce length and severity of outbreaks.	Most likely to be transmitted just before or after lesions appear.	Condoms, abstaining from sex before, during, and after outbreak.
Hepatitis B	Virus	Stomach virus, yellowing of the skin and eyes.	No cure. Rest and healthy diet are prescribed. A vaccine is available to prevent it.	100 times more contagious than HIV. May lead to permanent liver disease.	Avoid unprotected sex and contact with infected blood.
Human Immuno-deficiency Virus (HIV)	Virus that causes AIDS	There are many possible symptoms. Only an HIV test can diagnose HIV.	No cure. Various medications are available to lessen symptoms and prolong life.	Although medications can prolong life and prevent the onset of AIDS, the disease eventually kills.	Use condoms, make sure partner is uninfected.

every act of intercourse or oral sex. Note that only latex rubber condoms—not lambskin or other types of "natural membrane" condoms—provide this protection. Use a water-based lubricant (such as KY Jelly) to keep the condom from breaking.

Birth Control

SEE EXERCISE 10.1: WHAT'S YOUR DECISION?

Sexually active heterosexual students have to plan to prevent an unwanted pregnancy. Planning is the operative word. It doesn't do any good to think about it after the fact! What is the best method of contraception? It is any method that you use correctly and consistently each time you have intercourse. Table 10.2 compares the

(text continues on page 175)

Table 10.2 Methods of Contraception

Always discuss birth control with your partner so that you both feel comfortable with the option you have selected. For more information about a particular method, consult a pharmacist, your student health center, a local family planning clinic, the local health department, or your private physician. The important thing is to resolve to protect yourself and your partner *each and every time* you have sexual intercourse.

NORPLANT

Typical Use Effectiveness .05%
What It Is Six small silicone rubber capsules inserted into a woman's arm, which continually release a low dose of progesterone.
Advantages Highly effective. Works up to 5 years. Allows sexual spontaneity. Low hormone dose makes this medically safer than other hormonal methods.
Disadvantages Removal may be difficult. Very expensive to obtain initially. Insurance may not cover cost. Does not protect against STIs.
Comments High initial cost. Users may have typical side effects of hormonal methods, causing them to discontinue during the first year. Somewhat risky.

DEPO-PROVERA

Typical Use Effectiveness .3%
What It Is A hormone method, administered to women by injection every 3 months.
Advantages Highly effective. Allows for sexual spontaneity. Relatively low yearly cost.
Disadvantages A variety of side effects typical of progestin-type contraceptives may persist up to 6–8 months after termination. Does not protect against STIs.
Comments Easy and spontaneous, but users must remember to get their shots.

ORAL CONTRACEPTIVES

Typical Use Effectiveness .5%
What It Is Birth control pills.
Advantages Highly effective. Allows for sexual spontaneity. Most women have lighter or shorter periods.
Disadvantages Many minor side effects (nausea, weight gain), which cause a significant percentage of users to discontinue. Provides no protection against STIs.
Comments Available by prescription only, after a gynecological exam.

INTRAUTERINE DEVICE (IUD)

Typical Use Effectiveness 1–2%
What It Is Device inserted into the uterus by a physician.
Advantages May be left in for up to 10 years, depending on type. Less expensive than other long-term methods.
Disadvantages Increased risk of complications such as pelvic inflammatory disease and menstrual problems. Possible increased risk of contracting HIV, if exposed.
Comments Women who have not had a child may have a difficult time finding a doctor willing to prescribe this.

CONTRACEPTIVE PATCH

Typical Use Effectiveness N/A. Appears to be less effective in women weighing more than 198 pounds.
What It Is Skin patch worn on lower abdomen, buttocks, or upper body. Releases the hormones progestin and estrogen into the bloodstream.
Advantages Convenient. New patch applied once a week for 3 weeks. Patch not worn fourth week and woman has a menstrual period.
Disadvantages Similar to oral contraceptives. No protection from STIs.
Comments Available by prescription only.

CONDOM

Typical Use Effectiveness 14%
What It Is Rubber sheath that fits over penis.
Advantages Only birth control method that also provides good protection against STIs, including HIV. Actively involves male partner.
Disadvantages Less spontaneous than some other methods because must be put on right before intercourse. Some men believe it cuts down on pleasurable sensations.
Comments Experts believe that most condom failure is due to lack of consistent use rather than misuse or breakage.

FEMALE CONDOM

Typical Use Effectiveness 21%
What It Is A polyurethane sheath that lines vagina acting as barrier between genitals. Two rings hold it in place, one inside and one outside the vagina.

(continued)

Table 10.2 Methods of Contraception (*continued*)

Advantages Highly safe medically; does not require spermicide. Theoretically provides excellent protection against STIs—almost perfectly leak-proof and better than male condom in this regard.
Disadvantages Has not gained wide acceptance. Visible outer ring has been displeasing to some potential users.
Comments Although its effectiveness is not as high as for male condom, has the advantage of offering good STI protection that the woman remains in control of.

DIAPHRAGM

Typical Use Effectiveness 20%
What It Is Dome-shaped rubber cap inserted into the vagina that covers the cervix.
Advantages Safe method of birth control, virtually no side effects. May be inserted up to 2 hours prior to intercourse. May provide small measure of protection against STIs.
Disadvantages Wide variation in effectiveness depending on consistent use, fit of diaphragm, and frequency of intercourse. Multiple acts of intercourse require use of additional spermicide.
Comments Must be prescribed by a physician. Must always be used with a spermicidal jelly and left in 6–8 hours after intercourse.

CERVICAL CAP

Typical Use Effectiveness 20-40%
What It Is Cup-shaped device that fits over the cervix.
Advantages Similar to diaphragm, but may be worn longer—up to 48 hours. May provide small measure of protection against STIs.
Disadvantages Not widely available due to lack of practitioners trained in fitting them.
Comments Longer wearing time increases risk of vaginal infections.

SPERMICIDAL FOAMS, CREAMS, JELLIES, FILM, AND SUPPOSITORIES

Typical Use Effectiveness 26%
What It Is Sperm-killing chemicals inserted into vagina.
Advantages Easy to purchase and use. Provide some protection against STIs, including HIV.
Disadvantages Lower effectiveness than many methods. Can be messy. May increase likelihood of birth defects should pregnancy occur.
Comments As with condoms, it is suspected that failure is due to lack of consistent use. However, work better in combination with other methods, such as the diaphragm.

COITUS INTERRUPTUS

Typical Use Effectiveness 19%
What It Is Withdrawal.
Advantages Requires no devices or chemicals and can be used at any time, at no cost.
Disadvantages Relies heavily on man having enough control to remove himself from the vagina well in advance of ejaculation. May diminish pleasure for the couple.
Comments Ejaculation must be far enough away so that no semen can enter the vagina. Provides no protection against STIs.

PERIODIC ABSTINENCE

Typical Use Effectiveness 25%
What It Is Choosing not to have intercourse when ovulation is predicted; may be called natural family planning, calendar, or rhythm method.
Advantages Requires no devices or chemicals.
Disadvantages Requires period of abstinence each month, when ovulation is expected. Requires diligent record keeping. Provides no protection against STIs.
Comments For maximum effectiveness, consult a trained practitioner for guidance in using this method.

CHANCE OR NO METHOD

Typical Use Effectiveness 85%
What It Is Not using any form of contraception.
Advantages No monetary costs or side effects.
Disadvantages High risk for pregnancy and STIs.
Comments Some individuals choose not to use birth control for religious or moral reasons. Others may fear health risks. This decision should be thoroughly discussed with a health-care professional.

Source: Adapted from Rebecca J. Donatelle and Lorraine G. Davis, *Access to Health*, 6th ed., p. 175. Copyright © 2000 Allyn & Bacon.

Critical Thinking

CONTRACEPTION

Now that you have sufficient information on methods of birth control, evaluate the method you are using or would use. Now choose a method that is far safer than the one you just selected. What might be some of the reasons that you and other college students would avoid this method? Since it's a safer method, what could you say to convince yourself and others to try it?

major features of some common methods, presented in descending order of effectiveness. The "typical use effectiveness" numbers represent the percentage of women experiencing an unwanted pregnancy in one year per 100 uses of the method, with the normal number of human errors, memory lapses, and incomplete or incorrect use. A low number indicates the method is more effective, whereas a high number signals less effectiveness.

Making Decisions About Alcohol

Even if you don't drink, you should read this information because 50 percent of college students reported helping a drunken friend, classmate, or study partner in the past year. First, remember this: A number of surveys have confirmed that your peers aren't drinking as much as you think they are (see Figure 10.1), so there's no need for you to try and "catch up." Most students who try to estimate college drinking are off by almost half—and that's the truth. Second, remember that, in the final analysis, it's your decision to drink or not to drink alcoholic beverages; to drink moderately or to drink heavily; to know when to stop or to be labeled as a drunk who isn't fun to be around. You should know that between 10 and 20 percent of people in the United States become addicted to alcohol at some point in their lives. Alcohol can turn people into victims even though they don't drink: people killed by drunk drivers or

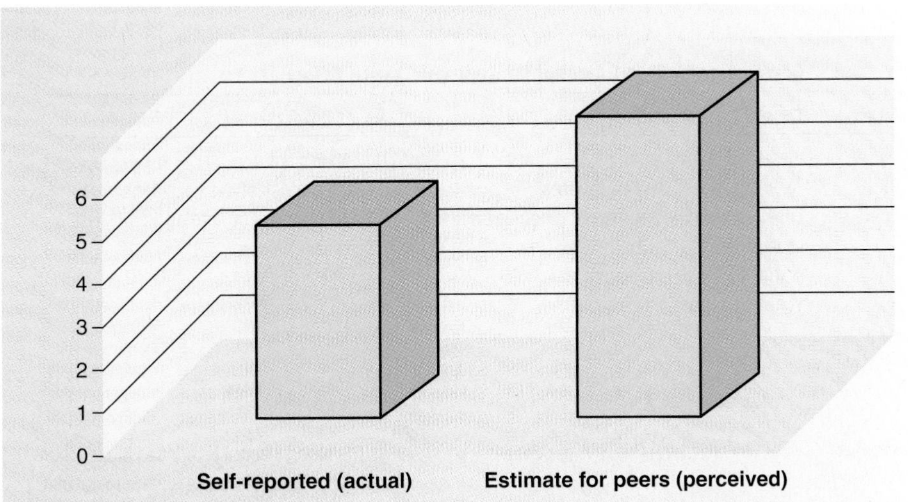

Source: B. Smith, G. Stamper, and R. Grant. A Peer-Led, Small-Groups Approach to Changing Perceptions of Drinking Norms Among College Students, 2001. Used by permission.

FIGURE 10.1 Number of Drinks Consumed per Drinking Occasion

family members who suffer from the behavior of an alcoholic. Over the course of one year, about 20 to 30 percent of students report serious problems related to excessive alcohol use. You may have heard news reports about college students who died or were seriously or permanently injured as a result of excessive drinking. Just one occasion of heavy or high-risk drinking can lead to problems.

Drinking and Blood Alcohol Content

How alcohol affects behavior depends on the dose of alcohol, which is best measured by the blood alcohol content or BAC (see Table 10.3). Most of the pleasurable effects of alcoholic beverages are experienced at lower BAC levels, when alcohol acts as a behavioral stimulant. For most people, the stimulant level is around one drink per hour. Usually, problems begin to emerge at doses higher than .05, when alcohol acts as a sedative and begins to slow down areas of the brain. Most people who have more than four or five drinks on one occasion feel "buzzed," show signs of impairment, and are likely to be higher risks for alcohol-related problems. However, significant impairment at lower doses can occur.

SEE WORKING TOGETHER EXERCISE: HELPING A FRIEND

How fast you drink makes a difference, too. Your body gets rid of alcohol at a rate of about one drink an hour. Drinking more than one drink an hour may cause a rise in BAC because the body is absorbing alcohol faster than it can eliminate it.

Professionals can estimate BAC from your behavior. When someone is stopped for drunk driving, police may videotape the person completing a series of tasks such as walking on a line and tipping his or her head back, or touching the nose with eyes closed. The degree of impairment shown in these tests can be presented as evidence in court.

Alcohol and Behavior

At BAC levels of .025 to .05, a drinker tends to feel animated and energized. At a BAC level of around .05, a drinker may feel rowdy or boisterous. This is where most people report feeling a buzz from alcohol. At a BAC level between .05 and .08, alcohol starts to act as a depressant. So as soon as you feel that buzz, remember that you are on the brink of losing coordination, clear thinking, and judgment!

Table 10.3 Correlation of Blood Alcohol Content (BAC) with Behavior

BAC Range	Common Effects on Behavior	Major Dangers
.00-.04	Increased energy, animation	No impairment
.05-.08	Feeling a "buzz;" slowed reflexes	4 times the risk of auto accident[a]
.09-.20	Impaired walking, poor social judgment, slurred speech, nausea, fighting, vandalism, sexual aggression, blackout	25 times the risk of auto accident[a], risk of indiscriminate sex
.20-.30	Vomiting, stupor, passing out	Death from suffocation or choking on vomit
.31-.45	Coma, shock from alcohol poisoning	Brain damage; death
.45 or higher	.45 is the fatal level for 50% of people	As the blood alcohol level rises higher than .45, death becomes more and more certain.

[a]Compared to a driver with a BAC less than .01.

Source: Robert Julien, *A Primer of Drug Action*, 9th ed., New York: Worth, 2001.

Driving is measurably impaired at BAC levels *lower* than the legal limit of .08. In fact, an accurate safe level for most people may be half the legal limit (.04). As BAC levels climb past .08, you will become progressively less coordinated and less able to make good decisions. Most people become severely uncoordinated with BAC levels higher than .08 and may begin falling asleep, falling down, or slurring their speech. Incidentally, this isn't funny.

Warning Signs, Saving Lives

Most people pass out or fall asleep when the BAC is above .25. Unfortunately, even after you pass out and stop drinking, your BAC can continue to rise as alcohol in your stomach is released to the intestine and absorbed into the bloodstream. Your body may try to get rid of alcohol by vomiting, but you can choke if you are unconscious, semiconscious, or severely uncoordinated.

Worse yet, at BAC levels higher than .30, most people will show signs of severe alcohol poisoning such as an inability to wake up, slowed breathing, fast but weak pulse, cool or damp skin, and pale or bluish skin. People exhibiting these symptoms need medical assistance *immediately*. If you ever find someone in such a state, remember to keep the person on his or her side with the head lower than the rest of the body. Check to see that the airway is clear, especially if the person is vomiting or if the tongue is blocking the back of the throat.

Heavy Drinking: The Danger Zone

Heavy drinking, sometimes called binge drinking, is commonly defined as five or more drinks for males and four or more drinks for females on a single occasion. Presumably, for a very large person who drinks slowly over a long period of time (several hours), four or five drinks may not lead to a BAC associated with impairment. However, research suggests that in many cases the BAC of heavy drinkers exceeds the legal limit for impairment (+.08).

The academic, medical, and social consequences of heavy drinking can seriously endanger quality of life. Research based on surveys conducted by the Core Institute at Southern Illinois University (*<http://www.siuc.edu/~coreinst>*) provides substantial evidence that heavy drinkers have significantly greater risk of adverse outcomes.

Among other problems, the Core data identify heavy drinking with increased risk of poor test performance, missed classes, unlawful behavior, violence, memory loss, drunk driving, regretful behavior, and vandalism, compared with all drinkers and all students. At the same time, college health centers nationwide are reporting increasing occurrences of serious medical conditions resulting from excessive alcohol use:

- Alcohol poisoning causing coma and shock
- Respiratory depression, choking, and respiratory arrest
- Head trauma and brain injury
- Lacerations
- Fractures
- Unwanted or unsafe sexual activity causing STIs and pregnancies
- Bleeding intestines
- Anxiety attacks and other psychological crises
- Worsening of underlying psychiatric conditions such as depression or anxiety

If you engage in heavy drinking so long that your body can tolerate large amounts, you may become an alcoholic. According to the medical definition, someone is alcohol-dependent or alcoholic if he or she exhibits three of the following symptoms:

TABLE 10.4 Comparison of Percentage of Students Reporting Alcohol-related Problems Experienced by Light to Moderate Drinkers, Heavy Drinkers, and Frequent Heavy Drinkers

Problem	Light to Moderate Drinkers	Heavy Drinkers	Frequent Heavy Drinkers
Got behind on schoolwork	9	25	48
Missed a class due to drinking	10	33	65
Argued with friends while drinking	10	24	47
Got hurt or injured	3	11	27
Damaged property	3	10	25
Got in trouble with campus police	2	5	15
Had 5 or more alcohol-related problems since the beginning of the school year	4	17	52

Source: Data from Henry Weschler et al., "Changes in Binge Drinking and Related Problems Among American College Students Between 1993 and 1997: Results of the Harvard School of Public Health College Alcohol Study," *Journal of American College Health* 47 (1998): 57-68.

1. A significant tolerance for alcohol
2. Withdrawal symptoms such as the shakes
3. Overuse of alcohol
4. Attempts to control or cut down on use
5. Preoccupation with drinking or becoming anxious when you do not have a "stash"
6. Making new friends who drink and staying away from friends who do not drink or who do not drink to get drunk
7. Continued heavy drinking despite experiencing alcohol-related social, academic, legal, or health problems (see Table 10.4)

Consequences for All

All Core Institute surveys conducted since the early 1990s have consistently shown a negative correlation between grades and the number of drinks per week—and not just for heavy drinkers (see Figure 10.2).

The message is very clear, yet many fail to "get it." If you choose to drink, drink just enough to feel relaxed. Then switch to a nonalcoholic beverage. Because if you drink any more, it's bound to be a no-win situation.

Tobacco—The Other Legal Drug

Tobacco use is clearly the cause of many serious medical conditions, including heart disease, cancer, and lung ailments. Over the years, tobacco has led to the deaths of hundreds of thousands of individuals.

Unfortunately, cigarette smoking is on the rise among college students. "The rise in this group is really an alarming sign," says Henry Wechsler of Harvard University. Wechsler compared surveys of more than 14,000 students at 116 colleges in 1993 and again in 1997 and found a 28 percent increase over those four years.

A 2000 national study on both cigarette and noncigarette tobacco use by college students found that nearly one-half of college students reported using tobacco products in the previous year. The study was conducted by researchers from the Massachusetts General Hospital and the Harvard School of Public Health (HSPH) College Alcohol Study.

Because more women than men now smoke, the rate of cancer in women is rapidly approaching or surpassing rates in men.

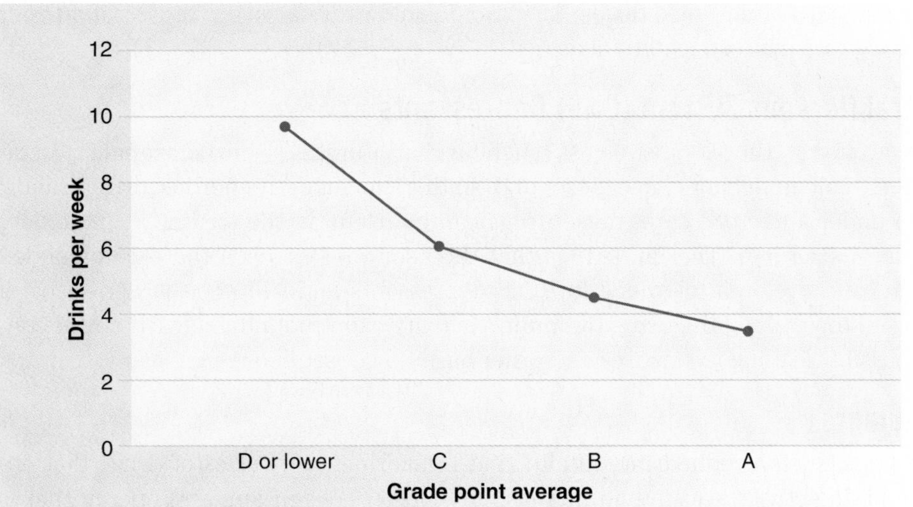

Source: Adapted with permission from C.A. Presley, P.W. Mellman, J.R. Cashin and R. Lyerla. *Alcohol and Drugs on American College Campuses: Use, Consequences, and Perceptions of the Campus Environment*, Vol. 4:1992–94. Carbondale, IL: The Core Institute, Southern Illinois University, Carbondale.

FIGURE 10.2 Negative Correlation Between Drinks per Week and Grade Point Average

Chemicals in tobacco are highly addictive, making it hard to quit. Although young people may not worry about long-term side effects, increased numbers of respiratory infections, worsening of asthma, bad breath, and stained teeth should be motivations to not start smoking at all. Again, the way to kick the habit is to find alternative and healthy ways to relax. Exercise is one of the best choices. Besides, it's hard to jog with tar in your lungs!

Prescription Drug Abuse and Addiction

An estimated 9 million people ages 12 and older used prescription drugs for nonmedical reasons in 1999, nearly triple the number for the previous year. Three classes of prescription drugs are the most commonly abused: opioids, central nervous system (CNS) depressants, and stimulants. It appears that college students' nonmedical use of pain relievers is on the rise and many individuals may engage in "doctor shopping" to get multiple prescriptions for the drugs they abuse.

Opioids

These pain relievers include morphine, codeine, and such branded drugs as OxyContin, Darvon, Vicodin, Demerol, and Dilaudid. Opioids work by blocking the transmission of pain messages to the brain. Chronic use can result in an addiction to higher

Speaking of Careers

To earn a license to provide treatment services for people having problems with alcohol and other drugs, explore a master's degree in social work (MSW) or a Ph.D. in psychology. Some people receive specialty training to work with those who have substance abuse problems without getting advanced graduate training. Such workers typically are college graduates who have trained to become certified alcohol counselors (CAC). Also, people who work in college or university student affairs programs typically have at least a master's degree in counseling or education and may be called to counsel students with alcohol problems.

doses. Taking a large single dose of an opioid could cause a severe reduction in your breathing rate that can lead to death.

Central Nervous System (CNS) Depressants

Each group of these substances (such as barbiturates, benzodiazepines, beta-blockers, calcium-channel blockers, and statins) includes numerous drug brands. Taken under a doctor's care, these drugs can be useful in the treatment of anxiety and sleep disorders. The flip side is that the user who exceeds the recommended dosage can develop a tolerance for CNS depressants and will need larger doses. If the user stops taking the drug, the brain's activity can rebound and race out of control, possibly leading to seizures and other harmful consequences.

Stimulants

Stimulants, such as ephedrine, Ritalin, and Dexadrine, are a class of drugs that enhance brain activity, causing an increase in alertness, attention, and energy that is accompanied by elevated blood pressure and increased heart rate. The legal use of stimulants to treat obesity, asthma, and other problems dropped off as their potential for abuse and addiction became apparent.[1]

Illegal Drugs

Illegal recreational drugs, such as marijuana, cocaine, methamphetamine, Ecstasy, and heroin, are used by a much smaller number of college students and far less frequently than alcohol. Yet these drugs are significant public health issues for college students, and we do hope that the comparative statistics shown in Table 10.5 and the brief additional information that follows will provoke further reading and discussion.

All drugs listed in Table 10.5, with the exception of alcohol and tobacco, are illegal (or illegal without a prescription), and the penalties associated with their possession or abuse tend to be much more severe than those associated with underage alcohol use.

Table 10.5 Annual Prevalence of Alcohol and Other Drugs on College Campuses

The following list gives the percentage of students who reported using each drug listed at least once within the year prior to completing the survey:

Drug	Percentage	Drug	Percentage
Tobacco	47.0%	Hallucinogens	6.6%
Alcohol	84.1%	Opiates	1.5%
Marijuana	33.6%	Inhalants	1.9%
Cocaine	5.0%	Designer drugs	9.1%
Amphetamines	7.6%	Steroids	0.8%
Sedatives	4.1%	Other	2.5%

Source: C.A. Presley, *2000 Statistics on Alcohol and Other Drug Use on American Campuses*, Carbondale, IL: The Core Institute, Southern Illinois University, Carbondale, 2000. Reprinted by permission.

[1]Adapted from "Prescription Drugs: Abuse and Addiction." National Institute on Drug Abuse, part of the National Institutes of Health, a division of the U.S. Department of Health and Human Services.

Athletic departments, potential employers, and government agencies do routine screenings for many of these drugs. Future employability, athletic scholarships, and insurability may be compromised if you have a positive drug test for any of these substances. A brief summary of five of the most prevalent drugs follows.

Marijuana

Marijuana has a half-life in the body of between three and seven days, depending on its potency and the smoker. Like alcohol, light use will produce a pleasant high. But chronic use of marijuana can lead to a lethargic state in which users may "forget" about current responsibilities (such as going to class). Long-term use carries the same risks of lung infections and cancer that are associated with smoking tobacco.

Ecstasy

MDMA, or Ecstasy, as it is known, is a synthetic—or manmade—drug. Although many young people believe that MDMA is safe and offers nothing but a pleasant high for the $25 cost of a single tablet (how bad can it be if it's that cheap?), the reality is far different. The effects of MDMA, when taken orally, last approximately four to six hours. Many users will take a second dose when the initial dose begins to fade. Some tablets contain not only MDMA but also other drugs, including amphetamine, caffeine, destromethorpin, ephedrine, and cocaine.

As MDMA significantly depletes serotonin—a substance in the brain that helps regulate mood, sleep, pain, emotion, and appetite, as well as other behaviors—it takes the brain time to rebuild the serotonin needed to perform important physiological and psychological functions. Of great concern is MDMA's adverse effects on the pumping efficiency of the heart. Heavy users may experience obsessive traits, anxiety, paranoia, and sleep disturbance. Another study indicates that MDMA can have long-lasting effects on memory.[2]

Heroin

Numerous reports have suggested a rise in heroin use among college students. A highly addictive drug with the potential to be more damaging and fatal than other opiates, heroin is the most abused and most rapidly acting of this group.

One of the most significant—and surest—effects of heroin use is addiction. The human body begins to develop tolerance to the drug on *first use.* Once this happens, the abuser must use more of the drug to achieve the same intensity. Within a short period of time, users must take the drug more and more often to alleviate the symptoms of addiction.

Heroin can be injected, smoked, or snorted. Injection is the most efficient way to administer low-purity heroin. However, the availability of high-purity heroin and the fear of infection by sharing needles have made snorting and smoking the drug more common. Some users believe that snorting or smoking heroin will not lead to addiction. They are 100 percent wrong.

Users typically experience an initial feeling of euphoria, a warm flushing of the skin, a dry mouth, and heavy extremities, followed by an alternately wakeful and drowsy state lasting for hours. Due to the depression of the central nervous system, mental functioning becomes clouded. Additionally, breathing may be slowed to the point of respiratory failure.

Chronic users may develop collapsed veins, infection of the heart lining and valves, abscesses, and liver disease. In addition, users are at risk for pulmonary complications, including various types of pneumonia. In addition to the effects of the drug itself, users who inject heroin also put themselves at risk for contracting HIV,

[2]Excerpted from "Ecstasy: What We Know and Don't Know About MDMA: A Scientific Review." National Institute on Drug Abuse, part of the National Institutes of Health (NIH), a division of the U.S. Department of Health and Human Services.

hepatitis B and C, and other blood-borne viruses. A heroin overdose may cause slow and shallow breathing, convulsions, coma, and possibly death.

Cocaine

Cocaine or crack produces an intense experience that heightens senses. A crack high lasts only a few minutes; then the good feelings are gone. The initial short-lived euphoria of cocaine will be followed by a "crash," involving anxiety, depression, irritability, extreme fatigue, and possibly paranoia. Physical health may deteriorate. An intense craving for more cocaine develops, as may tactile hallucinations of insects crawling underneath the skin.

Users are likely eventually to alienate family and friends and to become isolated and suspicious. Because addicts grow desperate for more cocaine, they will often lie, cheat, steal, and commit crimes of violence to get it.

Methamphetamine

Methamphetamine or meth (called speed, crank, crystal, glass, chalk, ice, etc.) is particularly dangerous because it costs so little and is so easy to make. Much of it is being produced in makeshift labs in homes or college residences, which not only means that the quality varies from batch to batch, but also that it's virtually impossible to tell what else is in the mixture.

The drug can initially produce euphoria, enhanced wakefulness, increased physical activity, and decreased appetite. Prolonged use can lead to binges, during which users take more meth every few hours for several days until they run out of the drug or become too disorganized to continue. Chronic abuse can lead to psychotic behavior, characterized by intense paranoia, visual and auditory hallucinations, and out-of-control rages that can be coupled with extremely violent behavior.

Researchers have found that many former meth users experience long-term brain damage, and it is unknown whether the damage can ever be reversed.

Stress

When you are stressed, your body undergoes rapid physiological, behavioral, and emotional changes. Your breathing may become more rapid and shallow. Your heart rate quickens, and your muscles begin to tighten. Your hands may become cold and/or sweaty. You may get a "butterfly" stomach, diarrhea, or constipation. Your mouth and lips may feel dry and hot, and you may notice that your hands and knees begin to shake or tremble. Your voice may quiver or even go up an octave.

You may also experience confusion, trouble concentrating, inability to remember things, and poor problem solving. You may feel fear, anxiety, depression, irritability, anger, or frustration, have insomnia, or wake up too early and not be able to go back to sleep.

Stress has many sources, but two seem to be prominent: life events and daily hassles. Life events are those that represent major adversity, such as the death of a parent or friend. Researchers believe that an accumulation of stress from life events, especially if many events occur over a short period of time, can cause physical and mental health problems. The College Readjustment Rating Scale (Exercise 10.4) is a life events scale designed especially for traditional college students. If you find that your score is 150 or higher, you have experienced a great deal of stress over the past year. You might consider what help you need or skills you must learn to be able to cope effectively.

The other major source of stress is daily hassles. These are the minor irritants that we experience every day, such as losing your keys, dropping your soft drink, having three tests on the same day, problems with your roommate, or worrying about money. For returning students, examples would be having to pay for an unexpected emergency repair, caring for a sick child, finding it difficult to juggle work and classes, and worrying about money.

Managing Stress and Depression

The best starting point for handling stress is to be in good shape physically and mentally. When your body and mind are healthy, it's like inoculating yourself against stress. This means you need to pay attention to diet, exercise, sleep, and mental health.

But what if you do all these things and still feel "down" and/or panicky? You may have a chronic case of depression and/or anxiety. A specialist can tell you if your symptoms are caused by chemical balances in your body—something that you may not be able to correct on your own. It's important to seek help, which may include psychotherapy, medication, or a combination of the two. If you don't have a local doctor, head for the campus health center.

Where to Go for Help

ON CAMPUS

Counseling center. Professionals here will offer individual and group assistance and lots of information. Remember, their support is confidential and you will not be judged.

Health center/infirmary. On most campuses the professionals who staff these are especially interested in educational outreach and practicing prevention. But you should be able to receive treatment as well.

Health education and wellness programs. Challenges with alcohol, other drugs, and sexual decision making and its consequences are part of the college universe. Fellow student peer health educators can provide support. Taking part in such peer leadership is also a great way to develop and practice your own communication skills.

Campus support groups. Many campuses provide student support groups led by professionals for students dealing with problems related to excessive alcohol and drug use, abusive sexual relationships, and so forth.

Courses in the curriculum. Learn more about it! Look for courses offered in such departments as health education, psychology, and sociology.

ONLINE

Read Dr. Ruth's thoughts on sex and drugs at **<http://www.studentnow.com/features/dr_ruth/sexanddrugs.html>**.

Check the National Clearinghouse for Alcohol and Drug Information at **<http://www.health.org/>** or by calling 800-729-6686.

Visit the Web site of the Centers for Disease Control, that provides objective information about STIs, drugs, and alcohol: **<http://www.cdc.gov/>**.

Check out DrugHelp at **<http://www.drughelp.org/>**.

Learn more about the dangers of methamphetamine at **<http://www.methamphetamineaddiction.com/methamphetamine.html>**.

ON INFOTRAC® COLLEGE EDITION

Read the following journal articles: Ralph Hingson, Timothy Heeren, Michael R. Winter, and Henry Wechsler, "Early Age of First Drunkenness as a Factor in College Students' Unplanned and Unprotected Sex Attributable to Drinking," *Pediatrics,* January 2003, 111, no. 1:34(8)

Arnold Mann, "Higher MDMA Doses Spike Heart Rate and BP" (Study of Eight Patients), *Clinical Psychiatry News,* November 2001, 29, no. 11:26(1)

Suicide

Suicide is the second leading cause of death among college students. About 1,100 college students kill themselves each year, for a number of reasons including general depression, loneliness, the breakup of a relationship, poor grades, a lack of close friends, or a combination of factors. Often, when someone decides to take his or her own life, that person dies without leaving a reason.

Most suicidal people send out signals to us; often, sadly, we simply don't believe or hear them. A potential suicide victim needs help as soon as possible. It may be difficult to convince someone—or yourself—that help is needed.

If someone you know is considering suicide, the most important things you can do are listen and stay with the person to make sure he or she is safe. Avoid arguments and the impulse to give advice. And when the time is right, escort the person to the campus medical or counseling center or a local hospital.

Some Warning Signs of Suicide

The list below is far from complete. Sometimes, you have to rely on your common sense when you believe either you or a friend is thinking about suicide. Speak up if you notice one or more symptoms in a friend. If you are feeling such symptoms, find a trusted friend and talk. Then head for the counseling or health center on campus.

SYMPTOMS OF SUICIDE

Depression
Feeling hopeless or helpless
Anger or hostility
Inability to feel pleasure
Feeling guilt
Isolation or withdrawal
Impulsive behavior
Thinking a lot about death
Talking about dying
Recent loss including loss of religious faith, loss of interest in friends, sex, hobbies, activities previously enjoyed
Change in personality
Change in sleep patterns
Change in eating habits
Diminished sexual interest
Low self-esteem
No hope for the future—believing things will never get better, that nothing will ever change
Giving things away that are valued
Ending important relationships or commitments
Promiscuity
Severe outbursts of temper
Drug use
Not going to work or school
Being unable to carry out normal tasks of daily life

Caffeine

Your caffeine consumption can have a big impact on your stress level. Consumed in larger quantities, caffeine may cause nervousness, headaches, irritability, stomach irritation, and insomnia—all symptoms of stress. Many heart patients have been told to avoid caffeine since it tends to speed up heart rates.

How much caffeine do you consume? Total your caffeine intake based on these figures:

1 cup brewed coffee 85 mg
1 cup instant coffee 60 mg
1 cup tea 30–50 mg
12-ounce cola drinks 35–65 mg
Many aspirin compounds 30–60 mg
Various cold preparations 30 mg
1 cup cocoa 2–10 mg
1 cup decaffeinated coffee 3 mg

Exercise

Exercise is an excellent stress management technique, the best way to stay fit, and a critical part of weight loss. The beta endorphins released during exercise can counteract stress and depression. Although any kind of recreation benefits your body and soul, the best exercise is aerobic. In aerobic exercise, you work until your pulse is in a "target zone" and keep it there for twenty to thirty minutes. You can reach your target heart rate through a variety of exercises: walking, jogging, running, swimming, biking, a treadmill, or a stair climber. Choose activities that you enjoy so you will look forward to your exercise time. To find your rate, subtract your age from 220 and multiply by 60. Then subtract your age again from 220 and multiply by 75. These are the high and low limits of what your heart rate (pulse) should be during exercise.

SEE EXERCISE 10.4: THE COLLEGE READJUSTMENT RATING SCALE

Sleep

Getting adequate sleep is another way to protect you from stress and help alleviate the symptoms of depression. Although college studies require hours of homework, it's unwise to stay up until the wee hours of the morning. Lack of sleep (a minimum of 6–8 hours) can lead to anxiety and depression. So plan ahead and decide how you are going to handle the situation. Getting enough rest makes you more efficient when you are awake. It also helps make a lot of other activities more enjoyable. If you have trouble sleeping on a regular basis, get medical advice. Sleep deprivation takes a terrible toll on your body.

Finally, remember there is no shame attached to having a mental health problem. Most depression and anxiety result from chemical imbalances in your system, imbalances that usually can be corrected. Proper counseling, medical attention, and perhaps legal prescription drugs carefully chosen by a doctor can turn your world toward the bright side.

Physical activity, especially when it's fun, can serve as a remedy for stress.

Staying Safe

With the stress you may be experiencing from other sources, one thing you want to avoid is becoming a victim of crime. Criminal activity occurs on campuses regularly. These suggestions may help you avoid a number of dangerous situations.

Personal property

- Record serial numbers of electronic equipment and keep numbers in a safe place.
- Mark books on a certain page with your name and driver's license number.
- Never leave personal possessions unprotected.
- Lock your room, even if you're returning soon.

- Never leave your key in a "safe place" for a friend.
- Report lost or stolen property to the campus police.
- Treat credit and debit cards like cash.

Automobile safety

- Keep vehicle locked at all times.
- Don't leave valuables in car where they can be seen.
- Park in well-lighted areas.
- Register your vehicle on campus. This makes it easier for police to trace it if it is stolen.

Personal safety

- Use campus escort service at night if available.
- Know the campus police number.
- Find out where emergency call boxes are on campus if your campus has them.
- Travel with at least one other person at night. Avoid dark areas.
- If you go away for a weekend, let someone know how to reach you.

Modifying Your Lifestyle

Modifying your lifestyle is yet another approach to stress management. You have the power to change your life so that it is less stressful. You may think that others, such as teachers, supervisors, parents, friends, or even your children, are controlling you. Of course, they do influence you, but ultimately you are in control of how you run your life. Lifestyle modification requires that you spend some time reflecting on your life, identifying the parts of your life that do not serve you well, and making plans for change. For instance, if you are always late for class and get stressed about this, get up ten minutes earlier. If you get nervous before a test when you talk to a certain classmate, avoid that person before a test. Learn test-taking skills so you can manage test anxiety better.

SEE EXERCISE 10.5: CHANGING PERCEPTIONS

Relaxation Techniques

You can use a number of relaxation techniques to reduce stress. The CD-ROM accompanying this book has more on this topic, as well as links to useful Web sites.

Learning them is just like learning any new skill. You need knowledge and practice. Check with your college counseling center, health clinic, or fitness center about classes that teach relaxation. These classes are often advertised in the student newspaper. Some colleges and universities have credit courses that teach relaxation techniques. You can also learn more about relaxation at any bookstore or library, where you'll find a large number of books on relaxation techniques. In addition, you can buy relaxation tapes and let an expert guide you through the process. The technique that you choose should be based on your personal preference. See the CD-ROM for a description of these techniques.

Nutrition and Body Weight

"You are what you eat" is more than a catchphrase; it's an important reminder of the vital role diet plays in our lives. You've probably read news stories telling how more and more young people are obese than ever before in our history. Many attribute this to the proliferation of fast-food restaurants, which place "flavor" and "filling" before "healthy." One chain even made its burgers larger in response to consumer research.

Setting Goals for Success

REDUCING STRESS

Look at the stressors you identified in Exercise 10.4. Write down your goals for dealing with at least one of these specific stressors. This will involve acquiring some new skills and practicing some sort of relaxation technique on a regular basis. Then, when a stressful situation arrives, you will be able to quiet the stress response. Use the goal-setting technique we outlined at the beginning of this book.

My goal is to reduce these stressors:

1. ____________________

2. ____________________

3. ____________________

I want to achieve this goal because: ____________________

I may encounter these obstacles: ____________________

My strategy for accomplishing this goal is to: ____________________

Eating more saturated fats—the kind found in hamburgers and other red meat products—than you should, for example, can lead to heart disease at a comparatively early age. Failing to consume a sufficient amount of fiber and grains may cause cancer. And the extra weight itself can rob you of good health.

So what to do? It's not easy at first, but if you commit to a new eating regime, you will not only feel better, but you'll also be healthier . . . and probably happier. Ask your student health center for more advice. If your college has a nursing program, that might be another source of information on diet. Meanwhile, here are some suggestions:

1. Restrict your intake of red meat, real butter, white rice, white bread, potatoes, and sweets. "White foods" are made with refined flour, which has few nutrients—so you're only getting empty carbs (translation: calories). Instead, go for fish, poultry, and soy products. *Note:* Grill a soy burger and you'll be surprised at the flavor, especially if you dress it with lettuce, tomato, and mustard or ketchup (not mayonnaise). Use whole wheat breads.
2. Eat enough vegetables and fruits daily. These are important building blocks for a balanced diet. Instead of fruit juices, which contain concentrated amounts of sugar (more empty calories), go for the fruit instead.
3. Avoid fried foods—french fries, fried chicken, and so forth. Choose grilled meats instead. Avoid foods with large amounts of sugar, such as donuts.
4. Keep your room stocked with healthy snacks, such as fruit, vegetables, yogurt, and graham crackers.
5. Eat a sensible amount of nuts and all the legumes (beans) you want to round out your fiber intake.
6. Make sure the oils you buy are either polyunsaturated or monounsaturated. Although oils are 100 percent fat, they don't mess with your cardiovascular system unless you use too much of them and start gaining weight. Avoid trans-fatty acids and saturated fats when shopping for oils. These are substances that can clog arteries.

7. Always read the government-required nutrition label on all packaged foods. Check sodium content (sodium will make you retain fluids and increase your weight) and the number of fat grams. A goal to strive for is a diet with only 20 percent fat. So if you read that a product has 160 calories per serving and only 3 grams of fat, it's a good choice. For a quick way to check, double the number of calories per serving, move the decimal point twice to the left, and compare the number to the fat grams per serving.

Figure 10.3, the Start Healthy Box, shows the Healthy Eating Pyramid, designed by Walter Willett, chairman of the department of nutrition at Harvard's School of Public Health. The Healthy Eating Pyramid puts exercise and weight control at the base, recommends eating whole-grain foods at most meals, and encourages eating vegetables "in abundance." This pyramid emphasizes eating lots of plant oils, like olive, canola, and soy, and gives fish and poultry a higher profile than red meat, which you should consider eating sparingly.

Obesity

People have been joking about the "freshman fifteen" forever, but it's no joke that new college students tend to gain an excessive amount of weight during their first term. There are a lot of reasons why students gain weight, some of them being increased stress, lifestyle changes, new food choices, changes in physical activity, and alcohol consumption. In addition to following the nutrition guidelines above, other ways to avoid obesity are eating smaller meals more often, getting regular exercise, keeping a food journal (to keep track of what you are actually consuming), and being realistic about dieting.

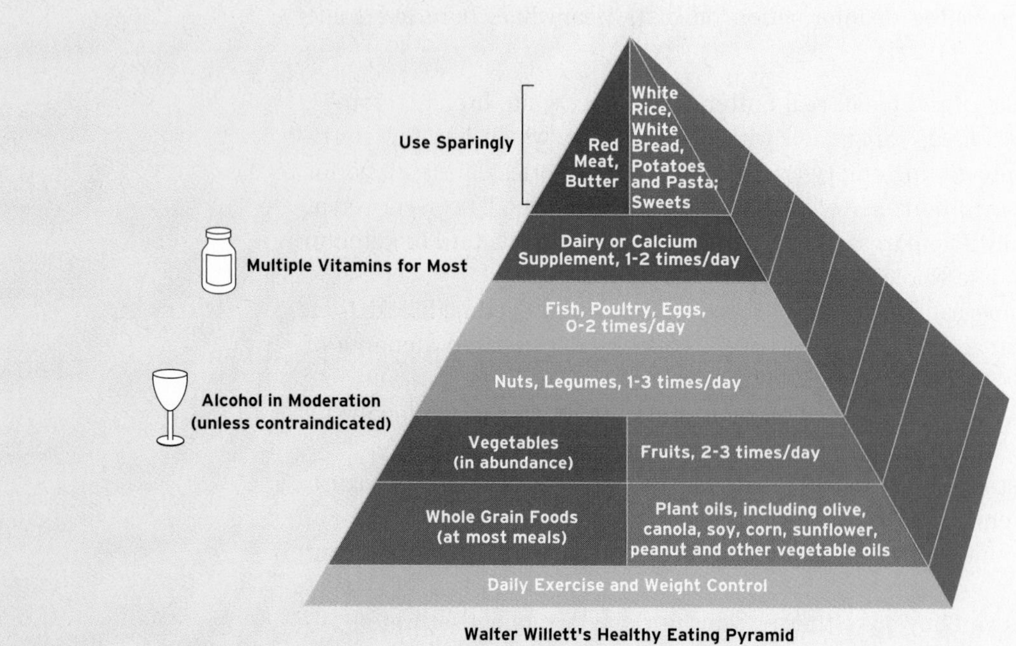

Figure 10.3 Eating Healthy

Source: Reprinted with permission of Simon & Schuster Adult Publishing Group from *Eat, Drink, and Be Healthy: The Harvard Medical School Guide to Healthy Eating* by Walter C. Willett, M.D. Copyright © 2001 by President and Fellows of Harvard College.

Examining Values

Reading about the topics of sexual health, substance abuse, and wellness is bound to make you think about the choices you make. Explore within yourself the particular choices you have made about having sex, drinking, taking drugs, smoking, and taking care of your body and mind. What pressures–or motivators–were behind those choices? Are you satisfied and proud of your choices? If not, are you considering making different choices?

Eating Disorders

Anorexia nervosa (anorexia) is an eating disorder made up of complex physical and emotional elements. A person with anorexia severely limits food intake, has a distorted body image, refuses to maintain a normal body weight, and is intensely afraid of gaining weight, despite being very underweight.

Anorexia primarily strikes women and girls. Anorexia usually begins during adolescence but can occur in early childhood or even adulthood.

There are several warning signs and symptoms to watch for in a person with anorexia:

- Participating in a sport—dance, gymnastics, track, or wrestling—just to lose weight
- Wearing loose-fitting clothing to hide the body and stay warm
- Incessantly drinking diet sodas
- Getting an unusually high number of colds
- Craving carbohydrates, such as potato chips or cookies
- Shopping at several stores to conceal purchases of food or laxatives[3]

Some people with anorexia make themselves vomit although they have not overeaten. Bulimia nervosa is the official name of the eating disorder characterized by binge-purge behavior.

A person with anorexia usually does not seek treatment because he or she does not think it is a problem. Weight loss is seen as an accomplishment. Friends and loved ones may become concerned about the weight loss before the person with anorexia acknowledges there is a problem. If you suspect that someone you know has anorexia, encourage him or her to seek medical and psychological treatment. Anorexia has the potential to become a lifelong illness, although appropriate treatment can cure this disorder. Long-term or severe anorexia can lead to serious health problems and even death.

Reassess Yourself

Let's go back to the self-assessment that appears at the beginning of this chapter. This is an opportunity for you to measure your progress, to check in with yourself and see how your approach to wellness may have changed as a result of reading this chapter. Which of the items on page 171 did you check? Would you change any of your answers as a result of reading this chapter? If so, which ones, and why?

[3]List excerpted from "Detective Work May Be Needed to Spot Eating Disorders: Clinical Pearls (Psychosomatic Medicine) by Robert Finn. *Clinical Psychiatry News,* Sept. 2003, v31, i9, p. 62(1).

Exercises

Each of these exercises will let you further explore the topic of this chapter. You'll find all these exercises, plus Internet and InfoTrac® College Edition exercises, on the CD-ROM that accompanies this book.

EXERCISE 10.1 What's Your Decision?

Although you might know about the strategies to keep yourself from contracting an STI, knowledge doesn't always translate into behavior. Use the following chart to brainstorm all the reasons you can think of that people *wouldn't* practice each of these prevention strategies: abstinence, monogamy, or condom use. Then go back over your list and consider whether each barrier would apply to you (yes, no, or maybe). In this way, you can better evaluate where you stand on the issue of safer sex and determine what areas you may need to work on to ensure that you protect yourself—always!

BARRIERS	DOES THIS APPLY TO YOU?
______________	______________
______________	______________
______________	______________
______________	______________
______________	______________

EXERCISE 10.2 Quality of Life

List five ways your or a friend's quality of life has been influenced by the drinking of others. In small groups, share some or all of these effects with others in the class. What did you find out when you compared your experiences with theirs?

EXERCISE 10.3 Monitoring Your Stress

Here's one way to learn to recognize how you feel when you are stressed. Following is a list of physical and emotional conditions that people may feel when stressed. Check the ones that best describe you. Then review those you have checked and write a paragraph describing how you feel and act under stress.

____My breathing is rapid and shallow.

____I feel a tightness in my chest.

____My pulse races.

____My muscles feel tense, especially around my shoulders, chest, forehead, and back of neck.

____My hands are cold or sweaty.

____I have "butterflies" in my stomach.

____I experience diarrhea or constipation.

____I have to urinate more frequently.

____My mouth is dry.

____I tremble or feel shaky.

____I have a quiver in my voice.

____Things easily confuse me.

____I have trouble remembering things.

____I have trouble solving problems.

____I feel irritable.

____I feel jittery.

____I have trouble concentrating.

____I feel overwhelmed.

____I am anxious about things I have to do.

____I feel depressed.

____I feel frustrated.

____I have insomnia.

____I wake up far too early and can't go back to sleep.

____I have noticed changes in my eating habits.

____I feel fatigued a good bit of the time.

EXERCISE 10.4 The College Readjustment Rating Scale

The College Readjustment Rating Scale is an adaptation of Holmes and Rahe's Life Events Scale.[4] It has been modified for traditional-age college students and should be considered as a rough indication of stress levels and possible health consequences.

In this scale, each event, such as one's first term in college, is assigned a value that represents the amount of readjustment a person has to make in life as a result of the change. In some studies, people with serious illnesses have been found to have high scores on similar scales. Persons with scores of 300 and higher have a high health risk. Persons scoring between 150 and 300 points have about a 50-50 chance of serious health change within two years. Subjects scoring 150 and below have a 1 in 3 chance of a serious health change.

To determine your stress score, circle the number of points corresponding to the events you have experienced in the past six months or are likely to experience in the next six months. Then add up the circled numbers.

Event	Points	Event	Points
Death of spouse	100	Male partner in unwed pregnancy	77
Female unwed pregnancy	92	Divorce	73
Death of parent	80		

[4]From T. H. Holmes and R. H. Rahe, "The Social Readjustment Scale," in Carol L. Otis and Roger Goldingay, *Campus Health Guide,* New York: CEEB, 1989.

Event	Points	Event	Points
Death of a close family member	70	Academic probation	39
Death of a close friend	65	Change in major	37
Divorce between parents	63	New love interest	36
Jail term	61	Increased workload in college	31
Major personal injury or illness	60	Outstanding personal acheivement	29
Flunk out of college	58	First term in college	28
Marriage	55	Serious conflict with instructor	27
Fired from job	50	Lower grades than expected	25
Loss of financial support for college (scholarship)	48	Change in colleges (transfer)	24
Failing grade in important or required course	47	Change in social activities	22
Sexual difficulties	45	Change in sleeping habits	21
Serious argument with significant other	40	Change in eating habits	19
		Minor violation of the law (e.g., traffic ticket)	15

If your score indicates potential health problems, it would be to your benefit to seriously review the stress inoculation and management techniques discussed in this chapter and select and implement some strategies to reduce your stress.

EXERCISE 10.5 Changing Perceptions

Practice managing stress by changing your perceptions:

1. Identify a stressor where perceptions can be altered.
2. Recognize the negative messages you are currently using in this situation.
3. Create two or three new messages that you will use to deal with the stressor.
4. Write down the new messages and keep them with you.
5. Practice saying the new messages to yourself.
6. Use the new messages when you encounter the stressors.
7. Practice, practice, practice. Change takes time.

EXERCISE 10.6 Doing a Weekly Check

For one week, keep a food journal in which you write down everything you eat. Divide the journal into these categories: saturated fats, poly- or monounsaturated fats, fruits and vegetables, red meat, poultry and fish, fried foods, pizza, and sweets. At the end of the week, review your journal. In which columns are most of your listings? If they happen to be in saturated fats, red meat, fried foods, pizza, and sweets, write down some substitute choices and try to follow them during the coming week. At the end of that week, write about your experiences. Did you feel better or worse during the second week? Was it easy or hard to make the changes? What will you do about your diet once this experiment is over?

Working Together Exercise
Helping a Friend

If you could make only three recommendations to a friend about safer partying, what would they be? Explain how each would help your friend enjoy the party without putting him or herself at risk. In groups of four, compare your list with those of other students and see if your group can agree on the three most important recommendations. Then see whether other groups in class had lists similar to yours or very different.

Photo Credits

This page constitutes an extension of the copyright page. We have made every effort to tract the ownership of all copyrighted material and to secure permission from copyright holders. In the event of any question arising as to the use of any material, we will be pleased to make the necessary corrections in future printings. Thanks are due to the following for permission to use the material indicated.

1: © Ariel Skelley/CORBIS; **3:** © Spencer Grant/PhotoEdit; **6:** © Digital Vision Ltd./AGE Fotostock America; **8:** © F. Schussler/PhotoLink/ Photodisc/Getty Images; **9:** © Will Hart/PhotoEdit; **10:** *top,* © Photodisc Collection/Getty Images; *bottom,* © Nick Koudis/ Photodisc/Getty Images; **12:** © Nick Koudis/Photodisc/ Getty Images; **13:** *top,* © Jacobs Stock Photography/Photodisc/Getty Images; *bottom,* © Nick Koudis/Photodisc/ Getty Images; **14:** © Benelux Press/ Index Stock Imagery; **18:** © Photodisc Collection/Getty Images; **30:** © Mel Curtis/Photodisc/Getty Images; **33:** *left,* © SW Productions/Photodisc/ Getty Images; **33:** *right,* © Pixtal/AGE Fotostock; **37:** © Bill Bachman/Index Stock Imagery; **45:** © Jeff Greenberg/ Index Stock Imagery; **47:** © Mike Mesgleski/Index Stock Imagery; **49:** © Sonda Dawes/The Image Works; **54:** © Comstock Images/Alamy; **60:** © Mark Richards/PhotoEdit; **64:** © Hermann Wostman/DPA/Landov; **69:** © Design Pics Inc./Alamy; **80:** © Royalty-Free/CORBIS; **91:** © Walter Bibikow/Index Stock Imagery; **95:** © Jess Stock/Getty Images; **113:** © Image Source/Alamy; **115:** © Image Source Limited/Index Stock Imagery; **119:** © Photo by Angela Mann; **123:** © Andersen Ross/Photodisc/Getty Images; **133:** © Richard Cummins/CORBIS; **150:** © Ian Shaw/Alamy; **154:** *top,* © David Young-Wolff/ PhotoEdit; *bottom,* © Courtesy of Earlham College; **155:** © Jonathan Nourok/PhotoEdit; **163:** © Roger Dollarhide; **169:** © Ryan McVay/Photodisc/Getty; **185:** © Seb Rogers/Alamy.

Glossary/Index

D

E

T

U

V

Values—views held on moral issues; what is most important to a person; abstractions such as truth, justice, and success.

W